Other Drama Classic Collections

CHEKHOV – FOUR PLAYS

The Seagull
Uncle Vanya
Three Sisters
The Cherry Orchard

IBSEN – THREE PLAYS

A Doll's House
Ghosts
Hedda Gabler

GREEK TRAGEDY

Antigone
Bacchae
Medea

RESTORATION COMEDY

WILLIAM WYCHERLEY
The Country Wife

APHRA BEHN
The Rover

WILLIAM CONGREVE
The Way of the World

edited and introduced by
TREVOR R. GRIFFITHS
and
SIMON TRUSSLER

NICK HERN BOOKS
London
www.nickhernbooks.co.uk

A Drama Classic Collection

This edition first published in Great Britain as a paperback
original in 2005 by Nick Hern Books Limited, 14 Larden Road,
London W3 7ST. Each play originally published individually
in the Drama Classics series.

The Country Wife: copyright in this edition of the text
© 2001 by Trevor R. Griffiths

The Rover: copyright in this edition of the text
© 1999 by Simon Trussler

The Way of the World: copyright in this edition of the text
© 1995 by Trevor R. Griffiths

Introduction copyright © 2005 by Nick Hern Books

Typeset by Country Setting, Kingsdown, Kent CT14 8ES
Printed by Bookmarque Ltd, Croydon, Surrey

ISBN-13   978 1 85459 848 6
ISBN-10   1 85459 848 1

Contents

Introduction: the Restoration

Restoration Society

When Charles II was invited back as king in 1660, eleven years after a republican government had executed his father, Charles I, the world had changed. The old social order had been based on a relatively static world view in which wealth and power derived from the ownership of land and where religion, rank, and social duty constituted a pyramid of interlocking social obligations, with the king at its apex. But the growth of trade and the rise of a wealthy merchant class had gradually imposed strains that ultimately led to the Civil War, the breakdown of the old absolutes and a search for a new order. The very fact that Charles I had been deposed, tried, and executed meant that the world could never be the same again.

The term 'Restoration' tends to be associated with a vision of the merry monarch surrounded by his courtiers, his spaniels and his bevy of mistresses, including the one-time orange-seller and actress Nell Gwyn, and a general atmosphere of libertinism. However, this grossly oversimplifies the complex interactions of a period which also saw the publication of John Milton's epic poems, John Bunyan's *Pilgrim's Progress*, John Locke's philosophy, Newton's physics and Thomas Hobbes's political theory – all attempts to map out the terrain of a new world in which old certainties had been displaced by new doubts.

Plays had been banned in the republican period of the Commonwealth and the theatres closed down. When they reopened officially at the Restoration there were two significant departures from the past: the old, large, open-air amphitheatres such as the Globe, where many of Shakespeare's plays had been staged, were finally abandoned in favour of much smaller, indoor theatres; and actresses were introduced for the first time to play female roles instead of the trained youths familiar from the Elizabethan and Jacobean theatre.

Restoration Comedy

The term 'Restoration Comedy' has sometimes been used very loosely to cover almost any comedy written between 1660 and 1737, the date of the Licensing Act that introduced effective pre-production censorship of plays. A modern equivalent might be to call all the dramatists writing from 1956 to the millennium 'Angry Young Men'. Nevertheless, there is enough common ground between, say, Etherege at one end of the period and Congreve and Vanburgh writing at the turn of the eighteenth century – in terms of shared approaches to the business of comedy, to characterisation, motifs and themes – to justify the use of the term 'Restoration Comedy' for the whole period.

The ending of the ban on organised theatre, the return of monarchical rule and the arrival of actresses encouraged a great sense of release, which expressed itself in the form of a cynical and sophisticated comedy of sexual intrigue. 'Restoration Comedies' deal almost obsessively with the sexual behaviour and moralities of a very narrow section of late seventeenth-century society, the fashionable, leisured gentlefolk found in a contemporary London of chocolate houses, parks, fashionable *soirées*, and theatres (in which they could watch versions of themselves on stage). The plays repeat themes, situations, character types (even actual characters), locations and images in such a down-to-earth manner that critics (though not always audiences) have regularly accused the drama of obscenity and pornographic intent or, alternatively, rescued it from such charges by deny-ing it any connection with reality. By 1700, social conditions had changed considerably from those of 1660, and the satirical excess of the immediate Restoration period was under considerable pressure from both inside and outside the theatre. Early Restoration Comedies tend to reflect the turmoil of the times, the feeling that the world doesn't make sense any more, the difficulties of finding a way to reconcile social pressure with personal desire, through satire. Later comedies, including *The Way of the World*, also attempt to suggest ways forward, to reconcile the conflicting desires to protect inherited wealth and to achieve personal fulfilment through love.

Comedy of Manners

In the English theatre, Restoration Comedy virtually inaugurated the genre of Comedy of Manners, preoccupied with showing the social behaviour of the contemporary rich and leisured class. From the Restoration onwards there is a rich vein of Comedies of Manners which runs through Sheridan and Goldsmith to Boucicault, Wilde, Coward, and Ayckbourn. Sometimes the plays simply reflect their society uncritically, sometimes they are savagely critical of its manners, as in *The Country Wife*. Many of the finest Comedies of Manners, including *The Way of the World*, explore social codes in ways that lead to a critique of society and the suggestion of modifying those codes to deal with the hypocrisies that the manners can hide.

Marriage in the Restoration

For the aristocracy and gentry who form the Dramatis Personae of most Restoration Comedies, and for their counterparts in the audience, marriage was not primarily, or even necessarily, a matter of romantic attachments between individuals. As the contemporary poet Samuel Butler wrote, 'Matrimony's but a bargain made/To serve the turns of interest and trade;/Not out of love or kindness, but designs/To settle lands and tenements like fines'. The transfer of wealth, property and land between families was a key factor in determining who married whom, and the romantic inclinations of the bride and groom were often entirely secondary to any financial or dynastic advantages that might arise from a marriage. This led to many loveless relationships and to cynicism about the institution of marriage as a whole. By concentrating on courtship and marriage, the comic dramatists of the Restoration were able to investigate discrepancies between the social code and underlying emotional realities. In a society effectively without divorce, how could marriage be arranged on anything other than a commercial basis?

The Restoration Theatre

'They altered at once the whole face of the stage by introducing scenes and women' – or so John Dennis claimed nostalgically, writing in 1725 of the events of 1660, when play-acting was once more permitted after being banned by the puritans since 1642. The court masques of the Jacobean and Caroline theatre had employed quite elaborate scenery, and the open-air theatres of the Elizabethans had long been giving way to indoor 'private' theatres, with greater potential for technical effects. The difference now was that the proscenium arch formed a 'picture-frame' for painted perspective scenery, which provided a formalised background to Restoration Comedy and Tragedy.

The scenery was made up of shutters that moved in grooves, so that scenes could be changed by opening and closing these shutters behind the actors. In *The Country Wife*, for example, the painted scenery for the first act would have represented Horner's lodgings and would have opened at the start of Act Two to reveal the next scene, Pinchwife's lodgings. In *The Way of the World*, the first act scenery would have represented the Chocolate House and would have opened for Act Two to reveal a picture of St James's Park. Actors entered through doors at either side of the proscenium arch, or from between the scenery shutters at the side, or, sometimes, were discovered as the shutters parted, the actors then coming forward onto the large forestage to act the scene. This meant that, although the performers still shared the same space as the audience, they were now acting against a background of pictures that in some way illustrated the play.

But it was only a background: the actors performed on the extensive apron stage in front of the proscenium, in a relationship with their audiences no less intimate and uncluttered than their forebears. Indeed, Restoration theatres, which seated from around five to eight hundred, were actually smaller than Elizabethan public playhouses, and their audiences, although not drawn quite so exclusively from a courtly elite as has sometimes been suggested, certainly felt themselves to be part of a social as much as a theatrical occasion. Also, since both the auditorium and the stage were evenly lit (by candelabra) throughout the performance, the audience could see each other as well as they could see the actors. This would have added an extra dimension to the sense of theatre as a reflection of contemporary life, and hence also that 'crossing of the boundary' between actor and character so clearly felt in many Restoration prologues and epilogues, where the player speaks simultaneously in character and in his or her own person.

How this affected the acting of the play itself is not certain: but the style would certainly have been presentational rather than realistic – at a time when rituals of 'presentation' were, of course, prominent in everyday behaviour as well. So, with directors unthought of, and playwrights far less involved in the practical business of mounting a play than their Elizabethan counterparts, the influence of the dancing-master was probably strong in matters of movement and stage grouping. As Jocelyn Powell aptly summed it up: 'The atmosphere of the Restoration theatre was that of a sophisticated cabaret.'

Of those managers seeking the 'patents' which would permit them to create theatrical companies amidst the political confusion of Charles's return, the two successful bidders were both men of influence at court, who had had experience of theatre before the Civil Wars: Sir William Davenant and Thomas Killigrew. Davenant had even succeeded in getting 'plays with music' produced under Cromwell's guard. After the Restoration, Davenant was given his royal patent to manage the Duke's Company (so called because it enjoyed the patronage of the Duke of York), which first played in a converted 'real' tennis court at Lincoln's Inn Fields – the older theatres having been pulled down or left derelict during the Civil Wars. They moved in 1671 to a playhouse purpose-built by Christopher Wren – the Dorset Garden Theatre, beside the Thames, where many of Aphra Behn's plays, including *The Rover*, were performed. Killigrew's company, known as the King's Company on account of enjoying the king's own patronage, played in another converted tennis court until the first Theatre Royal was completed in 1663, to be replaced after its destruction by fire by a new playhouse in 1674, which is where *The Country Wife* was first performed. (The foundations of this 1674 theatre are still visible under the stage of the present Theatre Royal Drury Lane.)

With just two companies of less than thirty players apiece – reduced to a single 'united' company from 1682 to 1695 – acting was thus an exclusive though not prestigious profession, its members as well-known personally to many in the audience as their own acquaintances in the pit or boxes. And, although the patents stressed that the introduction of actresses was a matter of morality – to correct the abuse of men appearing 'in the habits of women' – intimacy between these players and their audiences was not confined to closeness in the auditorium. It was probably inevitable that, in the absence of a traditional route for women into the profession, some actresses in a licentious age should have achieved their positions through sexual patronage – though it's also indisputable that Elizabeth Barry, despite her path being smoothed by the notorious rake Lord Rochester, became a truly great tragic actress, while Nell Gwyn, although she owed her early chances to being the mistress of a leading player, Charles Hart, became no less striking a comic actress before she caught the eye of the king.

Other actresses, such as the great Thomas Betterton's wife Mary, were nonetheless able to lead lives of untainted virtue at a time when such behaviour in courtly society was almost eccentric. The fine comic actress Anne Bracegirdle even managed to sustain a reputation for excessive prudishness in private life. This did not, however, prevent her being thought fair game for predatory males: as late as 1692, an assault on her honour was compounded by the murder of the actor William Mountford, who had tried to intervene on her behalf. Those guilty were not severely punished.

This was an age when Rochester might order Dryden to be beaten up in a back alley for an imagined satirical slight; when the king himself could instigate an assault upon a parliamentarian who had dared to criticise his mistresses; and when Rochester and Sedley could attempt the rape of an heiress in broad daylight. The mixture of violence and casual sexuality which Aphra Behn presents even less discreetly than most of her contemporaries – in Willmore, almost with pride – is thus a reflection on the stage of the very brittle veneer of politeness which barely concealed the viciousness of much high-society life.

The King, the Court, and the Courtesans

The character of Charles II might very easily have been conceived as the hero of a Wycherley play – dour, cynical, and introverted at heart, yet capable of a pretty wit, and sexually attractive beyond the advantages of force majeure. Whether his personality was shaped by exile, or simply well adapted to it, the fact remains that, before the Restoration, Charles enjoyed the semblance of both power and responsibility without the reality of either: life became, in short, a form of play-acting. Later, when the king strolled, supposedly incognito but recognised by all, into the House of Lords to listen to a debate, he would declare the entertainment as good as a play, and sardonically join in the laughter at veiled references to himself.

In exile, Charles had pursued his women with no less fervour then Willmore in *The Rover* – choosing his mistresses from among his own camp-followers, the nobility of the French court, or the brothels of Paris with the impartiality of a glutton for sex rather than a connoisseur of beauty. Back home, Charles's male companions were drawn largely from a promiscuous, hard-drinking, but highly literate set which included – besides the notorious Earl of Rochester – the Duke of Buckingham, Sir George Etherege and Charles Sedley, all playwrights, as much probably from fashion as inclination, just as in other ages courtiers might have been concerned to excel at hunting deer, jousting, or grouse-shooting.

These were men to whom casual violence came readily, and who trod with equanimity that uneasy tightrope between rape and seduction, between brutality and the defence of honour, which is so often reflected in the plays they wrote and watched. A regular attender at the theatres, Charles himself is said to have lent a hand in the writing of plays, and he also interested himself in matters of casting. He both encouraged and emulated the Restoration 'style', in dramatic art as in life – and apparently displayed it as freely among women of good breeding as among his male cronies or his concubines. It made for sexual equality, of a sort.

When the dynastic imperative finally cornered the king into marriage, he took to wife the unfortunate princess Catherine of Braganza – in part to safeguard the alliance with her native Portugal, in part to produce for the nation an unquestionably legitimate heir. This she failed to do – so perpetuating the long drawn-out crisis over the ever-likelier succession of Charles's Catholic brother, James. The king's treatment of his wife in many ways epitomised the double standards of Restoration Comedy. In private, he humiliated her by appointing his own mistresses – successively, Barbara Villiers, Countess of Castlemaine, and Louise de Kéroualle, Duchess of Portsmouth – as ladies of her bedchamber. Yet in public he allowed a curious sense of honour to guide his political instinct, and when the Whigs backed Titus Oates's allegations of Catherine's complicity in a plot to poison her husband, they misjudged their man. Charles refused to put away his wife, the allegations collapsed – and the Whigs, by then espousing the cause of Charles's illegitimate son, Monmouth, lost all credibility, along with their hopes of excluding James from the succession.

Aphra Behn flayed the Whigs with impunity in *The City Heiress* in 1682, but when she widened her target to include Monmouth himself, in her prologue to *Romulus and Hersilia* later that year, she was arrested, and at least severely reprimanded. Charles's affection for his unruly bastard son, or some perverse sense of his far-flung family's dignity, never entirely deserted him – nor, of course, did he forget his mistresses, of whom two of the most prominent came from the theatre. Mary Davis he took from the Duke's company, and the almost legendary Nell Gwyn from the King's – where her position was due to real talent and wit as well as to her undoubted beauty. When, at the height of the crisis over the succession to the throne, Nell's coach was mistaken for that of Charles's Catholic mistress, the Duchess of Portsmouth, Nell Gwyn famously won over a jostling mob by declaring from the window, 'Pray, good people, be civil. I am the protestant whore!' The line displays all the wry, self-aware sexuality of one of Aphra Behn's new women. Aphra and Nell were, in fact, close friends.

Even in death, Charles exhibited something like the last-act repentance of a rake from Restoration Comedy: at the prompting of Lady Portsmouth, he was attended by a priest, and made a deathbed conversion to Catholicism – the priest, by a fine irony, taking the covert, backstairs route to his bedchamber well-worn by so many of Charles's mistresses. And among his last words were those of commendation to his brother James: 'Let not poor Nelly starve.' In a room filled with as many illegitimate offspring as could be hastily assembled, neither Nell Gwyn nor any of his other women were permitted to pay their last respects. 'Poor Nelly' died of an apoplexy soon after. There is little in Restoration Comedy which exceeds Charles's personal excesses, or typifies better than his own conduct the mixture of calculation and generosity – and, to our sensibility, the sexual double-standards – which cloaked the Restoration 'wit'.

The Country Wife

William Wycherley (1641-1715)

William Wycherley was baptised on 8 April 1641 at Clive, near Shrewsbury. He was educated as a gentleman and sent to France to complete his education in 1656, returning to

England in 1660. He briefly attended Oxford University
before entering the Inner Temple, which offered the legal
equivalent of a university education. Wycherley probably
accompanied the British ambassador to Spain in January
1664 and served in a naval battle, probably the battle off
Harwich in 1665. His first published work was a satirical
poem, *Hero and Leander in Burlesque* (1669), but he achieved
considerable success with his first play, *Love in a Wood: or, St
James's Park* (1671). Its success led to an affair with the
Duchess of Cleveland that gained Wycherley entry to court
circles and established him as a wit alongside such figures as
the Earl of Rochester and Sir Charles Sedley. Wycherley's
second, less successful, play, *The Gentleman Dancing Master*
(1672), adapted from Calderón, was followed by what is now
generally regarded as his masterpiece, *The Country Wife* (1675).
His 1676 drama *The Plain Dealer* gained him the epithet
'Manly' after its leading character. His career was virtually
ended in 1678 by a severe illness, probably encephalitis, that
appears to have affected his memory and his writing skills. He
wrote no more plays and many of his subsequently published
poems may have been polished by the young Alexander
Pope, who befriended him in the early eighteenth century.

Although the last half of Wycherley's life was theatrically
unproductive, aspects of it were themselves highly theatrical,
offering proof that the world of Restoration drama was not as
remote from reality as some later critics have tried to claim.
In 1679 Wycherley married the Countess of Drogheda, who,
according to the seventeenth-century critic John Dennis,
insisted that if he went to the local tavern he should always
be visible from their lodgings across the road so that she
could check that there were no women with him. When she
died in 1681 her family made every effort to prevent
Wycherley from getting hold of her estate, and the various
claims and counter-claims were not settled until 1700.
Wycherley fell out of favour at court as a result of his marriage
and was even imprisoned for debt for several years. On his
eventual release he lived quietly at Clive until his father's
death in 1697 when he returned to London. Intrigue and
domestic drama re-entered his life just before his death
almost twenty years later. Apparently as part of a plot to

disinherit his nephew, Wycherley married a much younger woman, Elizabeth Jackson. After Wycherley's death she married Thomas Shrimpton, who had introduced her to Wycherley in the first place and whose mistress she had been. Wycherley's nephew subsequently alleged that he had been coerced into the marriage but lost his case. Wycherley died on New Year's Eve, 1715.

Comedy of Humours

Like many of his contemporaries, Wycherley draws heavily on Ben Jonson's satirical Comedy of Humours in choosing for his characters names that are an often ironic guide to dominant facets of their personalities. 'Horner', for example, suggests someone who gives cuckolds the horns that were metaphorically associated with their state. 'Pinchwife' indicates a man whose wife will be pinched, in the sense both of being sexually teased and of being stolen from him. 'Dainty' and 'Squeamish' belie their names in not being fastidious about anything except pretending to an outward appearance of sexual modesty and honourable behaviour (women's honour was conceived of as resting entirely in their sexual fidelity). 'Fidget' applies differentially to Sir Jaspar and Lady Fidget: he is always rushing off to another appointment, she is itching for sex. 'Sparkish' is formed from 'spark', a term for the kind of witty gentlemen also called 'wits', but he is only spark-ish because he is a pretender to wit, whereas Harcourt and Horner and the shadowy Dorilant are true wits. Even the doctor (Quack) who acts as Horner's confidant has a name that contributes to the general atmosphere of pretension and hypocrisy.

Such names point to a kind of debasement of values in the world of the play, but there are others that stand outside this mechanistic world. The name 'Alithea' suggests 'other goddess', and has associations with truth (and in the form 'Althea', with wholesomeness); it quite literally elevates her nominal status above the other characters whose names are almost all associated with physical activity. Since Alithea is Pinchwife's sister, her name is presumably Alithea Pinchwife, but she is never referred to by this name. This contrasts with the way that Margery Pinchwife tends to have her identity obscured by being thought of as 'the country wife', being dressed as her supposed brother, or being taken to Horner in the belief that she is Alithea. She seems to exist in terms of definitions imposed on her by others. Alithea, on the other hand, is much more of a free agent: she is known by her first name, thus defining herself as her own person rather than someone else's. Alithea as a name also indicates the character's separation from the majority of the other characters. Something similar happens with Frank Harcourt, who is indeed normally frank and open about his feelings but finds it hard to court Alithea because of her misplaced confidence that Sparkish's lack of jealousy is based on a genuine respect for her. Their names suggest that Alithea and Frank are a corrective to the materialistic/mechanical cynicism of the other characters.

Love, Marriage and Money

Many men and women were trapped in unions without affection, and the inevitable result was distrust, jealousy, and contempt. Sir Jaspar Fidget, for example, needs someone to entertain his wife without causing any scandal, a task Horner is apparently perfectly suited to since he is socially acceptable but, so he says, physically incapable of having sex with Lady Fidget. Sir Jaspar's bargain with Horner is purely economic, a kind of service contract in which Horner acts as a surrogate non-sexual husband in return for free meals. He is quite happy to purchase the outward appearance of a husband because he is unwilling to make the necessary commitment himself. It is this that makes Horner's sexual relationship with Sir Jaspar's wife an apt punishment for Sir Jaspar's posturing: Horner offers his wife more services than Sir Jaspar had bargained for, the substance as well as the appearance. The cuckolding of Sir Jaspar Fidget is a dramatic comment on the lack of any emotional ties in the marriage; and, of course, Lady Fidget is quite happy to follow her husband's example, providing her outward honour is not compromised.

Similarly, the Pinchwife marriage is a matter of convenience

rather than love. The ageing Pinchwife's motives for
marrying the young Margery are cynical, self-centred and
devoid of anything like emotional commitment. Pinchwife
marries a 'country wife' in order to avoid the pitfalls
associated with sophisticated London women and to profit
from the presumed innocence of a girl brought up in the
country. Pinchwife's first line to Margery is 'You're a fool'
(p. 23). He then instructs her to love him as a matter of duty,
and there is never a suggestion that the relationship should
be reciprocal. Since he knows that Margery has no reason to
be faithful, he becomes increasingly jealous, possessive and
violent, thus driving her ever faster into the arms of a lover.

Alithea is Pinchwife's sister and thus has first-hand experience
of a jealous man. She is taken in by Sparkish because he
appears to be constitutionally incapable of jealousy, whereas
he is simply stupid. Harcourt poses a problem not only
because Alithea finds herself attracted to him, but also
because Sparkish's obstinate refusal to be jealous of Harcourt
seems in itself to be a proof of his trust in her. Finally, when
Sparkish immediately believes Pinchwife's allegations against
her, Alithea feels free to respond to Harcourt, who has
consistently courted her on the basis that mutual love is
more important than mercenary considerations.

Marriage is, then, a vital component of the play. Only
Harcourt and Alithea's relationship seems to suggest a future
happy marriage because it is based on mutual esteem rather
than on the purely economic and social factors that define
the other relationships in the play. The ways in which *The
Country Wife* exposes the failings of one set of approaches to
human relationships transcends the immediate context to
suggest the dangers of any view of human relationships in
which partners are seen either in terms of the property they
bring with them or as sex objects.

Horner

Although the treatment of marriage is crucial, the satire of
pretensions to honour incarnated in Horner is the most
dynamic aspect of the play. Much of the pleasure in

watching or reading *The Country Wife* depends on dramatic irony, the way that the audience shares Horner's superior position. Because we share his perspective for much of the play, we tend to align ourselves with the satirical attack on those who hide a voracious sexual appetite behind a screen of hypocritical respectability. Horner is clearly the medium for Wycherley's satire, but is he himself the object of satirical attacks?

Perhaps Horner's obsession with collecting sexual scalps cuts him off from the kind of happiness that we might postulate for Harcourt and Alithea at the end of the play. Perhaps, isolated and reduced simply to a source of sexual gratification (as in the 'china' scene where his sexual supplies are soon exhausted), he becomes just as much a victim of his own stratagem as the Fidgets and the Pinchwifes. His revenge on husbands who treat their wives like objects is to reduce himself to an object, a kind of sex machine. He is not interested in the quality of the sex he gets but rather in its quantity, a glutton rather than a gourmet.

Horner does stand alone in the play: Harcourt and Dorilant are apparently his friends, yet he never shares his secret with them, allowing them to be completely misled, and he is apparently prepared to sacrifice Alithea and Harcourt to preserve his cover. Even at the end of the play, only the audience, Margery, the three hypocritical ladies and the quack know the nature of his pretence. He has quite deliberately cut himself off from other types of social intercourse, in favour of a kind of production-line orgasm. So it is just possible to see him as a kind of victim of his own trick, a man condemned to mechanical sexual encounters at the expense of a full life, but this is to ignore the ways in which Horner appears on stage in the course of the play in production.

Horner is the character who most engages our attention. While he may be a sexual glutton, he does appear to relish his successes. Moreover, he can scarcely be a tragic figure if he doesn't reach self-knowledge of his predicament or if it is not revealed to other characters. Within the world of the play, we enjoy watching a witty man triumph over ineffective opposition, but his amatory successes are achieved in a world he despises. The way in which we react to Horner parallels the way Wycherley presents his vision of a rotten society: we may well applaud Horner's technical skill in dealing with his society but simultaneously deplore the heartless nature of his and its behaviour. This polarity in our attitude to Horner reflects two central disjunctions in the society within the play: a) between marriage as practised by Fidget and Pinchwife and marriage as seen by Alithea and Harcourt, and b) between techniques or conventions on the one hand and the reality on the other. In other words, we can distinguish between two separate attitudes to Horner: on the one hand we admire his skill but, on the other, we deplore his approach to sex. This duality of response reflects the way in which this society has separated the outward from the inner reality. Horner not only exposes the other characters' corruption, but he also comments on their corruption. By contrast, no one ever comments on Horner; his satirical superiority to the other characters is unchallenged, and he remains consistent in his disguise. None of the other characters is able to penetrate his ruse without his help. Our attention is always being directed by him rather than at him.

The Visual and the Verbal

All the characters reveal the true nature that lies under their masks to Horner; the play's action is organised to manifest this linguistically as well as visually. It is particularly concerned with the questions of disguise and unmasking (as in the case of Margery being dressed as a boy) and with the demonstration of self-deception and hypocrisy (as in the 'china' scene where Horner conceals the Quack so that he can watch the process in action and comment on it like a chorus). At the end of 5.1 when Margery manages to pretend to be Alithea so that she can escape from Pinchwife, the jealous husband unwittingly brings his wife to the man who wants to make love to her because his jealousy has made him blind to the deception. The outward appearance that Margery is Alithea takes Pinchwife in, just as elsewhere in the play, people are taken in by Horner's outward

appearance of being a eunuch or by Lady Fidget's pretence
to honour. When Pinchwife cannot see beyond his sister's
gown to his wife beneath, we have an actual embodiment of
the kind of blinkered perception that prevents most of the
characters penetrating the others' surface pretensions to
honour and chastity.

The actual language of the play is important for the way in
which it consistently suggests differences between outward
appearance and inner realities. The many references to the
theatre, for example, remind us that what we are watching -
and tacitly assuming to be 'real' - is a fiction. The whole
play is also peppered with similes and analogies, particularly
between animal and human life. The use of nature imagery
tends to be reductive: when Harcourt and Horner talk of
drones, or Horner compares women and spaniels, or Alithea
and Margery talk of their existence in terms of being
caged birds, we are asked to see animal life as a degradation
of human potential. This reductive approach in nature
imagery is matched by a consistent reduction of human
emotions and values to questions of appetite, disease or
economic value. Everyone except Alithea and Harcourt sees
love, marriage, emotion and honour in strictly pragmatic
terms, as sex, contract, appetite and pretence. Alithea and
Harcourt stand somewhat outside this linguistic pattern, as
they stand somewhat outside the world of cuckoldry.
Harcourt refers to Alithea in terms which suggest her quasi-
divine status, and, in a comedy where disguises are rife, his
is as a priest.

Town and Country

Pinchwife is under the impression that the country is a
virtuous place just as the town is vicious. Often in
seventeenth-century literature the country was held up as a
superior place. This partly reflects the classical interest in
pastoral, partly the sense that towns were increasingly large
and complex places in contrast to which the country could
be seen as a kind of idyllic escape from urban pressures and
vices. In part it related to disquiet with the growth of trade

and a conservative nostalgia for a simpler life, in part to the complex interactions of the post-Commonwealth period. However, as Horner remarks, 'I have known a clap gotten in Wales', and the very innocence of the country is betrayed by the sexual pun in the word itself. The difference between country values and town values is the difference between Margery and Lady Fidget, between an honest delight in sex and a hypocritical one. Pinchwife is wrong in his assumptions about the merits of town and country because he does not understand that what matters is the human nature under the mask of manners; that it is the individual heart and mind that produce chastity, not the physical stress on chastity that produces chaste attitudes.

The Country Wife on Stage

In the nineteenth century, Macaulay wrote that Wycherley's 'indecency' 'protected him against critics in the same way that a skunk was protected against hunters: it is safe because it is too filthy to handle and too noisome even to approach'. In the theatre this view held from the mid-eighteenth century when Garrick produced his sanitised *The Country Girl*. *The Country Wife* itself was not revived until the 1920s, and its theatrical reputation has grown steadily ever since, even surviving a Glasgow Citizens' Theatre 1970s version reduced to mono-dimensional satire without the Alithea/Harcourt plot.

Although Macaulay's view still has some supporters, it confuses explicit interest in sex with pornography. *The Country Wife* does present human relationships reduced to the mechanical and materialistic, but its world is not a pornographic one: it is very clearly aware of the dangers of promiscuous sex in the form of venereal disease, since Horner's whole stratagem is based on being impotent as the result of treatment for just such a disease. Equally, Alithea and Harcourt offer a marked contrast to the mechanistic Newtonian attitudes of the Fidgets, the Pinchwifes and Horner.

The Country Wife survives as a challenging theatrical work because it explores a basic question of timeless relevance in a sophisticated and memorable way: how should men and women relate to one another? It adopts a memorable comic and satirical form to demonstrate how one society organised itself and what was wrong with that organisation. It does pose problems for those who want certainty from their plays: is Horner a hero, a villain, a satirical mouthpiece or a satirical butt? This very ambivalence is a measure of the way in which Wycherley has managed to produce an open-ended, sceptical play whose careful construction operates to make us ask ourselves the same fundamental question: how should I act? The mirror that Wycherley holds up to nature contains not only an image of his own times but a reflection of our own and any age that questions its own motivations and beliefs.

The Rover

Aphra Behn (1640–1689)

Aphra Amies, Johnson or Cooper (her maiden name is uncertain) is thought to have been born near Canterbury, in Kent, in the summer of 1640. In her early twenties her father was appointed Lieutenant-General of the then British colony of Surinam, in South America, but died on the voyage out to the Guianas. She stayed long enough to absorb the experiences which were later to shape her novel *Oronooko* but returned home to England in the spring of 1664. Within a year she was married to Mr Behn – an elusive figure, possibly a Dutch merchant with Guianese connections, who died soon afterwards, perhaps during the Great Plague of 1665. One of the managers of London's two theatre companies, Thomas Killigrew, an intimate of the recently restored king, Charles II, was evidently instrumental in Aphra Behn being briefly employed as a spy during the Dutch wars (which saw Surinam ceded to the Netherlands), but by 1667 she was again in London – and in the following year was imprisoned for debt, despite Killigrew's intercession on her behalf.

Until she reached the age of thirty, Behn's life was full of false starts and uncertainties. In that year, 1670, however, she not only established her career as a playwright – with a tragi-comedy called *The Forced Marriage*, which enjoyed a moderate success at the theatre in Lincoln's Inn Fields – but began a relationship with the dissolute lawyer John Hoyle, one of several supposed originals for Willmore in *The Rover*. For the following twelve years she became a fully professional playwright – an exceptional career for a woman at that time – writing some twenty plays, most of them comedies for the new Dorset Garden Theatre.

By the early 1680s, however, fashionable London was becoming more preoccupied with politics than with theatre. The then emerging Whig and Tory factions were at odds over the right of the king's Catholic brother, James, to succeed to the throne in the event of Charles remaining without a legitimate heir. In 1682 Aphra Behn contributed an allegedly 'abusive' and 'scandalous' prologue to an anonymous anti-Whig play, and found herself again under arrest. She was let off with a caution, but thereafter turned increasingly to the safer forms of fiction and poetry – though she enjoyed a final stage triumph in 1687 with a highly original, commedia-style farce, *The Emperor of the Moon*, before publishing what was for long her best-known work, the novel *Oronooko*, in 1688. The death of Charles in the same year, and the 'Bloodless Revolution' which saw off the hapless James, marked the end of the world Aphra Behn had known, and she died the following April, just before her forty-ninth birthday.

The Return of the Banished Cavaliers

The events which restored Charles II to the English throne in May 1660 were fast-moving: as late as September 1659, both Charles and his brother James had appeared to be making plans for an indefinite exile. Much had to be done during the new king's 'honeymoon' with his people, and it is a measure of the importance attached by Charles to theatrical matters that he seems to have given as much urgent attention to sorting out the squabbles between the various entrepreneurs vying to form new theatrical companies as to reconciling the old enemies of the civil wars.

After his apparently final defeat at Worcester in 1651, exile for Charles had been a relatively comfortable affair, passed mainly in the civilised if often conspiratorial surroundings of Paris and Brussels: but for many of the followers of the king and his 'martyred' father, the interregnum was spent in a constant struggle against hardship. Some laid low at home, their estates confiscated or sold off piecemeal to meet fines for their 'delinquency'. Others, like Belvile and Willmore in *The Rover*, became soldiers or sailors of fortune, accumulating mistresses, booty, or battle honours with equally offhand loyalty.

Most of the young Restoration gallants, now returning to England along with their king, would thus in all probability have spent a childhood or adolescence in the turbulent atmosphere of civil war, the early years of their adult life cut off from both family traditions and the sense of service which possession of land could still, on occasion, instil. Nor did the compromise between the old and new interests we call the 'Restoration settlement' return to the original owners the estates that had been sold off by persecuted royalists to puritan land-grabbers. Lacking roots, but often bearing a load of such grudges, these 'rovers' saw little reason not to pursue in England the kind of sexual and economic opportunism which had ruled their life-style in exile. Such opportunism was duly reflected in the plays they watched and wrote.

Besides, there was even a sort of moral justification for living out the belief that 'debauchery was loyalty, gravity rebellion': for inverting the detested values of puritanism was surely to be commended. And an open delight in sexual dalliance (as in theatricality) happily coincided with the tastes of the restored monarch. No wonder that Charles's court in Whitehall proved such a magnet, and that its values permeated the life and attitudes of 'the town' – the residential and shopping area of the fashionable West End, of which Covent Garden was then the youthful heart and the Strand the main artery.

By contrast, 'the city' was the City of London, further east, whose tradesmen and financiers, tainted with puritan

sympathies, became the 'cits' so often mocked in the
prologues, epilogues and cuckoldings of Restoration Comedy.
That the king, no less than his courtiers, was often dependent
on the financial assistance of these worthies made it, of course,
all the more necessary to display them as semi-illiterate
upstarts in the theatre – which the 'cits' nonetheless
attended, sometimes in such numbers as to spoil Samuel
Pepys's enjoyment. In the 'party' system now for the first
time emerging in British politics, it was from the 'cits' and
the interests of money that the Whigs drew their main
strength, with the 'Tories' representing the more traditional
and largely rural interests of 'land'.

The tensions of a nation and a capital which remained so
divided were reflected in its theatre. Although the setting of
The Rover is one of exile in a faraway country, its values are
those of men restored to their country, but not to their own.
Thus, the thwarting of an aged father's wish to marry his
daughter to a rich but geriatric suitor is an age-old theme of
comedy: but whereas the contemporary commedia made
prominent characters of its Pantaloons and their doddering
friends, it is significant that Behn keeps Florinda's stern
father and the dyspeptic Don Vincentio permanently off-
stage. The traditional struggles between the values of youth
and age, poverty and wealth, give way here to just the kind
of internecine sexual warfare in which the 'banished
cavaliers' of real life continued to drown – or to sublimate –
their sorrows.

The Professionalism of Aphra Behn

The theatre of the period differed from Shakespeare's in that
most playwrights were not formally attached to a particular
company. Dryden's contract to write three plays a year in
return for becoming a 'sharer' in the King's Company was
unusual – and unfulfilled. Generally, the professional writer
was dependent upon the benefit system, whereby the profits
of the third night's performance – and perhaps of the sixth,
and exceptionally of the ninth – were allocated to the author.
A good benefit could reap as much as £100, with a further

lump sum possible for publication: but there was no guarantee that any play would even reach the third night, and it was thus as important that a sympathetic audience should give a rousing reception on the first night as that a rich one (perhaps willing to pay well over the expected price for their seats) should fill the house on the third.

Those males scandalised by Aphra Behn, who dared to affront 'the modesty of her sex' by writing as bawdily as they, did not even deign to consider the element of economic necessity that drove her to satisfy the prevailing tastes of the town. She was among the more prolific of Restoration playwrights in part because she had to be – and the total of at least sixteen plays performed during her lifetime is thus in marked contrast with, say, Wycherley's four, or Congreve's six. When she declared in the preface to her late comedy *The Lucky Chance* (1686) that she was 'not content to write for a third night only', she may have been staking a conventional claim to be writing for posterity as well as for money: but her long association with Dorset Garden and the regularity of her output may suggest some more formal financial arrangement with the Duke's Company than the chances of the benefit system allowed.

In 1682, the two companies merged, in consequence of the decline in theatre attendances in the wake of the political crises of Charles's later years; and the United Company cut its costs still further by staging a higher proportion of revivals, whose dead authors made no claim upon diminishing receipts. Other playwrights, such as Behn's friends Thomas Otway and William Wycherley, fared no better, and John Dryden was forced to seek meagre government patronage. Classically educated males could at least turn to publishing translations as an alternative source of income – whereas Aphra Behn, in contributing to a version of Ovid, had to work from someone else's draft translation. Greek and Latin were no part of the expected female 'accomplishments'.

Aphra Behn enjoyed renewed stage success in later life – notably with *The Lucky Chance* and the strikingly original *The Emperor of the Moon*. But increasingly – and in not dissimilar

circumstances to her eighteenth-century successor, Henry
Fielding – she turned from plays to writing novels. In 1688,
the year before her death, she published *Oronooko*, the work
by which she probably remains best known – its anti-slavery
theme anticipating Harriet Beecher Stowe, and its element of
noble savagery even foreshadowing Rousseau. Whether or
not she was the first 'true' novelist, before such aspirants as
Defoe, Richardson and Fielding, depends on one's definition
of the novel – a form in which, however, women writers
were to overcome assumptions of male supremacy with
greater success than (until very recently) they challenged male
chauvinism in the theatre.

The Sexual Economics of the Restoration

The 'values of family life' may not have been a Victorian
invention, but in most earlier drama and literature little love
is expected to be lost between fathers and sons, elder and
younger brothers, or even (once trapped in marriage)
husbands and wives. The death of a wealthy father or elder
brother is usually a matter for congratulation among the
friends of the fortunate heir – while marriage, of course, has
everything to do with the businesslike arrangement of
property and dynasties, and very little to do with the
affections. True love, before marriage or after, is reserved for
a mistress – though in most romantic comedies, where love is
actually permitted to culminate in marriage, the hopeful
suitor by luck or judgement usually gets a respectable fortune
besides.

In real life, the young couple might not even have met
before their parents or go-betweens had finished arranging
the match. (Ordinary working folk could, ironically, better
'afford' to marry for love the less they could afford anything
else: but, until quite recently, ordinary working folk have not
much figured in great literature or theatre, other than as
comic relief.) And the matter was further complicated by the
'sexual revolution' which led Charles I to declare in 1664
that 'the passion of love is very much out of fashion in this
country'. Even the once-adored mistress was now regarded as

for sexual satisfaction only – an object of that curious combination of arousal and disgust which permeates the poems of such burnt-out rakes as Rochester. And the disgust is perhaps most readily heaped on those women who tried reciprocally to exercise the sexual freedom they had supposedly been granted.

Aphra Behn herself advocated a liberalised sexuality for women. But she acknowledged that the lack of an equivalent economic independence (combined with the fear or actuality of childbirth and the earlier loss of physical charms) constrained women from exercising their 'freedom' from a position of any other equality than that of their wits. And freedom of sexual movement was not freedom of social movement: the over-compliant mistress was still widely regarded as no better than a whore – to which status abandonment or decline could all too often reduce her. If Restoration actresses also called themselves 'Mrs', it was not because they had all been married, but because 'Miss' had come to be suggestive merely of sexual availability. Mrs Behn herself enjoyed the relative independence from male domination that only widowhood could bring – but not the inherited fortune that would have added security to freedom.

Aphra Behn was not above evading the problem in her plays – or rather, not above reconciling it, as many writers had done and would do again, by such a device as she used in *The Dutch Lover*, where, for all her heroine's vaunted rebellion against paternal choice, her preferred lover turns out to be her father's selected suitor as well. And if the very title of Behn's first play, *The Forced Marriage*, anticipates the importance of the theme to her writing, by her second, *The Amorous Prince*, she was falling back on the convention that the most promiscuous rake will assuredly reform when the final curtain looms.

The Town Fop showed the horrific consequences of a forced marriage, from which the participants are only released thanks to the hero's earlier, legally-binding pledge of marriage to his mistress. The father, meanwhile, has had time to see the consequences of his own preference – which include the hero spending half his unwanted wife's portion on a debauch. But no resolution is offered by Behn to the economic and sexual plight of the rejected wife – a 'loose end' not dissimilar to that in *The Rover* of the scorned Angellica, in whom the playwright seems to have invested a considerable, perhaps all too personal passion.

Aphra Behn, then, made no pretence of having resolved, dramatically or personally, all the problems posed by the combination of new attitudes to sexuality with very old attitudes to other kinds of freedom. In many ways she was no less equivocal or downright muddled about sex than most of her male counterparts – though she probably did recognise, as her biographer Angeline Goreau expresses it, that the 'liberated' wits of the Restoration were fearfully if unconsciously obsessed with 'the possibility that women might have sexual desires that were independent of their role as passive receptacles of male desire'.

That Hellena in *The Rover* falls in love with Willmore for all the wrong reasons may tell us more about Aphra Behn's own unfortunate liaisons than about Hellena: but neither the character nor her creator was a 'passive receptacle'. What Behn did achieve, in her writing if not in her life, was a triumphant assertion of women's rights to their own sexuality, and at least the tentative expression – if her plays were to remain commercial, it could be no more than tentative – of her belief that true sexual satisfaction for both men and women lay in close and reciprocal relationships, not in the yoking of sexuality to property rights and family trees.

'The Injuries of Age and Time'

For a woman whose plays make what appear to us quite proper claims for the independence of her sex, Aphra Behn numbered among her closest acquaintances many men – apart from the king himself, the likes of Sedley, Buckingham, and Rochester – who were liberated in their own sexuality, but unenlightened in their attitudes towards women. Rochester, like most of these courtly wits, was no 'mere' rake. Though credited with training one of his mistresses, Elizabeth Barry, for the stage, he undertook the exercise less

from interest in her own non-sexual attributes than to win a
bet with his male companions. Behn was indebted to
Rochester as a patron, but appears genuinely to have liked
and admired the man, with whom she exchanged bawdy
poems. A chronic drunkard as well as a poet, a ravisher of
pretty women and a fancier of young boys, Rochester, who is
often named as the model for the fashionable wit Dorimant
in Etherege's *The Man of Mode*, was capable of scandalising
even the king's sense of decency with some of his more
public outrages.

Rochester may well have been on Aphra Behn's mind when
she tried to make Willmore in *The Rover* so sexually magnetic.
But there were others in Behn's circle with a claim to be the
model for such a character. There was John Greenhill, the
highly talented portrait painter, who, like Rochester, died
probably of syphilis in his early thirties. Aphra Behn wrote
an elegy to his memory and sent a copy to Rochester: he
had at least been spared 'the injuries of age and time'. In
lighter-hearted vein, she made poetic mock of another male
acquaintance for his misfortune in contracting syphilis – not
an uncommon ailment in her circle, and one from which she
was possibly herself a sufferer in later years. If so, she
probably picked up the disease during the longest and
stormiest of her own love affairs, with the bisexual rake,
lawyer, man of letters, and chief claimant to be the original
of Willmore – John Hoyle.

Suspected of the republican sympathies which had led his
father to take his own life, Hoyle was in other respects
entirely a man of the Restoration. He was attractive to
women, and appears to have treated all his conquests with the
amused contempt which so exasperated Aphra Behn. Her
poems suggest that, despite her own previous liaisons, this
affair – which would have been at its tempestuous height
around the time she was writing *The Rover* – was the one in
which she felt the most complete consummation of her sexual
passion. Yet Hoyle kept Behn, like all his mistresses, at a distance, pursuing his other affairs while wishing her to remain
faithful to him alone; inflicting casual insults upon her, yet
highly sensitive to any imagined slights in her own behaviour.

Aphra Behn's remaining letters to Hoyle seem to be half-persuading, half-pleading for the kind of freedom, combined with commitment of the heart, to which Hellena in *The Rover* believes she had led Willmore. But Behn's biographer Angeline Goreau suggests that part of Hoyle's attraction was precisely the knowledge that she would never be called upon to act out the role of wife for him, any more than that of conventional mistress. She suffered, but she kept her freedom. So, presumably, did her Hellena – who conspicuously fails to appear in the undistinguished sequel to *The Rover*, The Second Part of *The Rover* (1680), in which Willmore has conveniently become a widower.

The death of Charles II in 1685 marked the close of an era that was already turning sour. John Hoyle was tried inconclusively for sodomy in 1687, by which time the affair with Behn was probably over. He outlived her only by three years, before being killed in a tavern brawl – for which his murderer successfully pleaded self-defence. Greenhill and Rochester were already dead, burned out by debauchery, and Buckingham was not only out of favour politically but 'worn to a thread with whoring'. Among Aphra Behn's playwriting friends, Wycherley was in a debtors' prison, Nathaniel Lee was on public exhibition in a madhouse, and Otway was starving to death in a slum – despite, it seems, some financial help from Behn, although she was herself in debt. She died – some said of a minor ailment ineptly treated – with a fine sense of timing, a few days after the coronation of William and Mary, whose accession ended the era with whose values Aphra Behn was so closely identified. *The Rover*, written in 1677, just a year before the 'Popish Plot', may in retrospect be seen as one of the last celebrations of the Restoration spirit, in which no real sense of doubt or danger lurks in the darker corners of bedchamber or tavern.

The Rover as Restoration Comedy

Critics of Aphra Behn's play find themselves in a paradoxical position. The works are inseparably linked with those social

and political conditions outlined in earlier sections, as they
are also with their author's personal feelings about those
conditions. Yet we know so few details of Behn's life, outside
her purely professional activities, that any conjectural
reconstruction inevitably leads us . . . back full circle to the
plays themselves.

Perhaps the chief gain from getting caught up in this critical
double-bind is the way in which characters in Behn's plays –
which one would otherwise tend to categorise as 'types' –
come to take on ampler dimensions. Fluent gallants have
been sparring in verbal duels with their pert mistresses in a
literary lineage which stretches from Shakespeare's Beatrice
and Benedick to Congreve's Mirabell and Millamant and
beyond – for example, to Bernard Shaw's Jack Tanner and
Ann Whitefield in *Man and Superman*. And critics have
conventionally 'placed' such couples with references to the
'enduring' psychological interest of love-hate relationships, or
the downright metaphysical workings of the life-force, rather
than to the social contexts within which such sexual
masquerades were conducted. But the duels of wit in *The
Rover* – as in the other examples cited, for that matter – are
fought within a complex web of sexual, social and economic
prejudices inseparable from their time.

Or, to take a different tangent: the character regarded by
most critics, even the most sympathetic, as an unsatisfactory
loose-end to the plot, Angellica Bianca (though sharing her
initials as well as her temperament with her creator),
becomes nothing so simple as an authorial mouthpiece, or as
theatrically irrelevant as a self-portrait, but a 'loose end' left
over by society itself. Angellica is the sexually attractive
woman who has rejected the loss of independence involved
in marriage: she has therefore exploited her only form of
inherited 'capital' – her looks – in part as revenge against
the male sex, which has reduced her to that expedient. But
the repudiation by Willmore represents for her not just the
scorning of real love painfully exposed, but a first reminder
that loss of beauty will leave her with a future of economic
uncertainty as well as personal loneliness.

When the critic L.C. Knights launched his influential attack on Restoration Comedy just before the Second World War, he was using the term in its commonly vague sense, to embrace the work of Congreve, Vanbrugh, and even Farquhar – all of whom wrote long after the values of the 'chronological' Restoration had been extinguished, and who were all too conscious of the moral critique of their work initiated in 1698 by Jeremy Collier. A century or so later, all that an apologetic Charles Lamb could suggest by way of excuse for these dissolute comedies was that they were 'artificial' – set in a 'Utopia of gallantry' with 'no reference whatsoever to the world that is'. Whether or not that is true of the later plays of Congreve and Vanbrugh, Aphra Behn helps us to view the actual world of the Restoration from a new angle which also gives added depth to the work of her closer contemporaries, Etherege, Otway, and Wycherley, and confirms that all are writing about a very 'real' if limited range of experience.

The Rover, of course, is unusual in that it is not set in the fashionable West End drawing-rooms and walks of Restoration London, but in a recent past to which a due proportion of its audiences in 1677 probably looked back a mite nostalgically (just as post-Second World War Londoners often looked back fondly to the camaraderie of the Blitz, despite its dangers and deprivations). True, this is still the world of 'the town', and the rustic simpleton Ned Blunt can expect to fall into its snares as surely as he would have done in London: but the advantage of 'foreignness' also means that Belvile and his companions are less sure-footed socially, just as they are free of the constraints of class expectations or family ties. In such freedoms from traditional constraints the 'actual' Restoration sensibility also had its roots.

And so, perhaps a trifle schematically, Aphra Behn shows her exiles spanning a whole spectrum of attitudes to women and to love – from the mere loutishness of Blunt, through the butterfly charm of Willmore and the almost accidental amours of Frederick, to the romantic single-heartedness of Belvile. Each has his theatrical ancestors, but each is also part of an historical moment. Each meets his match, and gets his sexual if not his moral desserts.

All moral judgements are relative. When Gilbert Burnet cautioned Rochester against womanising, his ostensibly Christian grounds of reproof were that it was wrong to rob a father or a husband of their property. When Hellena casts off her gypsy disguise and reveals that she has a fortune at her disposal, the only choice she has in deciding its and her own fate is between a nunnery and marriage. In declaring for Willmore, she is 'disposing' of her fortune indeed. It should not have been so, of course: but precisely because Behn's characters are not living in an 'artificial' world divorced from the social mores of their time, it would have been pointless for her to attempt any more 'morally appropriate' conclusion. The only alternative is the angry independence enjoyed by Angellica, and Aphra Behn does not attempt to suggest a conclusion to that.

Many of those parents who preferred to trust their own financial acumen rather than their daughter's emotional inclinations in choosing her a husband sincerely believed that lasting security was more important to a woman than perhaps fleeting sexual fulfilment. Restoration Comedy occasionally twisted the rules of the game by allowing the two to coincide – but it also accepted that 'rules' which did not generally relate love to marriage therefore permitted love outside marriage. The alleged hypocrisy of such plays is arguably the reverse – an openness, confessedly uncritical, about a state of sexual affairs which continued well into the Victorian era, although by that time openness had been overlain with hypocrisy.

Our own confused response to Restoration Comedy suggests that it continues to touch us near the quick. It was only permissible as a kind of make-believe once the Romantics had idealised sexual relationships without altering their economic base, but it came into a somewhat prettified version of its own during the nineteen twenties, when a fresh wave of the sexual revolution broke – but again touched only the upper classes. Once the 'bright young things' of the 'twenties were swept away, Restoration Comedy suffered stern critical rebuffs in the self-improving 'forties, until the 'permissive society' seemed to be spreading a gospel of sexual openness to all sections of society. Now, productions veer between those striving to uncover the social realities beneath the conventions, and those which take the plays out of time altogether. But none can ignore, even if they seek to avoid, what emerging feminist consciousness taught us in the nineteen seventies – that 'sexual openness' no more signified equality then than it had done three hundred years earlier.

As a feminist in her own time, that is one of the things that Aphra Behn had been saying all along. As a professional playwright with no alternative source of income, she could not, however, say it very loudly. That was her critical double-bind.

The Rover on Stage

Like so many of Aphra Behn's plays, *The Rover* was written for the Dorset Garden Theatre, which had opened with Thomas Betterton as joint manager in 1671. At the first recorded performance, on 24 March 1677, Charles II was present to see Betterton take the role of Belvile, with his wife Mary as Florinda. Betterton's friend, the versatile actor William Smith, played Willmore, and the brilliant low comedian Cave Underhill took the part of Ned Blunt. Elizabeth Barry, who was to become better known for her tragic roles, played Hellena.

Although the play was revived every few years until the turn of the century, it was in the first half of the eighteenth century that it became firmly established in the repertoire, from which it was absent for only a single season between 1703 and 1743. Following in the footsteps of Will Mountfort's Willmore – 'dangerous to see', according to Queen Mary, because 'he made vice so alluring' – Robert Wilks often took the role early in the new century. Mrs Barry had graduated to Angellica by 1707. A revival at Covent Garden in 1757, with Ned Shuter an outstanding Blunt, led to further productions in the following four seasons, but the play then disappeared from the repertoire until 1790, when a bowdlerisation entitled *Love in Many Masks* was put together by Kemble for Drury Lane. The changing moral climate which necessitated this treatment explains why the stage history of *The Rover* was then interrupted for the best part of two centuries.

When, at last, the play was restored to the stage, under the direction of John Barton at the Royal Shakespeare Company's new Swan Theatre in 1986, Barton felt it needful to revise the text, incorporating material of his own along with lines from one of Behn's sources, Killigew's *Thomaso*, and to reshape the structure (which he described as 'hazy and loose in places') to clarify an otherwise 'confusing' plot. His adaptation had the great merit – along with a slightly earlier revival of *The Lucky Chance* at the Royal Court – of reclaiming a rightful place for Aphra Behn among her acknowledged Restoration contemporaries: but subsequent revivals have effortlessly reverted to Behn's text, suggesting that her plotting is neither more nor less complicated than theirs (or Shakespeare's, for that matter), just less familiar. And where Barton's production had, consciously or otherwise, glossed over the play's darker side in favour of swaggering comedy, later productions have more openly addressed Willmore's abuse of women and his friends' casual contemplation of rape, blending comedy with ambiguity in an appropriate and challenging mix.

The Way of the World

William Congreve (1670-1729)

William Congreve was born in Bardsey, Yorkshire, on 24 January 1670. He spent much of his early life in Ireland, and his interest in theatre was probably fuelled by visits to the Smock Alley Theatre when he was a classical scholar at Trinity College Dublin. His family returned to England after the 'Glorious Revolution' of 1688 and he began to read law at the Middle Temple in 1691. The great poet and dramatist John Dryden encouraged his literary career. He and the dramatist Thomas Southerne recommended the young man's first play, *The Old Bachelor*, a comedy in the tradition of George Etherege and William Wycherley, to Drury Lane in 1693. It was a major success, with a phenomenally long run, for its time, of fourteen days.

The Double Dealer (1693), Congreve's second play, was more experimental, serious, and satirical, and less successful – owing, Congreve argued, to the audience not understanding what he was trying to do. *Love for Love* (1695) was a more conventional, and more successful, comedy, and then Congreve tried his hand at heroic tragedy with *The Mourning Bride*, in 1697. Heroic tragedy has not worn well, and Congreve's effort, unlike his comedies, is seldom revived today.

Although Congreve was only thirty when *The Way of the World* was staged at the Lincoln's Inn Fields theatre in 1700, it effectively marked the end of his career as a dramatist. Dryden states that it 'had but a moderate success', and it seems that Congreve may have been trying to do something too complex for contemporary audiences. He may also have been disheartened by attacks on the supposed immorality of Restoration drama by Jeremy Collier, a disaffected clergyman, whose sonorously titled *A Short View of the Immorality and Profaneness of the English Stage* had been published in 1698.

However, Congreve continued in theatrical management at Lincoln's Inn Fields until 1705, when he joined Vanburgh in managing the Queen's Theatre. He wrote a masque, *The Judgment of Paris* (1701), an opera libretto (*Semele*, printed 1710), and had a hand in *Squire Trelooby*, an adaptation from Molière, with Vanbrugh and William Walsh in 1704. He held a number of government posts, including Secretary for Jamaica, before his death on 19 January 1729.

While Congreve's dramatic work draws heavily on both his classical and his legal training, his personal life offers an illuminating insight into the social realities of his time and the plausibility of the plots of *The Way of the World*. As well as a long-standing relationship with the actress Anne

Bracegirdle (the original Millamant in *The Way of the World*),
Congreve also had an affair with the Duchess of
Marlborough. Congreve was (and is) generally assumed to
have been the father of the Duchess's daughter, who was
born in 1723. Contemporary gossip was silenced by the
revelation that the Duke was the executor of Congreve's will.
However, the Duchess's will provided for her to be buried
near her father in Westminster Abbey, rather than with her
husband. Since Congreve had already been buried in the
Abbey (at the Duchess's instigation) and since she left her
daughter 'all Mr Congreves Personal Estate that he left me',
as well as jewels bought with money Congreve had left her,
the inference is clear. These legal tactics ensured that the
disposition of bodies and legacies matched the realities of life
as they had lived it rather than as convention dictated. They
also suggest that the legal manoeuvres of *The Way of the World*
are more solidly grounded in reality than they might appear
to a modern audience.

The Comedy of *The Way of the World*

Congreve drew his inspiration from a variety of previous
dramatists as well as from contemporary life. As a classical
scholar he knew the plays of the Roman dramatist Terence,
which feature young men hunting for legacies. He was also
operating within a theatrical tradition that valued the satirical
comedy of Ben Jonson, as developed by his own immediate
predecessors such as Etherege and Wycherley, more highly
than the romantic comedy of Shakespeare. He draws heavily
on Jonson's Comedy of Humours for the names of his
characters, giving them names that are a guide to dominant
facets of their individual characters. Generally the more
peripheral and straightforwardly comic characters like
Petulant, Mincing, and Witwoud, who actually make little
impact on the plot, are more closely defined by their names
and prevailing character traits. Lady Wishfort is a clear
exception to this, since her whole comic force depends on
her inappropriate wish for an 'iteration of nuptials'.

In his Dedication to the play, Congreve himself differentiates

his methods from contemporary theatre practice. Satirical
comedies sometimes targeted the naturally foolish rather than
those who affected a greater wit or wisdom than they
actually possessed. But Congreve stressed that an audience
should react to natural fools reflectively, with compassion and
charity, and goes on to say, 'This reflection moved me to
design some characters which should appear ridiculous not
so much through natural folly (which is incorrigible and
therefore not proper for the stage) as through an affected
wit'. This approach may also reflect Congreve's response to
Collier's attacks on the supposed immorality of Restoration
drama. Although Congreve's ironic comment within the play
is to place Collier's book on Lady Wishfort's shelves as
suitably pious reading for his villainess Mrs Marwood, he
was stung by Collier, and published a riposte, his *Amendments
upon Mr Collier's False and Imperfect Citations*, in the same year
as Collier's diatribe.

Congreve's satirical attacks on affectation and his use of the
Humours tradition in naming characters may have suggested
to his original audience that the characters would be
caricatures with one broad defining characteristic, and this
certainly applies to someone like Mincing with her affected
and esoteric pronunciation and vocabulary. While the names
of the major characters do reveal less about their whole
personalities, they remain important pointers to how we are
meant to judge them. For example, it is hard to decide from
their initial dialogue alone whether Fainall or Mirabell is to
be the play's hero, but their names indicate that we are
meant to admire the 'admirable' character and distrust the
one who 'feigns all', although the information that gradually
emerges about Mirabell makes him a more complex figure
than his name might suggest. This refusal to settle for the
single viewpoint is an important factor in giving life to the
play, but its almost Chekhovian complexity of motivation and
allusiveness may have been an element in the initial
apparently disappointing response to the play. Of course the
characters are partly a product of the generic expectations of
Restoration comic form, but we are also asked to make
judgments on them as we would in everyday life, and those
judgments change as our picture of them builds up gradually

throughout the play. So there is a tension at the heart of the play between the generic expectations set up by names like Fainall and Wishfort and the more complex ways in which even some of the minor figures are presented.

Relationships and Structure

Congreve uses juxtapositions of different kinds of relationships as a central part of his dramatic method. His list of 'Dramatis Personae' offers a grid of such descriptions: Fainall is 'in love with Mrs Marwood', Millamant is 'niece to Lady Wishfort, and loves Mirabell'. Most complicated of all, Mrs Fainall is 'daughter to Lady Wishfort, and wife to Fainall, formerly friend to Mirabell'. Mrs Marwood, who is 'friend to Mr Fainall, and likes Mirabell' is a loose cannon who has no family affiliation other than being Fainall's mistress, but otherwise the patterns of kinship and of liking are equally complicated. As Fainall says to Mirabell about Sir Wilfull: 'He is half-brother to this Witwoud by a former wife, who was sister to my Lady Wishfort, my wife's mother. If you marry Millamant you must call us cousins too.' In general, the play moves on two planes at once, testing emotional realities against social realities, gradually revealing the discrepancy between underlying emotional commitments and outer social forms and equally gradually suggesting new social forms that might reflect the shifts in emotional commitments.

An example of this is the way in which family relationships are tested in each act against emotional ones. Act One is exclusively male, beginning with a conversation between the two gamblers who are to be at the centre of the plots, in a public arena (the Chocolate House); Act Two, set in the park, another public space, begins with a similar dialogue between the former mistress of one of the gamblers and the current mistress of the other (who also desires the first!). In both dialogues, the participants use hints and evasions to probe each other for signs of weakness and the true state of emotional affairs. Congreve organises matters like a formal dance: after the two scenes in which the Mirabell-Mrs Fainall axis is established against the Mr Fainall-Mrs Marwood axis, we see a further set of juxtaposed scenes in which Fainall and Mrs Marwood (the adulterous couple) are acrimonious, the ex-lovers, Mirabell and Mrs Fainall, are forgiving, and the current lovers, Mirabell and Millamant, are sparring.

The first two acts reveal discrepancies between external appearances and the underlying relationships in public places. Act Three takes us into the domestic arena of Lady Wishfort's house, where it remains for the rest of the play. Here the central event in the plot (Mrs Marwood over-hearing Foible's discussion with Mrs Fainall) reveals a key discrepancy between outward appearance and the reality: namely that the aristocratic suitor 'Sir Rowland' is actually Waitwell, Mirabell's servant. The rest of the play takes the open grid of relationships between those people who are linked through blood and marriage and the much more secret grid of those who are attached through passion rather than law, and works to rearrange the pattern so that, by the end, there is a much closer match between the emotional and the legal situations. Legal devices and legal vocabulary become a sustaining dramatic metaphor for human obligations and social relationships.

The 'Proviso' Scene

Congreve is explicit in insisting that only half Millamant's fortune is under her aunt's control. A real-life Millamant could easily have married on the remaining £6000 that she controls herself. So why are Mirabell's convoluted stratagems actually necessary? They are partly a demonstration of his seriousness as a lover, almost like the test of a medieval knight wooing his lady. Since both the Fainalls' existing marriage and the various marriages referred to and proposed within the play are scarcely models for a genuine union of kindred spirits, the action tests Mirabell's and Millamant's willingness and commitment to undertake such a hazardous enterprise. The underlying question of *The Way of the World* is how the sexes can find a way of living together that is not a purely economic arrangement, but one in which emotional and legal realities match and which is not characterised by excess. It is comic when Millamant says, 'If Mirabell should not make a good husband, I am a lost thing'; the underlying loss is not only an emotional one, but also that of financial independence.

Act Four consists largely of a series of marriage proposals of varying strengths and sincerity. The majority of these proposals are to Millamant, and the majority of her would-be suitors are at best perfunctory. Sir Wilfull, for example, woos her out of duty not love, but is unable to match her town sophistication with his uneducated country manners; Petulant's outburst is brief and brutal. As well as the internal contrast between the various proposals to Millamant, there is a further contrast when romance does appear in the artificially heightened language of Waitwell wooing Lady Wishfort as Sir Rowland. Even Lady Wishfort voices the play's scepticism about the relationship between high-sounding moral absolutes and the realities of *The Way of the World* when she describes Sir Rowland's language as excessive. All these proposals and the Fainalls' marriage offer negative models of the dangers that attend courtship and marriage. They provide a sharp contrast to Mirabell and Millamant's moving comic exorcism of those dangers as they agree mutual terms and ground rules for their marriage in what has come to be called 'the proviso scene' because of the conditions ('provisos') that they lay down for each other.

Although this is not the first such scene in Restoration Comedy, Mirabell and Millamant's declaration of love is a fine example of a typically understated reticent English love scene. The emotional core of their relationship is not expressed directly; instead social forms are made to match emotional reality as the characters use the methods of formal debate and cross-examination to agree a set of conditions for their relationship that allow them the possibility of uniting emotional and legal commitment. In the face of excesses of drunkenness, abruptness, gallantry and inarticulacy, the calm, rational, formal balance of Mirabell's and Millamant's alternating conditions – concisely captured when Mirabell completes Millamant's quoted couplet from a poem by

Edmund Waller – appears the most desirable way of living that is on offer within the world of the play.

Relationships, Power, Law and Knowledge

When there is a discrepancy between outward and inner orders, anyone who knows the facts has power over those who do not. Part of the pleasure of watching or reading *The Way of the World* lies in the way that the balance of power between the characters themselves and between characters and audience fluctuates depending on who knows what, when, and about whom; with the prizes going to those who can best exploit their knowledge of those discrepancies. This also partly explains the importance of irony and wit in these plays, since verbal control, or lack of it, is not only a source of comedy, but also stands as a kind of metaphor for the social and emotional control exerted by the truly witty characters.

In *The Way of the World*, anyone who is aware of a discrepancy has power over others, and the play is organised through a series of revelations and counter-revelations – a peeling away of layers of deceit and misapprehension. In these terms, the play is a power struggle over the control of legacies. Lady Wishfort controls half of Millamant's fortune; Fainall and Mirabell each want to persuade or force Lady Wishfort to make a disposition of her wealth in their own favour. The conflict is resolved by the appearance of a previously concealed legal document that gives Mirabell power over Mrs Fainall's fortune, in the same way as the marriage between Waitwell and Foible was intended to give Mirabell power over Lady Wishfort. Interestingly, however, in the last act, the revelation of Fainall's affair with Mrs Marwood, which the other characters assume will be practically as well as morally disabling, makes no difference at all to Fainall. He readily accepts the disjunction between the social and emotional order and when he is ultimately defeated, it is not by an action within the play, but by Mirabell's superior knowledge of a state of affairs prior to the play – the trump card of the writings in the black box.

Some Restoration Comedies appear both to share Fainall's acceptance of the discrepancy between outward appearance and inner states of affairs and to glorify in it. However, the action of *The Way of the World* involves a sense of cleansing, as the outward expressions of human relationships in the form of marriages and legal documents come to match more fully the inward states of human emotions. It is this that explains the true importance of the deed Mirabell enacts at the end of the play. At one level it is no more than a dramatic device to cut through a tightly knotted situation, but it is more than the final hidden secret at the centre of the pattern of revelations about the hidden emotional structures. Since it finally frees the characters who appear to be controlled by Lady Wishfort, it offers a fundamental basis on which to build a new social order.

A Transitional Comedy?

Ultimately, *The Way of the World* presents a comic vision of a world beset by doubts and uncertainties, in which individuals must seek their own stability without recourse to external moral systems. Like Shakespeare's *Twelfth Night* and *The Merchant of Venice* it cannot accommodate all its characters within its comic synthesis: Fainall and Mrs Marwood are excluded, and Mrs Fainall's future happiness, if not her wealth, is problematic.

The Way of the World is sometimes seen as marking a transition between the more overtly cynical work of the Restoration period and what came to be called Sentimental Comedy, in which the characters are sober and their sentiments fine, with the predictable result that the plays tend to be both morally uplifting and deeply dull. Mirabell is almost the last of the Restoration libertines, caught in a process of transition into a sententious (Millamant's accusation) eighteenth-century man of feeling: one could not easily imagine earlier Restoration heroes discussing how to bring up children with their future wives. While Mirabell is no heroic exemplar, he may, as Congreve said of the hero of his earlier comedy *Love for Love*, 'pass well enough for the best character in a comedy'. Yet, while Congreve was referring to the classical tradition that comedy shows human beings as worse than they are, there is something challengingly modern about the vision of *The Way of the World*, with its hero and heroine peering forward into an uncertain world, unsure of their bearings, but witty, resolute, and mutually supportive.

The Way of the World on Stage

The Way of the World was first performed at Lincoln's Inn Fields in March 1700. Although cast with the leading actors of the day – Betterton played Fainall and Mrs Bracegirdle was Millamant – the production was not a great success, and the play was not a regular feature in the repertory until the 1730s. The popular actress Kitty Clive played Millamant for her benefit in 1743, eventually moving on to play Lady Wishfort. Peg Woffington and Mrs Abingdon were other notable eighteenth-century Millamants, but the play was seldom staged in the nineteenth century because of its 'difficult' subject matter.

Nigel Playfair's 1924 Lyric Hammersmith production with Edith Evans as Millamant restored the play's fortunes, and Evans would go on to emulate Kitty Clive by playing Lady Wishfort (Old Vic,1948). John Gielgud played Mirabell in his own 1953 Lyric Hammersmith production, and the play is now revived fairly regularly, by the National Theatre in 1969 and 1995, the RSC in 1978, Chichester Festival Theatre in 1984, and by Peter Gill in 1992, again at the Lyric Hammersmith.

The Texts

These editions of *The Country Wife*, *The Rover* and *The Way of the World* are based on the 1675 Quarto, the 1677 Quarto and the 1700 Quarto respectively, with spelling and punctuation modernised.

Key Dates

c. 1640 Behn is born in Wye or Sturry, near Canterbury, Kent. Maiden name Amies, Johnson, or Cooper

1641 Wycherley is born in Clive, near Shrewsbury

1656-60 Wycherley lives in Paris.

1660 Wycherley attends Oxford University

1660 Wycherley enters the Inner Temple but never practises law

c. 1663 Behn's family moves to Surinam, but her father, who had been appointed Lieutenant-General, dies on the voyage. Behn stays on a local plantation

1664 Behn returns to London

c. 1665 Behn marries Mr. Behn, probably a Dutch merchant, who dies soon afterwards

1666 Behn is persuaded by Thomas Killigrew to serve as a spy in the Dutch Wars, but discovers little of value while in Antwerp, and remains unpaid for her services

1667 Behn returns to London

1668 Behn goes to prison for debt, despite petitions to Killigrew and the King. Date of release uncertain

1670 Congreve is born in Bardsey, Yorkshire. Behn's first play, the tragi-comic *The Forced Marriage*, is staged. Around this time, her long relationship with John Hoyle begins

1671 Wycherley's *Love in a Wood; or, St James's Park* and Behn's *The Amorous Prince* are staged

1672 Wycherley's *The Gentleman Dancing Master*, adapted from Calderón, is staged

1673 Behn's *The Dutch Lover* is staged – and fails

1674 Congreve is brought up in Ireland where his father is in the army

1675 Wycherley's *The Country Wife* is staged

1676 Wycherley's *The Plain Dealer* and Behn's *Abdelazer* and *The Town Fop* are staged

1677 Behn's *The Rover* is staged as are two other plays attributed to her, *The Debauchee* and *The Counterfeit Bridegroom*

1678 Behn's *Sir Patient Fancy*, adapted from Molière's *The Imaginary Invalid*, is staged

1679 The Exclusion Crisis, by which powers were sought to prevent the subsequent James II from coming to the throne, begins. Behn's *The Feigned Courtesans* and *The Young King* are staged. Wycherley marries the Countess of Drogheda

1680 Wycherley is banished from court because of his marriage

1681 Congreve attends Kilkenny School for four years. Behn's *The Second Part of The Rover, The False Count* and *The Roundheads* are staged. Wycherley's wife, the Countess of Drogheda, dies

1682 The two theatre companies merge into one 'United Company'. Behn's anti-Whig political lampoon *The City Heiress* is 'well received' on stage, but *Like Father, Like Son* fails on stage and remains unprinted. Increasing hostility from the Whigs leads to her arrest for the prologue she contributes to the anonymous *Romulus and Hersilia*. She largely abandons writing for the theatre. Wycherley is imprisoned for debt for four years

1683 Wycherley's *Epistles to the King and Duke*. Behn writes three of her posthumously published short novels

1684 Behn publishes her *Poems on Several Occasions*

1685 Charles II dies and his brother James II accedes to the throne. Behn publishes her poetic *Miscellany*

1686   Wycherley is released and given pension by James II.
Congreve enters Trinity College Dublin, as a
classical scholar. Behn publishes the prose work *La
Montre; or, The Lover's Watch*. Her *The Lucky Chance* is
staged

1687   One of Behn's greatest successes, *The Emperor of the
Moon*, is staged

1688   The 'Bloodless (or Glorious) Revolution' establishes
the protestant supremacy under William and Mary.
Congreve's family returns from Ireland. Behn
publishes the short novels *The Fair Jilt, Agnes de Castro*
and *Oroonoko*

1689   Behn dies 16 April and is buried in Westminster
Abbey. Posthumous production of her *The Widow
Ranter* fails

1691   Congreve enters the Middle Temple to train as a
lawyer

1692   Congreve translates Juvenal's *Eleventh Satire* and
publishes *Incognita*, a novel

1693   Congreve's *The Old Bachelor* is staged and achieves
unusually long run of fourteen days. His *The Double
Dealer* is staged, with less success

1695   Congreve's *Love for Love* is staged and runs for
thirteen days. He writes 'An Essay Concerning
Humour in Comedy'

1696   Posthumous production of Behn's *The Younger Brother*

1697   Congreve's *The Mourning Bride* is staged. He becomes
manager at the theatre in Lincoln's Inn Fields, until
1705. Wycherley returns to London

1698   Jeremy Collier publishes *A Short View of the Immorality
and Profaneness of the English Stage*. In response,
Congreve publishes *Amendments upon Mr Collier's False
and Imperfect Citations*

1700   Congreve's *The Way of the World* is staged

1701   Congreve's masque, *The Judgment of Paris*, is staged

1704   Congreve's *Squire Trelooby*, an adaptation from
       Molière, with Vanbrugh and William Walsh

1705   Congreve (with Vanbrugh) manages the Queen's
       Theatre until 1706

1710   Congreve's *Semele*, an opera libretto, is printed in his
       Works. Until his death, Congreve holds a number of
       government posts, including Commissioner of Wine
       Licences, Undersearcher of Customs, Secretary for
       Jamaica

1715   Wycherley marries Elizabeth Jackson; dies 31
       December

1717   Congreve edits *The Dramatic Works* of Dryden

1723   Mary Godolphin, daughter of Duchess of
       Marlborough, is born: Congreve is supposedly the
       father

1729   Congreve dies 19 January and is buried in
       Westminster Abbey

Further Reading

The Restoration

Liza Picard's *Restoration London* (Weidenfeld & Nicholson, 1997) is an encyclopaedic compendium of information on all aspects of Restoration life. Norman N. Holland's *The First Modern Comedies* (Harvard, 1959) is a thoughtful study of Restoration Comedy. Peter Holland's *The Ornament of Action* (Cambridge, 1979), Jocelyn Powell's *Restoration Theatre Production* (Routledge, 1984) and J. L. Styan's *Restoration Comedy in Performance* (Cambridge, 1986) are fine theatre-centred accounts of Restoration theatre and drama. R.W. Bevis, *English Drama: Restoration and Eighteenth Century, 1660-1789* (Longman, 1988) and Deborah Payne Fisk (ed) *The Cambridge Companion to English Restoration Theatre* (Cambridge University Press, 2000) are excellent introductions to the drama of the period with extensive bibliographies. David L. Hirst's *Comedy of Manners* (London, 1979) remains one of the best accounts of the genre.

Of the many general studies of Restoration theatre, the introduction to the definitive but massive 'calendar', *The London Stage*, has usefully been reprinted as a separate volume, *The London Stage 1660-1700: a Critical Introduction*, by Emmett L. Avery and Arthur H. Scouten (Carbondale, 1968), while the fifth volume of *The Revels History of Drama in English*, covering the period 1660 to 1750, edited by John Loftis and others (London, 1976), usefully blends theatre history with dramatic criticism.

Wycherley

Katharine M. Rogers's *William Wycherley* (Twayne, 1972) combines biographical and contextual material with criticism.

Behn

There are useful scholarly editions of *The Rover* edited by
Frederick M. Link in the Regents Restoration Drama series
(London, 1967), and by Marion Lomax in the New
Mermaids series (London, 1995). Selections of Aphra Behn's
plays include *Five Plays*, introduced by Maureen Duffy
(London, 1990) and *The Rover and Other Plays*, edited by Jane
Spencer (Oxford, 1995). Janet Todd's Penguin selection
(London, 1992) also includes Behn's novel, *Oroonoko*. The first
volume of Todd's six-volume *The Works of Aphra Behn*
(London, 1992–95) contains a valuable introduction.

Of the major modern biographies of Behn, Maureen Duffy's
The Passionate Shepherdess: Aphra Behn (London, 1977) is the
more pertinently critical about the works themselves, while
Angeline Goreau's *Reconstructing Aphra* (Oxford, 1980) is the
more helpful on the socio-political context. Frederick M.
Link's *Behn* (New York, 1968) was the first full-length critical
study. All three of these include extensive bibliographies of
work on Behn before the upsurge in feminist interest from
the 'eighties onwards. This is exemplified by Aphra Behn's
inclusion in Sara Heller Mendelson's *The Mental World of
Stuart Women* (Brighton, 1987), though Jacqueline Pearson's
*The Prostituted Muse: Images of Women and Women Dramatists
1642–1737* (Brighton, 1988) is more specifically dramatic in
orientation. A selection of other recent writings on her work,
Rereading Aphra Behn: History, Theory and Criticism, has been
edited by Heidi Hutner (Charlottesville, 1993).

Congreve

The standard biographical studies are John C. Hodges's
Congreve the Man (London, 1941) and his *William Congreve:
Letters and Documents* (London, 1964). Malcolm Kelsall's
Congreve: 'The Way of the World' (London, 1981) is an incisive,
brief study.

THE COUNTRY WIFE

Prologue

Spoken by Mr Hart

Poets, like cudgelled bullies, never do
At first or second blow submit to you;
But will provoke you still and ne'er have done,
Till you are weary first with laying on.
The late so baffled scribbler of this day,
Though he stands trembling, bids me boldly say,
What we before most plays are used to do,
For poets out of fear first draw on you;
In a fierce prologue the still pit defy,
And ere you speak, like Castril give the lie.
But though our Bayes's battles oft I've fought,
And with bruised knuckles their dear conquests bought;
Nay, never yet feared odds upon the stage,
In prologue dare not hector with the age,
But would take quarter from your saving hands,
Though Bayes within all yielding countermands,
Says you confederate wits no quarter give,
Therefore his play shan't ask your leave to live.
Well, let the vain rash fop, by huffing so,
Think to obtain the better terms of you;
But we, the actors, humbly will submit,
Now, and at any time, to a full pit;
Nay, often we anticipate your rage,
And murder poets for you on our stage.
We set no guards upon our tiring-room,
But when with flying colours there you come,
We patiently, you see, give up to you
Our poets, virgins, nay, our matrons too.

The Persons

MR HORNER
MR HARCOURT
MR DORILANT
MR PINCHWIFE
MR SPARKISH
SIR JASPAR FIDGET

MRS MARGERY PINCHWIFE
MRS ALITHEA
MY LADY FIDGET
MRS DAINTY FIDGET
MRS SQUEAMISH
OLD LADY SQUEAMISH

WAITERS, SERVANTS, AND ATTENDANTS
A BOY
A PARSON

A QUACK
LUCY, *Alithea's Maid*

CLASP

The Scene: *London*

ACT ONE

Enter HORNER, *and* QUACK *following him at a distance.*

HORNER (*aside*). A quack is as fit for a pimp as a midwife for a bawd; they are still but in their way both helpers of nature. – Well, my dear doctor, hast thou done what I desired?

QUACK. I have undone you for ever with the women, and reported you throughout the whole town as bad as an eunuch, with as much trouble as if I had made you one in earnest.

HORNER. But have you told all the midwives you know, the orange wenches at the playhouses, the city husbands, and old fumbling keepers of this end of the town? For they'll be the readiest to report it.

QUACK. I have told all the chamber-maids, waiting-women, tire-women, and old women of my acquaintance; nay, and whispered it as a secret to 'em, and to the whisperers of Whitehall, so that you need not doubt 'twill spread, and you will be as odious to the handsome young women as –

HORNER. As the smallpox. Well –

QUACK. And to the married women of this end of the town as –

HORNER. As the great ones; nay, as their own husbands.

QUACK. And to the city dames as Aniseed Robin of filthy and contemptible memory; and they will frighten their children with your name, especially their females.

HORNER. And cry, 'Horner's coming to carry you away!' I am only afraid 'twill not be believed. You told 'em 'twas by an English-French disaster, and an English-French surgeon, who has given me at once not only a cure but an antidote for the future against that damned malady, and that worse distemper, love, and all other women's evils.

QUACK. Your late journey into France has made it the more credible, and your being here a fortnight before you appeared in public looks as if you apprehended the shame, which I wonder you do not. Well, I have been hired by young gallants to belie 'em t'other way; but you are the first would be thought a man unfit for women.

HORNER. Dear Mr Doctor, let vain rogues be contented only to be thought abler men than they are, generally 'tis all the pleasure they have, but mine lies another way.

QUACK. You take, methinks, a very preposterous way to it, and as ridiculous as if we operators in physic should put forth bills to disparage our medicaments, with hopes to gain customers.

HORNER. Doctor, there are quacks in love, as well as physic, who get but the fewer and worse patients for their boasting. A good name is seldom got by giving it oneself, and women no more than honour are compassed by bragging. Come, come, doctor, the wisest lawyer never discovers the merits of his cause till the trial. The wealthiest man conceals his riches, and the cunning gamester his play. Shy husbands and keepers, like old rooks, are not to be cheated but by a new unpractised trick. False friendship will pass now no more than false dice upon 'em; no, not in the city.

Enter BOY.

BOY. There are two ladies and a gentleman coming up.

Exit BOY.

HORNER. A pox! Some unbelieving sisters of my former acquaintance who, I am afraid, expect their sense should be satisfied of the falsity of the report. No – this formal fool and women!

Enter SIR JASPAR, LADY FIDGET *and* MRS DAINTY FIDGET.

QUACK. His wife and sister.

SIR JASPAR. My coach breaking just now before your door, sir, I look upon as an occasional reprimand to me, sir, for not kissing your hands, sir, since your coming out of France, sir; and so my disaster, sir, has been my good fortune, sir; and this is my wife and sister, sir.

HORNER. What then, sir?

SIR JASPAR. My lady, and sister, sir. – Wife, this is Master Horner.

LADY FIDGET. Master Horner, husband!

SIR JASPAR. My lady, my Lady Fidget, sir.

HORNER. So, sir.

SIR JASPAR. Won't you be acquainted with her, sir? (*Aside.*) So the report is true, I find, by his coldness or aversion to the sex; but I'll play the wag with him. – Pray salute my wife, my lady, sir.

HORNER. I will kiss no man's wife, sir, for him, sir; I have taken my eternal leave, sir, of the sex already, sir.

SIR JASPAR (*aside*). Ha, ha, ha! I'll plague him yet. – Not know my wife, sir?

HORNER. I do know your wife, sir, she's a woman, sir, and consequently a monster, sir, a greater monster than a husband, sir.

SIR JASPAR. A husband! How, sir?

HORNER (*makes horns*). So, sir. But I make no more cuckolds, sir.

SIR JASPAR. Ha, ha, ha! Mercury, Mercury.

LADY FIDGET. Pray, Sir Jaspar, let us be gone from this rude fellow.

DAINTY. Who, by his breeding, would think he had ever been in France?

LADY FIDGET. Foh! he's but too much a French fellow,

such as hate women of quality and virtue for their love to their husbands, Sir Jaspar. A woman is hated by 'em as much for loving her husband as for loving their money. But pray let's be gone.

HORNER. You do well, madam, for I have nothing that you came for. I have brought over not so much as a bawdy picture, new postures, nor the second part of the *Ecole des Filles*, nor –

QUACK (*apart to* HORNER). Hold for shame, sir! What d'ye mean? You'll ruin yourself for ever with the sex –

SIR JASPAR. Ha, ha, ha! He hates women perfectly, I find.

DAINTY. What pity 'tis he should.

LADY FIDGET. Ay, he's a base rude fellow for't; but affectation makes not a woman more odious to them than virtue.

HORNER. Because your virtue is your greatest affectation, madam.

LADY FIDGET. How, you saucy fellow! Would you wrong my honour?

HORNER. If I could.

LADY FIDGET. How d'you mean, sir?

SIR JASPAR. Ha, ha, ha! No, he can't wrong your ladyship's honour, upon my honour; he, poor man – hark you in your ear – a mere eunuch.

LADY FIDGET. O filthy French beast! foh, foh! Why do we stay? Let's be gone. I can't endure the sight of him.

SIR JASPAR. Stay but till the chairs come. They'll be here presently.

LADY FIDGET. No, no.

SIR JASPAR. Nor can I stay longer. 'Tis – let me see – a quarter and a half quarter of a minute past eleven. The Council will be sat, I must away. Business must be preferred always before love and ceremony with the wise, Mr Horner.

HORNER. And the impotent, Sir Jaspar.

SIR JASPAR. Ay, ay, the impotent, Master Horner, ha, ha, ha!

LADY FIDGET. What, leave us with a filthy man alone in his lodgings?

SIR JASPAR. He's an innocent man now, you know. Pray stay, I'll hasten the chairs to you. – Mr Horner, your servant; I should be glad to see you at my house. Pray come and dine with me, and play at cards with my wife after dinner; you are fit for women at that game yet, ha, ha! (*Aside.*) 'Tis as much a husband's prudence to provide innocent diversion for a wife as to hinder her unlawful pleasures, and he had better employ her than let her employ herself. – Farewell.

Exit SIR JASPAR.

HORNER. Your servant, Sir Jaspar.

LADY FIDGET. I will not stay with him, foh!

HORNER. Nay, madam, I beseech you stay, if it be but to see I can be as civil to ladies yet as they would desire.

LADY FIDGET. No, no, foh! You cannot be civil to ladies.

DAINTY. You as civil as ladies would desire!

LADY FIDGET. No, no, no! foh, foh, foh!

Exeunt LADY FIDGET *and* DAINTY.

QUACK. Now I think, I, or you yourself, rather, have done your business with the women.

HORNER. Thou art an ass. Don't you see already, upon the report and my carriage, this grave man of business leaves his wife in my lodgings, invites me to his house and wife, who before would not be acquainted with me out of jealousy?

QUACK. Nay, by this means you may be the more acquainted with the husbands, but the less with the wives.

HORNER. Let me alone; if I can but abuse the husbands, I'll soon disabuse the wives! Stay – I'll reckon you up the advantages I am like to have by my stratagem. First, I shall be rid of all my old acquaintances, the most insatiable sorts of duns, that invade our lodgings in a morning. And next to the pleasure of making a new mistress is that of being rid of an old one, and of all old debts; love, when it comes to be so, is paid the most unwillingly.

QUACK. Well, you may be so rid of your old acquaintances, but how will you get any new ones?

HORNER. Doctor, thou wilt never make a good chemist, thou art so incredulous and impatient. Ask but all the young fellows of the town, if they do not lose more time, like huntsmen, in starting the game, than in running it down. One knows not where to find 'em, who will, or will not. Women of quality are so civil you can hardly distinguish love from good breeding, and a man is often mistaken. But now I can be sure she that shows an aversion to me loves the sport, as those women that are gone, whom I warrant to be right. And then the next thing is, your women of honour, as you call 'em, are only chary of their reputations, not their persons, and 'tis scandal they would avoid, not men. Now may I have, by the reputation of an eunuch, the privileges of one; and be seen in a lady's chamber in a morning as early as her husband; kiss virgins before their parents or lovers; and may be, in short, the *passe partout* of the town. Now doctor –

QUACK. Nay, now you shall be the doctor; and your process is so new that we do not know but it may succeed.

HORNER. Not so new neither. *Probatum est*, doctor.

QUACK. Well, I wish you luck and many patients whilst I go to mine.

Exit QUACK.

Enter HARCOURT *and* DORILANT *to* HORNER.

HARCOURT. Come, your appearance at the play yesterday has, I hope, hardened you for the future against the women's contempt and the men's raillery; and now you'll abroad as you were wont.

HORNER. Did I not bear it bravely?

DORILANT. With a most theatrical impudence; nay, more than the orange-wenches show there, or a drunken vizard-mask, or a great-bellied actress; nay, or the most impudent of creatures, an ill poet; or, what is yet more impudent, a second-hand critic.

HORNER. But what say the ladies? Have they no pity?

HARCOURT. What ladies? The vizard-masks, you know, never pity a man when all's gone, though in their service.

DORILANT. And for the women in the boxes, you'd never pity them when 'twas in your power.

HARCOURT. They say: 'tis pity, but all that deal with common women should be served so.

DORILANT. Nay, I dare swear, they won't admit you to play at cards with them, go to plays with 'em, or do the little duties which other shadows of men are wont to do for 'em.

HORNER. Who do you call shadows of men?

DORILANT. Half-men.

HORNER. What, boys?

DORILANT. Ay, your old boys, old *beaux garçons*, who like superannuated stallions are suffered to run, feed, and whinny with the mares as long as they live, though they can do nothing else.

HORNER. Well, a pox on love and wenching! Women serve but to keep a man from better company; though I can't enjoy them, I shall you the more. Good fellowship and friendship are lasting, rational, and manly pleasures.

HARCOURT. For all that, give me some of those pleasures you call effeminate too; they help to relish one another.

HORNER. They disturb one another.

HARCOURT. No, mistresses are like books. If you pore upon them too much they doze you and make you unfit for company; but if used discreetly you are the fitter for conversation by 'em.

DORILANT. A mistress should be like a little country retreat near the town, not to dwell in constantly, but only for a night and away, to taste the town the better when a man returns.

HORNER. I tell you, 'tis as hard to be a good fellow, a good friend, and a lover of women, as 'tis to be a good fellow, a good friend, and a lover of money. You cannot follow both, then choose your side. Wine gives you liberty, love takes it away.

DORILANT. Gad, he's in the right on't.

HORNER. Wine gives you joy; love, grief and tortures, besides the surgeon's. Wine makes us witty; love, only sots. Wine makes us sleep; love breaks it.

DORILANT. By the world, he has reason, Harcourt.

HORNER. Wine makes –

DORILANT. Ay wine makes us – makes us princes; love makes us beggars, poor rogues, i'gad – and wine –

HORNER. So, there's one converted – No, no, love and wine, oil and vinegar.

HARCOURT. I grant it; love will still be uppermost.

HORNER. Come, for my part I will have only those glorious, manly pleasures of being drunk and very slovenly.

Enter BOY.

BOY. Mr Sparkish is below, sir.

Exit BOY.

HARCOURT. What, my dear friend! A rogue that is fond of me only, I think, for abusing him.

DORILANT. No, he can no more think the men laugh at him than that women jilt him, his opinion of himself is so good.

HORNER. Well, there's another pleasure by drinking I thought not of; I shall lose his acquaintance, because he cannot drink. And you know 'tis a very hard thing to be rid of him, for he's one of those nauseous offerers at wit, who, like the worst fiddlers, run themselves into all companies.

HARCOURT. One that, by being in the company of men of sense, would pass for one.

HORNER. And may so to the short-sighted world, as a false jewel amongst true ones is not discerned at a distance. His company is as troublesome to us as a cuckold's when you have a mind to his wife's.

HARCOURT. No, the rogue will not let us enjoy one another, but ravishes our conversation, though he signifies no more to't than Sir Martin Mar-all's gaping and awkward thrumming upon the lute does to his man's voice and music.

DORILANT. And to pass for a wit in town shows himself a fool every night to us, that are guilty of the plot.

HORNER. Such wits as he are, to a company of reasonable men, like rooks to the gamesters, who only fill a room at the table, but are so far from contributing to the play that they only serve to spoil the fancy of those that do.

DORILANT. Nay, they are used like rooks too, snubbed, checked, and abused; yet the rogues will hang on.

HORNER. A pox upon 'em, and all that force nature, and would be still what she forbids 'em! Affectation is her greatest monster.

HARCOURT. Most men are the contraries to that they would seem. Your bully, you see, is a coward with a long sword; the little, humbly fawning physician with his ebony cane is he that destroys men.

DORILANT. The usurer, a poor rogue possessed of mouldy bonds and mortgages; and we they call spendthrifts are only wealthy, who lay out his money upon daily new purchases of pleasure.

HORNER. Ay, your arrantest cheat is your trustee, or executor; your jealous man, the greatest cuckold; your churchman, the greatest atheist; and your noisy, pert rogue of a wit, the greatest fop, dullest ass, and worst company, as you shall see. For here he comes.

Enter SPARKISH *to them.*

SPARKISH. How is't, sparks, how is't? Well, faith, Harry, I must rally thee a little, ha, ha, ha! Upon the report in town of thee, ha, ha, ha! I can't hold i'faith; shall I speak?

HORNER. Yes, but you'll be so bitter then.

SPARKISH. Honest Dick and Frank here shall answer for me, I will not be extreme bitter, by the universe.

HARCOURT. We will be bound in ten thousand pound bond, he shall not be bitter at all.

DORILANT. Nor sharp, nor sweet.

HORNER. What, not downright insipid?

SPARKISH. Nay then, since you are so brisk and provoke me, take what follows. You must know, I was discoursing and rallying with some ladies yesterday, and they happened to talk of the fine new signs in town.

HORNER. Very fine ladies, I believe.

SPARKISH. Said I, 'I know where the best new sign is'. 'Where?' says one of the ladies. 'In Covent Garden', I replied. Said another, 'In what street?' 'In Russell Street', answered I. 'Lord', says another, 'I'm sure there was ne'er a fine new sign there yesterday'. 'Yes, but there was', said I again, 'and it came out of France, and has been there a fortnight'.

DORILANT. A pox! I can hear no more, prithee.

HORNER. No, hear him out; let him tune his crowd a while.

HARCOURT. The worst music, the greatest preparation.

SPARKISH. Nay, faith, I'll make you laugh. 'It cannot be', says a third lady. 'Yes, yes', quoth I again. Says a fourth lady –

HORNER. Look to't, we'll have no more ladies.

SPARKISH. No – then mark, mark, now. Said I to the fourth, 'Did you never see Mr Horner? He lodges in Russell Street, and he's a sign of a man, you know, since he came out of France!' He, ha, he!

HORNER. But the devil take me, if thine be the sign of a jest.

SPARKISH. With that they all fell a-laughing, till they bepissed themselves. What, but it does not move you, methinks? Well, I see one has as good go to law without a witness, as break a jest without a laugher on one's side. Come, come sparks, but where do we dine? I have left at Whitehall an earl to dine with you.

DORILANT. Why, I thought thou hadst loved a man with a title better than a suit with a French trimming to't.

HARCOURT. Go to him again.

SPARKISH. No, sir, a wit to me is the greatest title in the world.

HORNER. But go dine with your earl, sir; he may be exceptious. We are your friends, and will not take it ill to be left, I do assure you.

HARCOURT. Nay, faith, he shall go to him.

SPARKISH. Nay, pray, gentlemen.

DORILANT. We'll thrust you out, if you won't. What, disappoint anybody for us?

SPARKISH. Nay, dear gentlemen, hear me.

HORNER. No, no, sir, by no means; pray go, sir.

SPARKISH. Why, dear rogues –

DORILANT. No, no.

They all thrust him out of the room.

ALL. Ha, ha, ha!

SPARKISH *returns.*

SPARKISH. But, sparks, pray hear me. What, d'ye think
I'll eat then with gay shallow fops and silent coxcombs?
I think wit as necessary at dinner as a glass of good wine,
and that's the reason I never have any stomach when
I eat alone. – Come, but where do we dine?

HORNER. Even where you will.

SPARKISH. At Chateline's?

DORILANT. Yes, if you will.

SPARKISH. Or at the Cock?

DORILANT. Yes, if you please.

SPARKISH. Or at the Dog and Partridge?

HORNER. Ay, if you have a mind to't, for we shall dine at
neither.

SPARKISH. Pshaw! with your fooling we shall lose the new
play; and I would no more miss seeing a new play the
first day than I would miss sitting in the wits' row.
Therefore I'll go fetch my mistress and away.

Exit SPARKISH. *Manent* HORNER, HARCOURT,
DORILANT. *Enter to them* MR PINCHWIFE.

HORNER. Who have we here? Pinchwife?

PINCHWIFE. Gentlemen, your humble servant.

HORNER. Well, Jack, by thy long absence from the town,
the grumness of thy countenance, and the slovenliness of
thy habit, I should give thee joy, should I not, of
marriage?

PINCHWIFE (*aside*). Death! Does he know I'm married too?
I thought to have concealed it from him at least. – My
long stay in the country will excuse my dress, and I have

a suit of law, that brings me up to town, that puts me out of humour. Besides, I must give Sparkish tomorrow five thousand pounds to lie with my sister.

HORNER. Nay, you country gentlemen, rather than not purchase, will buy anything; and he is a cracked title, if we may quibble. Well, but am I to give thee joy? I heard thou wert married.

PINCHWIFE. What then?

HORNER. Why, the next thing that is to be heard is, thou'rt a cuckold.

PINCHWIFE (*aside*). Insupportable name!

HORNER. But I did not expect marriage from such a whoremaster as you, one that knew the town so much, and women so well.

PINCHWIFE. Why, I have married no London wife.

HORNER. Pshaw! that's all one. That grave circumspection in marrying a country wife is like refusing a deceitful, pampered Smithfield jade to go and be cheated by a friend in the country.

PINCHWIFE (*aside*). A pox on him and his simile! – At least we are a little surer of the breed there, know what her keeping has been, whether foiled or unsound.

HORNER. Come, come, I have known a clap gotten in Wales. And there are cousins, justices, clerks, and chaplains in the country, I won't say coachmen! But she's handsome and young?

PINCHWIFE (*aside*). I'll answer as I should do. – No, no, she has no beauty but her youth; no attraction but her modesty; wholesome, homely, and housewifely, that's all.

DORILANT. He talks as like a grazier as he looks.

PINCHWIFE. She's too awkward, ill-favoured, and silly to bring to town.

HARCOURT. Then methinks you should bring her, to be taught breeding.

PINCHWIFE. To be taught! No, sir, I thank you. Good wives and private soldiers should be ignorant. (*Aside*.) I'll keep her from your instructions, I warrant you.

HARCOURT (*aside*). The rogue is as jealous as if his wife were not ignorant.

HORNER. Why, if she be ill-favoured, there will be less danger here for you than by leaving her in the country; we have such variety of dainties that we are seldom hungry.

DORILANT. But they always have coarse, constant, swingeing stomachs in the country.

HARCOURT. Foul feeders indeed.

DORILANT. And your hospitality is great there.

HARCOURT. Open house, every man's welcome!

PINCHWIFE. So, so, gentlemen.

HORNER. But, prithee, why would'st thou marry her? If she be ugly, ill-bred, and silly, she must be rich then?

PINCHWIFE. As rich as if she brought me twenty thousand pound out of this town; for she'll be as sure not to spend her moderate portion as a London baggage would be to spend hers, let it be what it would; so 'tis all one. Then, because she's ugly, she's the likelier to be my own; and being ill-bred, she'll hate conversation; and since silly and innocent, will not know the difference betwixt a man of one-and-twenty and one of forty.

HORNER. Nine – to my knowledge; but if she be silly, she'll expect as much from a man of forty-nine as from him of one-and-twenty. But methinks wit is more necessary than beauty; and I think no young woman ugly that has it, and no handsome woman agreeable without it.

PINCHWIFE. 'tis my maxim he's a fool that marries, but he's a greater that does not marry a fool. What is wit in a wife good for, but to make a man a cuckold?

HORNER. Yes, to keep it from his knowledge.

PINCHWIFE. A fool cannot contrive to make her husband a
  cuckold.

HORNER. No, but she'll club with a man that can; and
  what is worse, if she cannot make her husband a cuckold,
  she'll make him jealous, and pass for one, and then 'tis all
  one.

PINCHWIFE. Well, well, I'll take care for one, my wife shall
  make me no cuckold, though she had your help,
  Mr Horner; I understand the town, sir.

DORILANT (aside). His help!

HARCOURT (aside). He's come newly to town, it seems, and
  has not heard how things are with him.

HORNER. But tell me, has marriage cured thee of whoring,
  which it seldom does?

HARCOURT. 'Tis more than age can do.

HORNER. No, the word is, I'll marry and live honest.
  But a marriage vow is like a penitent gamester's oath, and
  entering into bonds and penalties to stint himself to such
  a particular small sum at play for the future, which makes
  him but the more eager, and not being able to hold out,
  loses his money again, and his forfeit to boot.

DORILANT. Ay, ay, a gamester will be a gamester whilst his
  money lasts, and a whoremaster whilst his vigour.

HARCOURT. Nay, I have known 'em, when they are broke
  and can lose no more, a-fumbling with the box in their
  hands to fool with only, and hinder other gamesters.

DORILANT. That had wherewithal to make lusty stakes.

PINCHWIFE. Well, gentlemen, you may laugh at me, but
  you shall never lie with my wife; I know the town.

HORNER. But prithee, was not the way you were in better?
  Is not keeping better than marriage?

PINCHWIFE. A pox on't! The jades would jilt me; I could
  never keep a whore to myself.

HORNER. So, then, you only married to keep a whore to yourself. Well, but let me tell you, women, as you say, are like soldiers, made constant and loyal by good pay rather than by oaths and covenants. Therefore I'd advise my friends to keep rather than marry, since too I find, by your example, it does not serve one's turn – for I saw you yesterday in the eighteenpenny place with a pretty country wench.

PINCHWIFE (*aside*). How the devil! Did he see my wife then? I sat there that she might not be seen. But she shall never go to a play again.

HORNER. What, dost thou blush at nine-and-forty for having been seen with a wench?

DORILANT. No, faith, I warrant 'twas his wife, which he seated there out of sight, for he's a cunning rogue, and understands the town.

HARCOURT. He blushes! Then 'twas his wife – for men are now more ashamed to be seen with them in public than with a wench.

PINCHWIFE (*aside*). Hell and damnation! I'm undone, since Horner has seen her, and they know 'twas she.

HORNER. But prithee, was it thy wife? She was exceedingly pretty; I was in love with her at that distance.

PINCHWIFE. You are like never to be nearer to her. Your servant, gentlemen. (*Offers to go.*)

HORNER. Nay, prithee stay.

PINCHWIFE. I cannot, I will not.

HORNER. Come, you shall dine with us.

PINCHWIFE. I have dined already.

HORNER. Come, I know thou hast not. I'll treat thee, dear rogue. Thou shan't spend none of thy Hampshire money today.

PINCHWIFE (*aside*). Treat me! So, he uses me already like his cuckold!

HORNER. Nay, you shall not go.

PINCHWIFE. I must, I have business at home.

Exit PINCHWIFE.

HARCOURT. To beat his wife; he's as jealous of her as a
Cheapside husband of a Covent Garden wife.

HORNER. Why, 'tis as hard to find an old whoremaster
without jealousy and the gout, as a young one without
fear or the pox.

As gout in age from pox in youth proceeds,
So wenching past, then jealousy succeeds:
The worst disease that love and wenching breeds.

ACT TWO

MRS MARGERY PINCHWIFE *and* ALITHEA; MR
PINCHWIFE *peeping behind at the door.*

MRS PINCHWIFE. Pray, sister, where are the best fields
and woods to walk in, in London?

ALITHEA. A pretty question! Why, sister, Mulberry Garden
and St James's Park; and for close walks, the New
Exchange.

MRS PINCHWIFE. Pray, sister, tell me why my husband
looks so grum here in town, and keeps me up so close,
and will not let me go a-walking, nor let me wear my best
gown yesterday?

ALITHEA. Oh, he's jealous, sister.

MRS PINCHWIFE. Jealous? What's that?

ALITHEA. He's afraid you should love another man.

MRS PINCHWIFE. How should he be afraid of my loving
another man, when he will not let me see any but
himself.

ALITHEA. Did he not carry you yesterday to a play?

MRS PINCHWIFE. Ay, but we sat amongst ugly people. He
would not let me come near the gentry, who sat under us,
so that I could not see 'em. He told me none but naughty
women sat there, whom they toused and moused. But I
would have ventured for all that.

ALITHEA. But how did you like the play?

MRS PINCHWIFE. Indeed I was a-weary of the play, but
I liked hugeously the actors; they are the goodliest,
properest men, sister.

ALITHEA. Oh, but you must not like the actors, sister.

MRS PINCHWIFE. Ay, how should I help it, sister? Pray, sister, when my husband comes in, will you ask leave for me to go a-walking?

ALITHEA (*aside*). A-walking! Ha, ha! Lord, a country gentlewoman's leisure is the drudgery of a foot-post; and she requires as much airing as her husband's horses.

Enter MR PINCHWIFE *to them.*

But here comes your husband; I'll ask, though I'm sure he'll not grant it.

MRS PINCHWIFE. He says he won't let me go abroad for fear of catching the pox.

ALITHEA. Fie, the smallpox you should say.

MRS PINCHWIFE. Oh my dear, dear bud, welcome home! Why dost thou look so fropish? Who has nangered thee?

PINCHWIFE. You're a fool!

MRS PINCHWIFE *goes aside and cries.*

ALITHEA. Faith, so she is, for crying for no fault, poor tender creature!

PINCHWIFE. What, you would have her as impudent as yourself, as arrant a jill-flirt, a gadder, a magpie, and to say all – a mere notorious town-woman?

ALITHEA. Brother, you are my only censurer; and the honour of your family shall sooner suffer in your wife there than in me, though I take the innocent liberty of the town.

PINCHWIFE. Hark you, mistress, do not talk so before my wife. The innocent liberty of the town!

ALITHEA. Why, pray, who boasts of any intrigue with me? What lampoon has made my name notorious? What ill women frequent my lodgings? I keep no company with any women of scandalous reputations.

PINCHWIFE. No, you keep the men of scandalous
    reputations company.

ALITHEA. Where? Would you not have me civil? Answer
    'em in a box at the plays, in the drawing room at
    Whitehall, in St James's Park, Mulberry Garden, or –

PINCHWIFE. Hold, hold! Do not teach my wife where the
    men are to be found! I believe she's the worse for your
    town documents already. I bid you keep her in ignorance,
    as I do.

MRS PINCHWIFE. Indeed, be not angry with her, bud.
    She will tell me nothing of the town though I ask her a
    thousand times a day.

PINCHWIFE. Then you are very inquisitive to know, I find!

MRS PINCHWIFE. Not I, indeed, dear. I hate London.
    Our placehouse in the country is worth a thousand of't.
    Would I were there again!

PINCHWIFE. So you shall, I warrant. But were you not
    talking of plays and players when I came in? (*To*
    ALITHEA.) You are her encourager in such discourses.

MRS PINCHWIFE. No, indeed, dear; she chid me just now
    for liking the player-men.

PINCHWIFE (*aside*). Nay, if she be so innocent as to own to
    me her liking them, there is no hurt in't. – Come, my
    poor rogue, but thou lik'st none better than me?

MRS PINCHWIFE. Yes, indeed, but I do; the player-men
    are finer folks.

PINCHWIFE. But you love none better than me?

MRS PINCHWIFE. You are mine own dear bud, and I
    know you; I hate a stranger.

PINCHWIFE. Ay, my dear, you must love me only, and not
    be like the naughty town-women, who only hate their
    husbands and love every man else; love plays, visits, fine
    coaches, fine clothes, fiddles, balls, treats, and so lead a
    wicked town-life.

MRS PINCHWIFE. Nay, if to enjoy all these things be a town-life, London is not so bad a place, dear.

PINCHWIFE. How! If you love me, you must hate London.

ALITHEA (*aside*). The fool has forbid me discovering to her the pleasures of the town, and he is now setting her agog upon them himself.

MRS PINCHWIFE. But, husband, do the town-women love the player-men too?

PINCHWIFE. Yes, I warrant you.

MRS PINCHWIFE. Ay, I warrant you.

PINCHWIFE. Why, you do not, I hope?

MRS PINCHWIFE. No, no, bud; but why have we no player-men in the country?

PINCHWIFE. Ha! – Mistress Minx, ask me no more to go to a play.

MRS PINCHWIFE. Nay, why love? I did not care for going; but when you forbid me, you make me, as't were, desire it.

ALITHEA (*aside*). So 'twill be in other things, I warrant.

MRS PINCHWIFE. Pray, let me go to a play, dear.

PINCHWIFE. Hold your peace, I wo'not.

MRS PINCHWIFE. Why, love?

PINCHWIFE. Why, I'll tell you.

ALITHEA (*aside*). Nay, if he tell her, she'll give him more cause to forbid her that place.

MRS PINCHWIFE. Pray, why, dear?

PINCHWIFE. First, you like the actors, and the gallants may like you.

MRS PINCHWIFE. What, a homely country girl? No, bud, nobody will like me.

PINCHWIFE. I tell you, yes, they may.

MRS PINCHWIFE. No, no, you jest – I won't believe you, I will go.

PINCHWIFE. I tell you then, that one of the lewdest fellows in town, who saw you there, told me he was in love with you.

MRS PINCHWIFE. Indeed! Who, who, pray who was't?

PINCHWIFE (*aside*). I've gone too far, and slipped before I was aware. How overjoyed she is!

MRS PINCHWIFE. Was it any Hampshire gallant, any of our neighbours? I promise you, I am beholding to him.

PINCHWIFE. I promise you, you lie; for he would but ruin you, as he has done hundreds. He has no other love for women, but that; such as he look upon women, like basilisks, but to destroy 'em.

MRS PINCHWIFE. Ay, but if he loves me, why should he ruin me? Answer me to that. Methinks he should not; I would do him no harm.

ALITHEA. Ha, ha, ha!

PINCHWIFE. 'Tis very well; but I'll keep him from doing you any harm, or me either.

Enter SPARKISH *and* HARCOURT.

But here comes company; get you in, get you in.

MRS PINCHWIFE. But pray, husband, is he a pretty gentleman that loves me?

PINCHWIFE. In, baggage, in! (*Thrusts her in; shuts the door.*) (*Aside.*) What, all the lewd libertines of the town brought to my lodging by this easy coxcomb! S'death, I'll not suffer it.

SPARKISH. Here Harcourt, do you approve my choice? (*To* ALITHEA.) Dear little rogue, I told you I'd bring you acquainted with all my friends, the wits, and –

HARCOURT *salutes her.*

PINCHWIFE (*aside*). Ay, they shall know her, as well as you yourself will, I warrant you.

SPARKISH. This is one of those, my pretty rogue, that are to dance at your wedding tomorrow; and him you must bid welcome ever to what you and I have.

PINCHWIFE (*aside*). Monstrous!

SPARKISH. Harcourt, how dost thou like her, faith? – Nay, dear, do not look down; I should hate to have a wife of mine out of countenance at any thing.

PINCHWIFE (*aside*). Wonderful!

SPARKISH. Tell me, I say, Harcourt, how dost thou like her? Thou hast stared upon her enough to resolve me.

HARCOURT. So infinitely well that I could wish I had a mistress too, that might differ from her in nothing but her love and engagement to you.

ALITHEA. Sir, Master Sparkish has often told me that his acquaintance were all wits and railleurs and now I find it.

SPARKISH. No, by the universe, madam, he does not rally now; you may believe him. I do assure you, he is the honestest, worthiest, true-hearted gentleman – a man of such perfect honour, he would say nothing to a lady he does not mean.

PINCHWIFE (*aside*). Praising another man to his mistress!

HARCOURT. Sir, you are so beyond expectation obliging, that –

SPARKISH. Nay, egad, I am sure you do admire her extremely; I see't in your eyes. – He does admire you, madam. – By the world, don't you?

HARCOURT. Yes, above the world, or the most glorious part of it, her whole sex; and till now I never thought I should have envied you or any man about to marry, but you have the best excuse for marriage I ever knew.

ALITHEA. Nay, now, sir, I'm satisfied you are of the society of the wits and railleurs, since you cannot spare your

friend, even when he is but too civil to you. But the surest
sign is, since you are an enemy to marriage, for that,
I hear, you hate as much as business or bad wine.

HARCOURT. Truly, madam, I never was an enemy to
marriage till now, because marriage was never an enemy
to me before.

ALITHEA. But why, sir, is marriage an enemy to you now?
Because it robs you of your friend here? For you look
upon a friend married as one gone into a monastery, that
is dead to the world.

HARCOURT. 'Tis indeed, because you marry him; I see,
madam, you can guess my meaning. I do confess heartily
and openly, I wish it were in my power to break the
match. By heavens I would!

SPARKISH. Poor Frank.

ALITHEA. Would you be so unkind to me?

HARCOURT. No, no, 'tis not because I would be unkind to
you.

SPARKISH. Poor Frank! No, gad, 'tis only his kindness to
me.

PINCHWIFE (*aside*). Great kindness to you indeed! Insensible
fop, let a man make love to his wife to his face!

SPARKISH. Come, dear Frank, for all my wife there that
shall be, thou shalt enjoy me sometimes, dear rogue.
By my honour, we men of wit condole for our deceased
brother in marriage as much as for one dead in earnest. –
I think that was prettily said of me, ha, Harcourt? – But
come, Frank, be not melancholy for me.

HARCOURT. No, I assure you I am not melancholy for
you.

SPARKISH. Prithee, Frank, dost think my wife that shall be,
there, a fine person?

HARCOURT. I could gaze upon her till I became as blind
as you are.

SPARKISH. How, as I am? How?

HARCOURT. Because you are a lover, and true lovers are blind, stock blind.

SPARKISH. True, true; but by the world, she has wit too, as well as beauty. Go, go with her into a corner, and try if she has wit; talk to her anything; she's bashful before me.

HARCOURT. Indeed, if a woman wants wit in a corner, she has it nowhere.

ALITHEA (*aside to* SPARKISH). Sir, you dispose of me a little before your time –

SPARKISH. Nay, nay, madam, let me have an earnest of your obedience, or – Go, go, madam –

HARCOURT courts ALITHEA aside.

PINCHWIFE. How, sir! If you are not concerned for the honour of a wife, I am for that of a sister; he shall not debauch her. Be a pander to your own wife, bring men to her, let 'em make love before your face, thrust 'em into a corner together, then leave 'em in private! Is this your town wit and conduct?

SPARKISH. Ha, ha, ha! A silly wise rogue would make one laugh more than a stark fool, ha, ha! I shall burst. Nay, you shall not disturb 'em; I'll vex thee, by the world.

Struggles with PINCHWIFE to keep him from HARCOURT and ALITHEA.

ALITHEA. The writings are drawn, sir, settlements made; 'tis too late, sir, and past all revocation.

HARCOURT. Then so is my death.

ALITHEA. I would not be unjust to him.

HARCOURT. Then why to me so?

ALITHEA. I have no obligation to you.

HARCOURT. My love.

ALITHEA. I had his before.

HARCOURT. You never had it; he wants, you see, jealousy, the only infallible sign of it.

ALITHEA. Love proceeds from esteem; he cannot distrust my virtue. Besides he loves me, or he would not marry me.

HARCOURT. Marrying you is no more sign of his love, than bribing your woman, that he may marry you, is a sign of his generosity. Marriage is rather a sign of interest than love; and he that marries a fortune, covets a mistress, not loves her. But if you take marriage for a sign of love, take it from me immediately.

ALITHEA. No, now you have put a scruple in my head. But in short, sir, to end our dispute, I must marry him, my reputation would suffer in the world else.

HARCOURT. No, if you do marry him, with your pardon, madam, your reputation suffers in the world, and you would be thought in necessity for a cloak.

ALITHEA. Nay, now you are rude, sir. – Mr Sparkish, pray come hither, your friend here is very troublesome, and very loving.

HARCOURT (*aside to* ALITHEA). Hold, hold! –

PINCHWIFE. D'ye hear that?

SPARKISH. Why, d'ye think I'll seem to be jealous, like a country bumpkin?

PINCHWIFE. No, rather be a cuckold, like a credulous cit.

HARCOURT. Madam, you would not have been so little generous as to have told him?

ALITHEA. Yes, since you could be so little generous as to wrong him.

HARCOURT. Wrong him! No man can do't, he's beneath an injury; a bubble, a coward, a senseless idiot, a wretch so contemptible to all the world but you that –

ALITHEA. Hold, do not rail at him, for since he is like to be my husband, I am resolved to like him. Nay, I think I am obliged to tell him you are not his friend. – Master Sparkish, Master Sparkish!

SPARKISH. What, what? Now, dear rogue, has not she wit?

HARCOURT (*speaks surlily*). Not as much as I thought, and hoped she had.

ALITHEA. Mr Sparkish, do you bring people to rail at you?

HARCOURT. Madam –

SPARKISH. How! No, but if he does rail at me, 'tis but in jest, I warrant; what we wits do for one another, and never take any notice of it.

ALITHEA. He spoke so scurrilously of you, I had no patience to hear him; besides, he has been making love to me.

HARCOURT (*aside*). True, damned, tell-tale woman.

SPARKISH. Pshaw, to show his parts – we wits rail and make love often but to show our parts; as we have no affections, so we have no malice; we –

ALITHEA. He said you were a wretch, below an injury.

SPARKISH. Pshaw!

HARCOURT (*aside*). Damned, senseless, impudent, virtuous jade! Well, since she won't let me have her, she'll do as good, she'll make me hate her.

ALITHEA. A common bubble.

SPARKISH. Pshaw!

ALITHEA. A coward.

SPARKISH. Pshaw, pshaw!

ALITHEA. A senseless, drivelling idiot.

SPARKISH. How! Did he disparage my parts? Nay, then my honour's concerned; I can't put up that, sir, by the world. Brother, help me to kill him. (*Aside.*) I may draw now, since we have the odds of him! 'Tis a good occasion, too, before my mistress – (*Offers to draw.*)

ALITHEA. Hold, hold!

SPARKISH. What, what?

ALITHEA (*aside*). I must not let 'em kill the gentleman neither, for his kindness to me; I am so far from hating him that I wish my gallant had his person and understanding. – Nay, if my honour –

SPARKISH. I'll be thy death.

ALITHEA. Hold, hold! Indeed, to tell the truth, the gentleman said after all that what he spoke was but out of friendship to you.

SPARKISH. How! Say, I am – I am a fool, that is, no wit, out of friendship to me?

ALITHEA. Yes, to try whether I was concerned enough for you, and made love to me only to be satisfied of my virtue, for your sake.

HARCOURT (*aside*). Kind however –

SPARKISH. Nay, if it were so, my dear rogue, I ask thee pardon; but why would not you tell me so, faith?

HARCOURT. Because I did not think on't, faith.

SPARKISH. Come, Horner does not come; Harcourt, let's be gone to the new play. – Come, madam.

ALITHEA. I will not go, if you intend to leave me alone in the box and run into the pit, as you use to do.

SPARKISH. Pshaw! I'll leave Harcourt with you in the box to entertain you, and that's as good; if I sat in the box, I should be thought no judge, but of trimmings. – Come away, Harcourt, lead her down.

Exeunt SPARKISH, HARCOURT *and* ALITHEA.

PINCHWIFE. Well, go thy ways, for the flower of the true town fops, such as spend their estates before they come to

'em, and are cuckolds before they're married. But let me
go look to my own freehold – How!

Enter MY LADY FIDGET, MISTRESS DAINTY
FIDGET *and* MISTRESS SQUEAMISH.

LADY FIDGET. Your servant, sir; where is your lady? We
are come to wait upon her to the new play.

PINCHWIFE. New play!

LADY FIDGET. And my husband will wait upon you
presently.

PINCHWIFE (*aside*). Damn your civility. – Madam, by no
means; I will not see Sir Jaspar here till I have waited
upon him at home; nor shall my wife see you till she has
waited upon your ladyship at your lodgings.

LADY FIDGET. Now we are here, sir –

PINCHWIFE. No, madam.

DAINTY. Pray, let us see her.

SQUEAMISH. We will not stir till we see her.

PINCHWIFE (*aside*). A pox on you all! (*Goes to the door and
returns.*) She has locked the door, and is gone abroad.

LADY FIDGET. No, you have locked the door, and she's
within.

DAINTY. They told us below, she was here.

PINCHWIFE (*aside*). Will nothing do? – Well, it must out
then. To tell you the truth, ladies, which I was afraid to
let you know before, lest it might endanger your lives, my
wife has just now the smallpox come out upon her. Do not
be frightened; but pray, be gone, ladies; you shall not stay
here in danger of your lives; pray get you gone, ladies.

LADY FIDGET. No, no, we have all had 'em.

SQUEAMISH. Alack, alack!

DAINTY. Come, come, we must see how it goes with her;
I understand the disease.

LADY FIDGET. Come.

PINCHWIFE (*aside*). Well, there is no being too hard for women at their own weapon, lying; therefore I'll quit the field.

Exit PINCHWIFE.

SQUEAMISH. Here's an example of jealousy.

LADY FIDGET. Indeed, as the world goes, I wonder there are no more jealous, since wives are so neglected.

DAINTY. Pshaw! as the world goes, to what end should they be jealous?

LADY FIDGET. Foh! 'tis a nasty world.

SQUEAMISH. That men of parts, great acquaintance, and quality should take up with and spend themselves and fortunes in keeping little playhouse creatures, foh!

LADY FIDGET. Nay, that women of understanding, great acquaintance and good quality should fall a-keeping, too, of little creatures, foh!

SQUEAMISH. Why, 'tis the men of quality's fault; they never visit women of honour and reputation as they used to do; and have not so much as common civility for ladies of our rank, but use us with the same indifferency and ill-breeding as if we were all married to 'em.

LADY FIDGET. She says true; 'tis an arrant shame women of quality should be so slighted. Methinks, birth — birth should go for something. I have known men admired, courted, and followed for their titles only.

SQUEAMISH. Ay, one would think men of honour should not love, no more than marry, out of their own rank.

DAINTY. Fie, fie upon 'em! They are come to think cross-breeding for themselves best, as well as for their dogs and horses.

LADY FIDGET. They are dogs, and horses for't.

SQUEAMISH. One would think, if not for love, for vanity a little.

DAINTY. Nay, they do satisfy their vanity upon us sometimes; and are kind to us in their report, tell all the world they lie with us.

LADY FIDGET. Damned rascals! That we should be only wronged by 'em. To report a man has had a person, when he has not had a person, is the greatest wrong in the whole world that can be done to a person.

SQUEAMISH. Well, 'tis an arrant shame noble persons should be so wronged and neglected.

LADY FIDGET. But still 'tis an arranter shame for a noble person to neglect her own honour, and defame her own noble person with little inconsiderable fellows, foh!

DAINTY. I suppose the crime against our honour is the same with a man of quality as with another.

LADY FIDGET. How! No, sure, the man of quality is likest one's husband, and therefore the fault should be the less.

DAINTY. But then the pleasure should be the less!

LADY FIDGET. Fie, fie, fie, for shame, sister! Whither shall we ramble? Be continent in your discourse, or I shall hate you.

DAINTY. Besides, an intrigue is so much the more notorious for the man's quality.

SQUEAMISH. 'Tis true, nobody takes notice of a private man, and therefore with him 'tis more secret, and the crime's the less when 'tis not known.

LADY FIDGET. You say true; i'faith, I think you are in the right on't. 'Tis not an injury to a husband till it be an injury to our honours; so that a woman of honour loses no honour with a private person; and to say truth –

DAINTY (*apart to* SQUEAMISH). So, the little fellow is grown a private person – with her –

LADY FIDGET. But still my dear, dear honour.

Enter SIR JASPAR, HORNER, DORILANT.

SIR JASPAR. Ay, my dear, dear of honour, thou hast still so much honour in thy mouth –

HORNER (*aside*). That she has none elsewhere.

LADY FIDGET. Oh, what d'ye mean to bring in these upon us?

DAINTY. Foh, these are as bad as wits.

SQUEAMISH. Foh!

LADY FIDGET. Let us leave the room.

SIR JASPAR. Stay, stay; faith, to tell you the naked truth –

LADY FIDGET. Fie, Sir Jaspar, do not use that word 'naked'.

SIR JASPAR. Well, well, in short, I have business at Whitehall, and cannot go to the play with you, therefore would have you go –

LADY FIDGET. With those two to a play?

SIR JASPAR. No, not with t'other, but with Mr Horner. There can be no more scandal to go with him than with Mr Tattle, or Master Limberham.

LADY FIDGET. With that nasty fellow! No – no!

SIR JASPAR. Nay, prithee dear, hear me.

Whispers to LADY FIDGET.

HORNER. Ladies –

HORNER, DORILANT *drawing near* SQUEAMISH *and* DAINTY.

DAINTY. Stand off.

SQUEAMISH. Do not approach us.

DAINTY. You herd with the wits, you are obscenity all over.

SQUEAMISH. And I would as soon look upon a picture of Adam and Eve, without fig leaves, as any of you, if I could help it; therefore keep off, and do not make us sick.

DORILANT. What a devil are these?

HORNER. Why, these are pretenders to honour, as critics to wit, only by censuring others; and as every raw, peevish, out-of-humoured, affected, dull, tea-drinking, arithmetical fop sets up for a wit, by railing at men of sense, so these for honour by railing at the court and ladies of as great honour as quality.

SIR JASPAR. Come, Mr Horner, I must desire you to go with these ladies to the play, sir.

HORNER. I, sir?

SIR JASPAR. Ay, ay, come, sir.

HORNER. I must beg your pardon, sir, and theirs; I will not be seen in women's company in public again for the world.

SIR JASPAR. Ha, ha, strange aversion!

SQUEAMISH. No, he's for women's company in private.

SIR JASPAR. He – poor man – he! Ha, ha, ha!

DAINTY. 'Tis a greater shame amongst lewd fellows to be seen in virtuous women's company than for the women to be seen with them.

HORNER. Indeed, madam, the time was I only hated virtuous women, but now I hate the other too; I beg your pardon, ladies.

LADY FIDGET. You are very obliging, sir, because we would not be troubled with you.

SIR JASPAR. In sober sadness, he shall go.

DORILANT. Nay, if he wo'not, I am ready to wait upon the ladies; and I think I am the fitter man.

SIR JASPAR. You, sir, no, I thank you for that – Master Horner is a privileged man amongst the virtuous ladies; 'twill be a great while before you are so, he, he, he! He's my wife's gallant, he, he, he! No, pray withdraw, sir, for as I take it, the virtuous ladies have no business with you.

DORILANT. And I am sure he can have none with them.
'Tis strange a man can't come amongst virtuous women
now but upon the same terms as men are admitted into
the great Turk's seraglio; but heavens keep me from being
an ombre player with 'em! But where is Pinchwife?

Exit DORILANT.

SIR JASPAR. Come, come, man; what, avoid the sweet
society of womankind? That sweet, soft, gentle, tame,
noble creature, woman, made for man's companion –

HORNER. So is that soft, gentle, tame, and more noble
creature a spaniel and has all their tricks – can fawn, lie
down, suffer beating, and fawn the more; barks at your
friends when they come to see you; makes your bed hard;
gives you fleas, and the mange sometimes. And all the
difference is, the spaniel's the more faithful animal and
fawns but upon one master.

SIR JASPAR. He, he, he!

SQUEAMISH. Oh, the rude beast!

DAINTY. Insolent brute!

LADY FIDGET. Brute! Stinking, mortified, rotten French
wether, to dare –

SIR JASPAR. Hold, an't please your ladyship. – For shame,
Master Horner, your mother was a woman. – (*Aside.*) Now
shall I never reconcile 'em. – Hark you, madam, take my
advice in your anger. You know you often want one to
make up your drolling pack of ombre players; and you
may cheat him easily, for he's an ill gamester, and
consequently loves play. Besides, you know, you have
but two old civil gentlemen (with stinking breaths too)
to wait upon you abroad; take in the third into your
service. The other are but crazy; and a lady should have
a supernumerary gentleman-usher, as a supernumerary
coachhorse, lest sometimes you should be forced to stay at
home.

LADY FIDGET. But are you sure he loves play, and has
money?

SIR JASPAR. He loves play as much as you, and has money as much as I.

LADY FIDGET. Then I am contented to make him pay for his scurrility; money makes up in a measure all other wants in men. (*Aside.*) Those whom we cannot make hold for gallants, we make fine.

SIR JASPAR (*aside*). So, so; now to mollify, to wheedle him. – Master Horner, will you never keep civil company? Methinks 'tis time now, since you are only fit for them. Come, come, man, you must e'en fall to visiting our wives, eating at our tables, drinking tea with our virtuous relations after dinner, dealing cards to 'em, reading plays and gazettes to 'em, picking fleas out of their shocks for 'em, collecting receipts, new songs, women, pages, and footmen for 'em.

HORNER. I hope they'll afford me better employment, sir.

SIR JASPAR. He, he, he! 'Tis fit you know your work before you come into your place; and since you are unprovided of a lady to flatter, and a good house to eat at, pray frequent mine, and call my wife mistress, and she shall call you gallant, according to the custom.

HORNER. Who, I?

SIR JASPAR. Faith, thou shalt for my sake; come, for my sake only.

HORNER. For your sake –

SIR JASPAR. Come, come, here's a gamester for you; let him be a little familiar sometimes; nay, what if a little rude? Gamesters may be rude with ladies, you know.

LADY FIDGET. Yes, losing gamesters have a privilege with women.

HORNER. I always thought the contrary, that the winning gamester had most privilege with women; for when you have lost your money to a man, you'll lose anything you have, all you have, they say, and he may use you as he pleases.

SIR JASPAR. He, he, he! Well, win or lose, you shall have your liberty with her.

LADY FIDGET. As he behaves himself; and for your sake I'll give him admittance and freedom.

HORNER. All sorts of freedom, madam?

SIR JASPAR. Ay, ay, ay, all sorts of freedom thou canst take, and so go to her, begin thy new employment; wheedle her, jest with her, and be better acquainted one with another.

HORNER (*aside*). I think I know her already, therefore may venture with her, my secret for hers.

HORNER *and* LADY FIDGET *whisper.*

SIR JASPAR. Sister, coz, I have provided an innocent playfellow for you there.

DAINTY. Who, he!

SQUEAMISH. There's a playfellow indeed!

SIR JASPAR. Yes, sure, what, he is good enough to play at cards, blindman's buff, or the fool with sometimes.

SQUEAMISH. Foh, we'll have no such playfellows.

DAINTY. No, sir, you shan't choose playfellows for us, we thank you.

SIR JASPAR. Nay, pray hear me.

Whispering to them.

LADY FIDGET. But, poor gentleman, could you be so generous, so truly a man of honour, as for the sakes of us women of honour, to cause yourself to be reported no man? No man! And to suffer yourself the greatest shame that could fall upon a man, that none might fall upon us women by your conversation? But indeed, sir, as perfectly, perfectly, the same man as before going into France, sir? As perfectly, perfectly, sir?

HORNER. As perfectly, perfectly, madam. Nay, I scorn you should take my word; I desire to be tried only, madam.

LADY FIDGET. Well, that's spoken again like a man of
honour; all men of honour desire to come to the test. But,
indeed, generally you men report such things of
yourselves, one does not know how or whom to believe;
and it is come to that pass we dare not take your words,
no more than your tailor's, without some staid servant of
yours be bound with you. But I have so strong a faith in
your honour, dear, dear, noble sir, that I'd forfeit mine for
yours at any time, dear sir.

HORNER. No, madam, you should not need to forfeit it for
me; I have given you security already to save you
harmless, my late reputation being so well known in the
world, madam.

LADY FIDGET. But if upon any future falling out, or upon
a suspicion of my taking the trust out of your hands,
to employ some other, you yourself should betray your
trust, dear sir? I mean, if you'll give me leave to speak
obscenely, you might tell, dear sir.

HORNER. If I did, nobody would believe me; the
reputation of impotency is as hardly recovered again in
the world as that of cowardice, dear madam.

LADY FIDGET. Nay, then, as one may say, you may do
your worst, dear, dear, sir.

SIR JASPAR. Come, is your ladyship reconciled to him yet?
Have you agreed on matters? For I must be gone to
Whitehall.

LADY FIDGET. Why, indeed, Sir Jaspar, Master Horner is
a thousand, thousand times a better man than I thought
him. Cousin Squeamish, Sister Dainty, I can name him
now, truly; not long ago, you know, I thought his very
name obscenity, and I would as soon have lain with him
as have named him.

SIR JASPAR. Very likely, poor madam.

DAINTY. I believe it.

SQUEAMISH. No doubt on't.

SIR JASPAR. Well, well – that your ladyship is as virtuous as any she, I know, and him all the town knows – he, he, he! Therefore, now you like him, get you gone to your business together; go, go, to your business, I say, pleasure, whilst I go to my pleasure, business.

LADY FIDGET. Come then, dear gallant.

HORNER. Come away, my dearest mistress.

SIR JASPAR. So, so; why 'tis as I'd have it.

Exit SIR JASPAR.

HORNER. And as I'd have it!

LADY FIDGET.
Who for his business from his wife will run,
Takes the best care to have her business done.

Exeunt omnes.

ACT THREE

Scene One

ALITHEA *and* MRS PINCHWIFE.

ALITHEA. Sister, what ails you? You are grown melancholy.

MRS PINCHWIFE. Would it not make anyone melancholy, to see you go every day fluttering about abroad, whilst I must stay at home like a poor, lonely, sullen bird in a cage?

ALITHEA. Ay, sister, but you came young and just from the nest to your cage, so that I thought you liked it; and could be as cheerful in't as others that took their flight themselves early, and are hopping abroad in the open air.

MRS PINCHWIFE. Nay, I confess I was quiet enough till my husband told me what pure lives the London ladies live abroad, with their dancing, meetings, and junketings, and dressed every day in their best gowns; and I warrant you, play at ninepins every day of the week, so they do.

Enter MR PINCHWIFE.

PINCHWIFE. Come, what's here to do? You are putting the town pleasures in her head, and setting her a-longing.

ALITHEA. Yes, after ninepins; you suffer none to give her those longings, you mean, but yourself.

PINCHWIFE. I tell her of the vanities of the town like a confessor.

ALITHEA. A confessor! Just such a confessor as he that, by forbidding a silly ostler to grease the horse's teeth, taught him to do't.

PINCHWIFE. Come, Mistress Flippant, good precepts are lost when bad examples are still before us. The liberty you take abroad makes her hanker after it, and out of humour at home. Poor wretch, she desired not to come to London; I would bring her.

ALITHEA. Very well.

PINCHWIFE. She has been this week in town, and never desired, till this afternoon, to go abroad.

ALITHEA. Was she not at a play yesterday?

PINCHWIFE. Yes, but she ne'er asked me. I was myself the cause of her going.

ALITHEA. Then, if she ask you again, you are the cause of her asking, and not my example.

PINCHWIFE. Well, tomorrow night I shall be rid of you; and the next day, before 'tis light, she and I'll be rid of the town, and my dreadful apprehensions. Come, be not melancholy, for thou shalt go into the country after tomorrow, dearest.

ALITHEA. Great comfort!

MRS PINCHWIFE. Pish! What d'ye tell me of the country for?

PINCHWIFE. How's this! What, pish at the country?

MRS PINCHWIFE. Let me alone, I am not well.

PINCHWIFE. O, if that be all − what ails my dearest?

MRS PINCHWIFE. Truly I don't know; but I have not been well since you told me there was a gallant at the play in love with me.

PINCHWIFE. Ha! −

ALITHEA. That's by my example too!

PINCHWIFE. Nay, if you are not well, but are so concerned because a lewd fellow chanced to lie, and say he liked you, you'll make me sick too.

MRS PINCHWIFE. Of what sickness?

PINCHWIFE. O, of that which is worse than the plague, jealousy.

MRS PINCHWIFE. Pish, you jeer! I'm sure there's no such disease in our receipt-book at home.

PINCHWIFE. No, thou never met'st with it, poor innocent. (*Aside.*) Well, if thou cuckold me, 'twill be my own fault – for cuckolds and bastards are generally makers of their own fortune.

MRS PINCHWIFE. Well, but pray, bud, let's go to a play tonight.

PINCHWIFE. 'Tis just done, she comes from it; but why are you so eager to see a play?

MRS PINCHWIFE. Faith, dear, not that I care one pin for their talk there; but I like to look upon the player-men, and would see, if I could, the gallant you say loves me; that's all, dear bud.

PINCHWIFE. Is that all, dear bud?

ALITHEA. This proceeds from my example.

MRS PINCHWIFE. But if the play be done, let's go abroad, however, dear bud.

PINCHWIFE. Come, have a little patience, and thou shalt go into the country on Friday.

MRS PINCHWIFE. Therefore I would see first some sights, to tell my neighbours of. Nay, I will go abroad, that's once.

ALITHEA. I'm the cause of this desire too.

PINCHWIFE. But now I think on't, who was the cause of Horner's coming to my lodging today? That was you.

ALITHEA. No, you, because you would not let him see your handsome wife out of your lodging.

MRS PINCHWIFE. Why, O lord! Did the gentleman come hither to see me indeed?

PINCHWIFE. No, no. – You are not cause of that damned question too, Mistress Alithea? (*Aside.*) Well, she's in the right of it. He is in love with my wife – and comes after her – 'tis so – but I'll nip his love in the bud; lest he should follow us into the country, and break his chariot-wheel near our house on purpose for an excuse to come to't. But I think I know the town.

MRS PINCHWIFE. Come, pray bud, let's go abroad before 'tis late; for I will go, that's flat and plain.

PINCHWIFE (*aside*). So! the obstinacy already of a town-wife, and I must, whilst she's here, humour her like one. – Sister, how shall we do that she may not be seen or known?

ALITHEA. Let her put on her mask.

PINCHWIFE. Pshaw! A mask makes people but the more inquisitive, and is as ridiculous a disguise as a stage beard; her shape, stature, habit will be known. And if we should meet with Horner, he would be sure to take acquaintance with us, must wish her joy, kiss her, talk to her, leer upon her, and the devil and all. No, I'll not use her to a mask, 'tis dangerous; for masks have made more cuckolds than the best faces that ever were known.

ALITHEA. How will you do then?

MRS PINCHWIFE. Nay, shall we go? The Exchange will be shut, and I have a mind to see that.

PINCHWIFE. So – I have it – I'll dress her up in the suit we are to carry down to her brother, little Sir James; nay, I understand the town tricks. Come, let's go dress her. A mask! No – a woman masked, like a covered dish, gives a man curiosity and appetite, when, it may be, uncovered, 'twould turn his stomach; no, no.

ALITHEA. Indeed your comparison is something a greasy one. But I had a gentle gallant used to say, 'A beauty masked, like the sun in eclipse, gathers together more gazers than if it shined out'.

Exeunt.

Scene Two

The scene changes to the New Exchange.

Enter HORNER, HARCOURT, DORILANT.

DORILANT. Engaged to women, and not sup with us?

HORNER. Ay, a pox on 'em all.

HARCOURT. You were much a more reasonable man in the morning, and had as noble resolutions against 'em as a widower of a week's liberty.

DORILANT. Did I ever think to see you keep company with women in vain?

HORNER. In vain! No − 'tis, since I can't love 'em, to be revenged on 'em.

HARCOURT. Now your sting is gone, you looked in the box, amongst all those women, like a drone in the hive, all upon you; shoved and ill-used by 'em all, and thrust from one side to t'other.

DORILANT. Yet he must be buzzing amongst 'em still, like other old beetle-headed, liquorish drones. Avoid 'em, and hate 'em as they hate you.

HORNER. Because I do hate 'em and would hate 'em yet more, I'll frequent 'em. You may see by marriage, nothing makes a man hate a woman more than her constant conversation. In short, I converse with 'em, as you do with rich fools, to laugh at 'em and use 'em ill.

DORILANT. But I would no more sup with women, unless I could lie with 'em, than sup with a rich coxcomb, unless I could cheat him.

HORNER. Yes, I have known thee sup with a fool for his drinking; if he could set out your hand that way only, you were satisfied, and if he were a wine-swallowing mouth 'twas enough.

HARCOURT. Yes, a man drinks often with a fool, as he tosses with a marker, only to keep his hand in ure. But do the ladies drink?

HORNER. Yes, sir, and I shall have the pleasure at least of laying 'em flat with a bottle, and bring as much scandal that way upon 'em as formerly t'other.

HARCOURT. Perhaps you may prove as weak a brother amongst 'em that way as t'other.

DORILANT. Foh! Drinking with women is as unnatural as scolding with 'em; but 'tis a pleasure of decayed fornicators, and the basest way of quenching love.

HARCOURT. Nay, 'tis drowning love instead of quenching it. But leave us for civil women too!

DORILANT. Ay, when he can't be the better for 'em. We hardly pardon a man that leaves his friend for a wench, and that's a pretty lawful call.

HORNER. Faith, I would not leave you for 'em, if they would not drink.

DORILANT. Who would disappoint his company at Lewis's for a gossiping?

HARCOURT. Foh! Wine and women, good apart, together as nauseous as sack and sugar. But hark you, sir, before you go, a little of your advice; an old maimed general, when unfit for action, is fittest for counsel. I have other designs upon women than eating and drinking with them. I am in love with Sparkish's mistress, whom he is to marry tomorrow. Now how shall I get her?

Enter SPARKISH, *looking about.*

HORNER. Why, here comes one will help you to her.

HARCOURT. He! He, I tell you, is my rival, and will hinder my love.

HORNER. No, a foolish rival and a jealous husband assist their rival's designs; for they are sure to make their women hate them, which is the first step to their love for another man.

HARCOURT. But I cannot come near his mistress but in his company.

HORNER. Still the better for you, for fools are most easily cheated when they themselves are accessories; and he is to be bubbled of his mistress, as of his money, the common mistress, by keeping him company.

SPARKISH. Who is that, that is to be bubbled? Faith, let me snack, I han't met with a bubble since Christmas. Gad, I think bubbles are like their brother woodcocks, go out with the cold weather.

HARCOURT (*apart to* HORNER). A pox! He did not hear all I hope.

SPARKISH. Come, you bubbling rogues you, where do we sup? – Oh, Harcourt, my mistress tells me you have been making fierce love to her all the play long, ha, ha! – But I –

HARCOURT. I make love to her?

SPARKISH. Nay, I forgive thee; for I think I know thee, and I know her, but I am sure I know myself.

HARCOURT. Did she tell you so? I see all women are like these of the Exchange, who, to enhance the price of their commodities, report to their fond customers offers which were never made 'em.

HORNER. Ay, women are as apt to tell before the intrigue as men after it, and so show themselves the vainer sex. But hast thou a mistress, Sparkish? 'Tis as hard for me to believe it as that thou ever hadst a bubble, as you bragged just now.

SPARKISH. Oh, your servant, sir; are you at your raillery, sir? But we were some of us beforehand with you today at the play. The wits were something bold with you, sir; did you not hear us laugh?

HARCOURT. Yes, but I thought you had gone to plays to laugh at the poet's wit, not at your own.

SPARKISH. Your servant, sir; no, I thank you. Gad, I go to
a play as to a country treat; I carry my own wine to one,
and my own wit to t'other, or else I'm sure I should not
be merry at either. And the reason why we are so often
louder than the players is because we think we speak
more wit, and so become the poet's rivals in his audience.
For to tell you the truth, we hate the silly rogues; nay, so
much that we find fault even with their bawdy upon the
stage, whilst we talk nothing else in the pit as loud.

HORNER. But, why should'st thou hate the silly poets?
Thou hast too much wit to be one, and they, like whores,
are only hated by each other. And thou dost scorn
writing, I'm sure.

SPARKISH. Yes, I'd have you to know, I scorn writing;
but women, women, that make men do all foolish things,
make 'em write songs too; everybody does it. 'Tis even
as common with lovers as playing with fans; and you can
no more help rhyming to your Phyllis than drinking to
your Phyllis.

HARCOURT. Nay, poetry in love is no more to be avoided
than jealousy.

DORILANT. But the poets damned your songs, did they?

SPARKISH. Damn the poets! They turned 'em into
burlesque, as they call it. That burlesque is a hocus-pocus
trick they have got, which by the virtue of *hictius doctius*,
topsy-turvy, they make a wise and witty man in the world
a fool upon the stage, you know not how. And 'tis
therefore I hate 'em too, for I know not but it may be my
own case; for they'll put a man into a play for looking
asquint. Their predecessors were contented to make
serving-men only their stage-fools, but these rogues must
have gentlemen, with a pox to 'em, nay knights. And,
indeed, you shall hardly see a fool upon the stage but he's
a knight; and to tell you the truth, they have kept me
these six years from being a knight in earnest, for fear of
being knighted in a play, and dubbed a fool.

DORILANT. Blame 'em not, they must follow their copy,
the age.

HARCOURT. But why should'st thou be afraid of being in a play, who expose yourself every day in the playhouses, and as public places?

HORNER. 'Tis but being on the stage, instead of standing on a bench in the pit.

DORILANT. Don't you give money to painters to draw you like? And are you afraid of your pictures at length in a playhouse, where all your mistresses may see you?

SPARKISH. A pox! Painters don't draw the smallpox or pimples in one's face. Come, damn all your silly authors whatever, all books and booksellers, by the world, and all readers, courteous or uncourteous.

HARCOURT. But, who comes here, Sparkish?

Enter MR PINCHWIFE *and his wife in man's clothes,* ALITHEA, LUCY *her maid.*

SPARKISH. Oh hide me! There's my mistress too.

SPARKISH *hides himself behind* HARCOURT.

HARCOURT. She sees you.

SPARKISH. But I will not see her. 'Tis time to go to Whitehall, and I must not fail the drawing-room.

HARCOURT. Pray, first carry me, and reconcile me to her.

SPARKISH. Another time; faith, the king will have supped.

HARCOURT. Not with the worse stomach for thy absence; thou art one of those fools that think their attendance at the king's meals as necessary as his physicians', when you are more troublesome to him than his doctors, or his dogs.

SPARKISH. Pshaw! I know my interest, sir; prithee, hide me.

HORNER. Your servant, Pinchwife. – What, he knows us not!

PINCHWIFE (*to his wife, aside*). Come along.

MRS PINCHWIFE. Pray, have you any ballads? Give me sixpenny worth?

CLASP. We have no ballads.

MRS PINCHWIFE. Then give me *Covent Garden Drollery*, and a play or two – Oh, here's *Tarugo's Wiles*, and *The Slighted Maiden*; I'll have them.

PINCHWIFE (*apart to her*). No, plays are not for your reading. Come along; will you discover yourself?

HORNER. Who is that pretty youth with him, Sparkish?

SPARKISH. I believe his wife's brother, because he's something like her; but I never saw her but once.

HORNER. Extremely handsome; I have seen a face like it too. Let us follow 'em.

Exeunt PINCHWIFE, MISTRESS PINCHWIFE, ALITHEA, LUCY; HORNER, DORILANT *following them.*

HARCOURT. Come, Sparkish, your mistress saw you, and will be angry you go not to her. Besides I would fain be reconciled to her, which none but you can do, dear friend.

SPARKISH. Well, that's a better reason, dear friend. I would not go near her now, for hers or my own sake, but I can deny you nothing; for though I have known thee a great while, never go, if I do not love thee as well as a new acquaintance.

HARCOURT. I am obliged to you indeed, dear friend. I would be well with her, only to be well with thee still; for these ties to wives usually dissolve all ties to friends. I would be contented she should enjoy you a-nights, but I would have you to myself a-days, as I have had, dear friend.

SPARKISH. And thou shalt enjoy me a-days, dear, dear friend, never stir; and I'll be divorced from her, sooner than from thee. Come along –

HARCOURT (*aside*). So we are hard put to't, when we
make our rival our procurer; but neither she nor her
brother would let me come near her now. When all's
done, a rival is the best cloak to steal to a mistress under,
without suspicion; and when we have once got to her as
we desire, we throw him off like other cloaks.

Exit SPARKISH, *and* HARCOURT *following him.*

Re-enter MR PINCHWIFE, MISTRESS PINCHWIFE *in
man's clothes.*

PINCHWIFE (*to* ALITHEA, *off-stage*). Sister, if you will not
go, we must leave you. (*Aside.*) The fool her gallant and
she will muster up all the young saunterers of this place,
and they will leave their dear seamstresses to follow us.
What a swarm of cuckolds and cuckold-makers are here! –
Come, let's be gone, Mistress Margery.

MRS PINCHWIFE. Don't you believe that, I han't half my
bellyfull of sights yet.

PINCHWIFE. Then walk this way.

MRS PINCHWIFE. Lord, what a power of brave signs are
here! Stay – the Bull's Head, the Ram's Head, and the
Stag's Head! Dear –

PINCHWIFE. Nay, if every husband's proper sign here were
visible, they would be all alike.

MRS PINCHWIFE. What d'ye mean by that, bud?

PINCHWIFE. 'Tis no matter – no matter, bud.

MRS PINCHWIFE. Pray tell me; nay, I will know.

PINCHWIFE. They would all be bulls', stags', and rams'
heads!

Exeunt MR PINCHWIFE, MRS PINCHWIFE.

Re-enter SPARKISH, HARCOURT, ALITHEA, LUCY
at t'other door.

SPARKISH. Come, dear madam, for my sake you shall be
reconciled to him.

ALITHEA. For your sake I hate him.

HARCOURT. That's something too cruel, madam, to hate me for his sake.

SPARKISH. Ay indeed, madam, too, too cruel to me, to hate my friend for my sake.

ALITHEA. I hate him because he is your enemy; and you ought to hate him too, for making love to me, if you love me.

SPARKISH. That's a good one; I hate a man for loving you! If he did love you, 'tis but what he can't help; and 'tis your fault not his, if he admires you. I hate a man for being of my opinion; I'll ne'er do't, by the world.

ALITHEA. Is it for your honour or mine, to suffer a man to make love to me, who am to marry you tomorrow?

SPARKISH. Is it for your honour or mine, to have me jealous? That he makes love to you is a sign you are handsome; and that I am not jealous, is a sign you are virtuous. That, I think, is for your honour.

ALITHEA. But, 'tis your honour too I am concerned for.

HARCOURT. But why, dearest madam, will you be more concerned for his honour than he is himself? Let his honour alone, for my sake and his. He, he has no honour –

SPARKISH. How's that?

HARCOURT. But what my dear friend can guard himself.

SPARKISH. O ho – that's right again.

HARCOURT. Your care of his honour argues his neglect of it, which is no honour to my dear friend here; therefore once more, let his honour go which way it will, dear madam.

SPARKISH. Ay, ay, were it for my honour to marry a woman whose virtue I suspected, and could not trust her in a friend's hands?

ALITHEA. Are you not afraid to lose me?

HARCOURT. He afraid to lose you, madam! No, no – you may see how the most estimable and most glorious creature in the world is valued by him. Will you not see it?

SPARKISH. Right, honest Frank, I have that noble value for her that I cannot be jealous of her.

ALITHEA. You mistake him. He means you care not for me nor who has me.

SPARKISH. Lord, madam, I see you are jealous! Will you wrest a poor man's meaning from his words?

ALITHEA. You astonish me, sir, with your want of jealousy.

SPARKISH. And you make me giddy, madam, with your jealousy and fears, and virtue and honour. Gad, I see virtue makes a woman as troublesome as a little reading or learning.

ALITHEA. Monstrous!

LUCY (*behind*). Well, to see what easy husbands these women of quality can meet with; a poor chambermaid can never have such ladylike luck. Besides, he's thrown away upon her; she'll make no use of her fortune, her blessing; none to a gentleman for a pure cuckold, for it requires good breeding to be a cuckold.

ALITHEA. I tell you then plainly, he pursues me to marry me.

SPARKISH. Pshaw!

HARCOURT. Come, madam, you see you strive in vain to make him jealous of me. My dear friend is the kindest creature in the world to me.

SPARKISH. Poor fellow.

HARCOURT. But his kindness only is not enough for me, without your favour; your good opinion, dear madam, 'tis that must perfect my happiness. Good gentleman, he believes all I say; would you would do so. Jealous of me! I would not wrong him nor you for the world.

ALITHEA walks carelessly to and fro.

SPARKISH. Look you there; hear him, hear him, and do not walk away so.

HARCOURT. I love you, madam, so –

SPARKISH. How's that! Nay – now you begin to go too far indeed.

HARCOURT. So much, I confess, I say I love you, that I would not have you miserable, and cast yourself away upon so unworthy and inconsiderable a thing as what you see here.

Clapping his hand on his breast, points at SPARKISH.

SPARKISH. No, faith, I believe thou would'st not; now his meaning is plain. But I knew before thou would'st not wrong me nor her.

HARCOURT. No, no, heavens forbid the glory of her sex should fall so low as into the embraces of such a contemptible wretch, the last of mankind – my dear friend here – I injure him.

Embracing SPARKISH.

ALITHEA. Very well.

SPARKISH. No, no, dear friend, I knew it. Madam, you see he will rather wrong himself than me, in giving himself such names.

ALITHEA. Do not you understand him yet?

SPARKISH. Yes, how modestly he speaks of himself, poor fellow.

ALITHEA. Methinks he speaks impudently of yourself, since – before yourself too; insomuch that I can no longer suffer his scurrilous abusiveness to you, no more than his love to me.

Offers to go.

SPARKISH. Nay, nay, madam, pray stay. His love to you! Lord, madam, has he not spoke yet plain enough?

ALITHEA. Yes indeed, I should think so.

SPARKISH. Well then, by the world, a man can't speak civilly to a woman now but presently she says he makes love to her! Nay, madam, you shall stay, with your pardon, since you have not yet understood him, till he has made an *éclaircissement* of his love to you, that is, what kind of love it is. (*To* HARCOURT.) Answer to thy catechism: friend, do you love my mistress here?

HARCOURT. Yes, I wish she would not doubt it.

SPARKISH. But how do you love her?

HARCOURT. With all my soul.

ALITHEA. I thank him; methinks he speaks plain enough now.

SPARKISH (*to* ALITHEA). You are out still. – But with what kind of love, Harcourt?

HARCOURT. With the best and truest love in the world.

SPARKISH. Look you there then, that is with no matrimonial love, I'm sure.

ALITHEA. How's that? Do you say matrimonial love is not best?

SPARKISH (*aside*). Gad, I went too far ere I was aware. – But speak for thyself, Harcourt; you said you would not wrong me nor her.

HARCOURT. No, no, madam, e'en take him for heaven's sake –

SPARKISH. Look you there, madam.

HARCOURT. Who should in all justice be yours, he that loves you most.

Claps his hand on his breast.

ALITHEA. Look you there, Mr Sparkish, who's that?

SPARKISH. Who should it be? – Go on, Harcourt.

HARCOURT. Who loves you more than women titles, or fortune fools.

Points at SPARKISH.

SPARKISH. Look you there, he means me still, for he points at me.

ALITHEA. Ridiculous!

HARCOURT. Who can only match your faith and constancy in love.

SPARKISH. Ay.

HARCOURT. Who knows, if it be possible, how to value so much beauty and virtue.

SPARKISH. Ay.

HARCOURT. Whose love can no more be equalled in the world than that heavenly form of yours.

SPARKISH. No.

HARCOURT. Who could no more suffer a rival than your absence, and yet could no more suspect your virtue than his own constancy in his love to you.

SPARKISH. No.

HARCOURT. Who, in fine, loves you better than his eyes, that first made him love you.

SPARKISH. Ay – nay, madam, faith, you shan't go, till –

ALITHEA. Have a care, lest you make me stay too long –

SPARKISH. But till he has saluted you; that I may be assured you are friends, after his honest advice and declaration. Come, pray, madam, be friends with him.

Enter PINCHWIFE *and* MRS PINCHWIFE.

ALITHEA. You must pardon me, sir, that I am not yet so obedient to you.

PINCHWIFE. What, invite your wife to kiss men?
Monstrous! Are you not ashamed? I will never forgive
you.

SPARKISH. Are you not ashamed that I should have more
confidence in the chastity of your family than you have?
You must not teach me, I am a man of honour, sir,
though I am frank and free. I am frank, sir –

PINCHWIFE. Very frank, sir, to share your wife with your
friends.

SPARKISH. He is an humble, menial friend, such as
reconciles the differences of the marriage bed. You know
man and wife do not always agree; I design him for that
use, therefore would have him well with my wife.

PINCHWIFE. A menial friend! – You will get a great many
menial friends by showing your wife as you do.

SPARKISH. What then? It may be I have a pleasure in't, as
I have to show fine clothes at a playhouse the first day,
and count money before poor rogues.

PINCHWIFE. He that shows his wife or money will be in
danger of having them borrowed sometimes.

SPARKISH. I love to be envied, and would not marry a
wife that I alone could love; loving alone is as dull as
eating alone. Is it not a frank age? And I am a frank
person. And to tell you the truth, it may be I love to have
rivals in a wife; they make her seem to a man still but as
a kept mistress. And so good night, for I must to
Whitehall. Madam, I hope you are now reconciled to
my friend; and so I wish you a good night, madam, and
sleep if you can, for tomorrow you know I must visit
you early with a canonical gentleman. Good night, dear
Harcourt.

Exit SPARKISH.

HARCOURT. Madam, I hope you will not refuse my visit
tomorrow, if it should be earlier with a canonical
gentleman than Mr Sparkish's.

PINCHWIFE (*coming between* ALITHEA *and* HARCOURT).
This gentlewoman is yet under my care; therefore you
must yet forbear your freedom with her, sir.

HARCOURT. Must, sir!

PINCHWIFE. Yes, sir, she is my sister.

HARCOURT. 'Tis well she is, sir – for I must be her
servant, sir. Madam –

PINCHWIFE. Come away, sister; we had been gone if it
had not been for you, and so avoided these lewd
rakehells, who seem to haunt us.

Enter HORNER, DORILANT *to them.*

HORNER. How now, Pinchwife!

PINCHWIFE. Your servant.

HORNER. What! I see a little time in the country makes a
man turn wild and unsociable, and only fit to converse
with his horses, dogs, and his herds.

PINCHWIFE. I have business, sir, and must mind it; your
business is pleasure, therefore you and I must go different
ways.

HORNER. Well, you may go on, but this pretty young
gentleman –

Takes hold of MRS PINCHWIFE.

HARCOURT. The lady –

DORILANT. And the maid –

HORNER. Shall stay with us, for I suppose their business is
the same with ours, pleasure.

PINCHWIFE (*aside*). 'Sdeath, he knows her, she carries it so
sillily! Yet if he does not, I should be more silly to
discover it first.

ALITHEA. Pray, let us go, sir.

PINCHWIFE. Come, come –

HORNER (*to* MRS PINCHWIFE). Had you not rather stay
with us? – Prithee, Pinchwife, who is this pretty young
gentleman?

PINCHWIFE. One to whom I'm a guardian. (*Aside.*) I wish I
could keep her out of your hands.

HORNER. Who is he? I never saw anything so pretty in all
my life.

PINCHWIFE. Pshaw, do not look upon him so much; he's a
poor bashful youth, you'll put him out of countenance.
Come away, brother.

Offers to take her away.

HORNER. Oh, your brother?

PINCHWIFE. Yes, my wife's brother. Come, come, she'll
stay supper for us.

HORNER. I thought so, for he is very like her I saw you at
the play with, whom I told you I was in love with.

MRS PINCHWIFE (*aside*). O Jeminy! Is this he that was in
love with me? I am glad on't, I vow, for he's a curious
fine gentleman, and I love him already too. (*To* MR
PINCHWIFE.) Is this he, bud?

PINCHWIFE (*to his wife*). Come away, come away!

HORNER. Why, what haste are you in? Why won't you let
me talk with him?

PINCHWIFE. Because you'll debauch him. He's yet young
and innocent, and I would not have him debauched for
anything in the world. (*Aside.*) How she gazes on him!
the devil –

HORNER. Harcourt, Dorilant, look you here; this is the
likeness of that dowdy he told us of, his wife. Did you
ever see a lovelier creature? The rogue has reason to be
jealous of his wife, since she is like him, for she would
make all that see her in love with her.

HARCOURT. And as I remember now, she is as like him
here as can be.

DORILANT. She is indeed very pretty, if she be like him.

HORNER. Very pretty? A very pretty commendation – She is a glorious creature, beautiful beyond all things I ever beheld.

PINCHWIFE. So, so.

HARCOURT. More beautiful than a poet's first mistress of imagination.

HORNER. Or another man's last mistress of flesh and blood.

MRS PINCHWIFE. Nay, now you jeer sir; pray don't jeer me.

PINCHWIFE. Come, come. (*Aside.*) By heavens, she'll discover herself.

HORNER. I speak of your sister, sir.

PINCHWIFE. Ay, but saying she was handsome, if like him, made him blush. (*Aside.*) I am upon a rack!

HORNER. Methinks he is so handsome he should not be a man.

PINCHWIFE (*aside*). Oh, there 'tis out, he has discovered her. I am not able to suffer any longer. (*To his wife.*) Come, come away, I say –

HORNER. Nay, by your leave, sir, he shall not go yet. (*To them.*) Harcourt, Dorilant, let us torment this jealous rogue a little.

HARCOURT *and* DORILANT. How?

HORNER. I'll show you.

PINCHWIFE. Come, pray let him go, I cannot stay fooling any longer; I tell you his sister stays supper for us.

HORNER. Does she? Come then, we'll all go sup with her and thee.

PINCHWIFE. No, now I think on't, having stayed so long for us, I warrant she's gone to bed. (*Aside.*) I wish she and

I were well out of their hands. – Come, I must rise early tomorrow, come.

HORNER. Well then, if she be gone to bed, I wish her and you a good night. But pray, young gentleman, present my humble service to her.

MRS PINCHWIFE. Thank you heartily, sir.

PINCHWIFE (*aside*). 'Sdeath, she will discover herself yet in spite of me. – He is something more civil to you, for your kindness to his sister, than I am, it seems.

HORNER. Tell her, dear sweet little gentleman, for all your brother there, that you have revived the love I had for her at first sight in the playhouse.

MRS PINCHWIFE. But did you love her indeed, and indeed?

PINCHWIFE (*aside*). So, so. – Away, I say.

HORNER. Nay, stay. Yes, indeed, and indeed, pray do you tell her so, and give her this kiss from me.

Kisses her.

PINCHWIFE (*aside*). O heavens! What do I suffer! Now 'tis too plain he knows her, and yet –

HORNER. And this, and this –

Kisses her again.

MRS PINCHWIFE. What do you kiss me for? I am no woman.

PINCHWIFE (*aside*). So – there, 'tis out. – Come, I cannot, nor will stay any longer.

HORNER. Nay, they shall send your lady a kiss too. Here, Harcourt, Dorilant, will you not?

They kiss her.

PINCHWIFE (*aside*). How, do I suffer this? Was I not accusing another just now for this rascally patience, in permitting his wife to be kissed before his face? Ten thousand ulcers gnaw away their lips! – Come, come.

HORNER. Good night, dear little gentleman; madam, goodnight; farewell, Pinchwife. (*Apart to* HARCOURT *and* DORILANT.) Did not I tell you I would raise his jealous gall?

Exeunt HORNER, HARCOURT *and* DORILANT.

PINCHWIFE. So, they are gone at last! Stay, let me see first if the coach be at this door. (*Exit.*)

HORNER, HARCOURT *and* DORILANT *return.*

HORNER. What, not gone yet? Will you be sure to do as I desired you, sweet sir?

MRS PINCHWIFE. Sweet sir, but what will you give me then?

HORNER. Anything. Come away into the next walk.

Exit HORNER, *haling away* MRS PINCHWIFE.

ALITHEA. Hold, hold! What d'ye do?

LUCY. Stay, stay, hold –

HARCOURT. Hold, madam, hold! Let him present him, he'll come presently; nay, I will never let you go till you answer my question.

ALITHEA, LUCY, *struggling with* HARCOURT *and* DORILANT.

LUCY. For god's sake, sir, I must follow 'em.

DORILANT. No, I have something to present you with too; you shan't follow them.

PINCHWIFE *returns.*

PINCHWIFE. Where? – how? – what's become of? – gone! – whither?

LUCY. He's only gone with the gentleman, who will give him something, an't please your worship.

PINCHWIFE. Something! – Give him something, with a pox! – Where are they?

ALITHEA. In the next walk only, brother.

PINCHWIFE. Only, only! Where, where?

Exit PINCHWIFE *and returns presently then goes out again.*

HARCOURT. What's the matter with him? Why so much concerned? But dearest madam –

ALITHEA. Pray, let me go, sir; I have said and suffered enough already.

HARCOURT. Then you will not look upon, nor pity, my sufferings?

ALITHEA. To look upon 'em, when I cannot help 'em, were cruelty not pity; therefore I will never see you more.

HARCOURT. Let me then, madam, have my privilege of a banished lover, complaining or railing, and giving you but a farewell reason why, if you cannot condescend to marry me, you should not take that wretch, my rival.

ALITHEA. He only, not you, since my honour is engaged so far to him, can give me a reason, why I should not marry him. But if he be true, and what I think him to me, I must be so to him. Your servant, sir.

HARCOURT. Have women only constancy when 'tis a vice, and, like fortune, only true to fools?

DORILANT (*to* LUCY, *who struggles to get from him*). Thou sha't not stir, thou robust creature! You see I can deal with you, therefore you should stay the rather, and be kind.

Enter PINCHWIFE.

PINCHWIFE. Gone, gone, not to be found! Quite gone! Ten thousand plagues go with 'em! Which way went they?

ALITHEA. But into t'other walk, brother.

LUCY. Their business will be done presently sure, an't please your worship; it can't be long in doing, I'm sure on't.

ALITHEA. Are they not there?

PINCHWIFE. No; you know where they are, you infamous wretch, eternal shame of your family, which you do not dishonour enough yourself, you think, but you must help her to do it too, thou legion of bawds!

ALITHEA. Good brother –

PINCHWIFE. Damned, damned sister!

ALITHEA. Look you here, she's coming.

Enter MRS PINCHWIFE *in man's clothes, running, with her hat under her arm, full of oranges and dried fruit;* HORNER *following.*

MRS PINCHWIFE. O dear bud, look you here what I have got, see.

PINCHWIFE (*aside, rubbing his forehead*). And what have I got here too, which you can't see.

MRS PINCHWIFE. The fine gentleman has given me better things yet.

PINCHWIFE. Has he so? (*Aside.*) Out of breath and coloured! I must hold yet.

HORNER. I have only given your little brother an orange, sir.

PINCHWIFE (*to* HORNER). Thank you, sir. (*Aside.*) You have only squeezed my orange, I suppose, and give it me again. Yet I must have a city patience. (*To his wife.*) Come, come away.

MRS PINCHWIFE. Stay, till I have put up my fine things, bud.

Enter SIR JASPAR FIDGET.

SIR JASPAR. O Master Horner, come, come, the ladies stay for you; your mistress, my wife, wonders you make not more haste to her.

HORNER. I have stayed this half hour for you here, and 'tis your fault I am not now with your wife.

SIR JASPAR. But pray, don't let her know so much. The truth on't is, I was advancing a certain project to his majesty about – I'll tell you.

HORNER. No, let's go and hear it at your house. Good night, sweet little gentleman. One kiss more; you'll remember me now, I hope.

Kisses her.

DORILANT. What, Sir Jaspar, will you separate friends? He promised to sup with us; and if you take him to your house, you'll be in danger of our company too.

SIR JASPAR. Alas, gentlemen, my house is not fit for you; there are none but civil women there, which are not for your turn. He, you know, can bear with the society of civil women now, ha, ha, ha! Besides, he's one of my family – he's – he, he, he!

DORILANT. What is he?

SIR JASPAR. Faith, my eunuch, since you'll have it, he, he, he!

Exeunt SIR JASPAR FIDGET *and* HORNER.

DORILANT. I rather wish thou wert his, or my, cuckold. Harcourt, what a good cuckold is lost there for want of a man to make him one! Thee and I cannot have Horner's privilege, who can make use of it.

HARCOURT. Ay, to poor Horner 'tis like coming to an estate at threescore, when a man can't be the better for't.

PINCHWIFE. Come.

MRS PINCHWIFE. Presently, bud.

DORILANT. Come, let us go too. (*To* ALITHEA.) Madam, your servant. (*To* LUCY.) Good night, strapper.

HARCOURT. Madam, though you will not let me have a good day or night, I wish you one; but dare not name the other half of my wish.

ALITHEA. Good night, sir, for ever.

MRS PINCHWIFE. I don't know where to put this here, dear bud. You shall eat it. Nay, you shall have part of the fine gentleman's good things, or treat, as you call it, when we come home.

PINCHWIFE. Indeed, I deserve it, since I furnished the best part of it. (*Strikes away the orange.*)

The gallant treats, presents, and gives the ball;
But 'tis the absent cuckold, pays for all.

ACT FOUR

Scene One

In PINCHWIFE'*s house in the morning.* LUCY, ALITHEA *dressed in new clothes.*

LUCY. Well, madam, now have I dressed you, and set you out with so many ornaments, and spent upon you ounces of essence and pulvilio; and all this for no other purpose but as people adorn and perfume a corpse for a stinking second-hand grave; such or as bad I think Master Sparkish's bed.

ALITHEA. Hold your peace.

LUCY. Nay, madam, I will ask you the reason why you would banish poor Master Harcourt for ever from your sight? How could you be so hard-hearted?

ALITHEA. 'Twas because I was not hard-hearted.

LUCY. No, no; 'twas stark love and kindness, I warrant.

ALITHEA. It was so; I would see him no more because I love him.

LUCY. Hey-day, a very pretty reason!

ALITHEA. You do not understand me.

LUCY. I wish you may yourself.

ALITHEA. I was engaged to marry, you see, another man, whom my justice will not suffer me to deceive or injure.

LUCY. Can there be a greater cheat or wrong done to a man than to give him your person without your heart? I should make a conscience of it.

ALITHEA. I'll retrieve it for him after I am married a while.

LUCY. The woman that marries to love better will be as much mistaken as the wencher that marries to live better. No, madam, marrying to increase love is like gaming to become rich; alas, you only lose what little stock you had before.

ALITHEA. I find by your rhetoric you have been bribed to betray me.

LUCY. Only by his merit, that has bribed your heart, you see, against your word and rigid honour. But what a devil is this honour? 'Tis sure a disease in the head, like the megrim, or falling sickness, that always hurries people away to do themselves mischief. Men lose their lives by it; women what's dearer to 'em, their love, the life of life.

ALITHEA. Come, pray talk you no more of honour, nor Master Harcourt. I wish the other would come to secure my fidelity to him and his right in me.

LUCY. You will marry him then?

ALITHEA. Certainly. I have given him already my word, and will my hand too, to make it good, when he comes.

LUCY. Well, I wish I may never stick pin more if he be not an arrant natural to t'other fine gentleman.

ALITHEA. I own he wants the wit of Harcourt, which I will dispense withal for another want he has, which is want of jealousy which men of wit seldom want.

LUCY. Lord, madam, what should you do with a fool to your husband? You intend to be honest, don't you? Then that husbandly virtue, credulity, is thrown away upon you.

ALITHEA. He only that could suspect my virtue should have cause to do it. 'Tis Sparkish's confidence in my truth that obliges me to be so faithful to him.

LUCY. You are not sure his opinion may last.

ALITHEA. I am satisfied 'tis impossible for him to be jealous after the proofs I have had of him. Jealousy in a husband – heaven defend me from it! It begets a

thousand plagues to a poor woman, the loss of her
honour, her quiet, and her –

LUCY. And her pleasure.

ALITHEA. What d'ye mean, impertinent?

LUCY. Liberty is a great pleasure, madam.

ALITHEA. I say, loss of her honour, her quiet, nay, her life
sometimes; and what's as bad almost, the loss of this
town; that is, she is sent into the country, which is the last
ill usage of a husband to a wife, I think.

LUCY (aside). Oh, does the wind lie there? – Then of
necessity, madam, you think a man must carry his wife
into the country, if he be wise. The country is as terrible,
I find, to our young English ladies as a monastery to
those abroad; and on my virginity, I think they would
rather marry a London jailer than a high sheriff of a
county, since neither can stir from his employment.
Formerly women of wit married fools for a great estate, a
fine seat, or the like; but now 'tis for a pretty seat only in
Lincoln's Inn Fields, St James's Fields, or the Pall Mall.

Enter to them SPARKISH, *and* HARCOURT *dressed like a
parson.*

SPARKISH. Madam, your humble servant, a happy day to
you, and to us all.

HARCOURT. Amen.

ALITHEA. Who have we here?

SPARKISH. My chaplain, faith. O madam, poor Harcourt
remembers his humble service to you, and in obedience to
your last commands, refrains coming into your sight.

ALITHEA. Is not that he?

SPARKISH. No, fie, no; but to show that he ne'er intended
to hinder our match, has sent his brother here to join
our hands. When I get a wife, I must get her a chaplain,
according to the custom. This is his brother, and my
chaplain.

ALITHEA. His brother?

LUCY (*aside*). And your chaplain, to preach in your pulpit, then!

ALITHEA. His brother!

SPARKISH. Nay, I knew you would not believe it. – I told you, sir, she would take you for your brother Frank.

ALITHEA. Believe it!

LUCY (*aside*). His brother! ha, ha, he! He has a trick left still, it seems.

SPARKISH. Come, my dearest, pray let us go to church before the canonical hour is past.

ALITHEA. For shame, you are abused still.

SPARKISH. By the world, 'tis strange now you are so incredulous.

ALITHEA. 'Tis strange you are so credulous.

SPARKISH. Dearest of my life, hear me. I tell you this is Ned Harcourt of Cambridge, by the world; you see he has a sneaking college look. 'Tis true he's something like his brother Frank, and they differ from each other no more than in their age, for they were twins.

LUCY. Ha, ha, he!

ALITHEA. Your servant, sir; I cannot be so deceived, though you are. But come, let's hear, how do you know what you affirm so confidently?

SPARKISH. Why, I'll tell you all. Frank Harcourt, coming to me this morning to wish me joy and present his service to you, I asked him if he could help me to a parson; whereupon he told me he had a brother in town who was in orders, and he went straight away and sent him, you see there, to me.

ALITHEA. Yes, Frank goes and puts on a black coat, then tells you he is Ned; that's all you have for't!

SPARKISH. Pshaw, Pshaw! I tell you by the same token, the midwife put her garter about Frank's neck to know 'em asunder, they were so like.

ALITHEA. Frank tells you this too?

SPARKISH. Ay, and Ned there too; nay, they are both in a story.

ALITHEA. So, so; very foolish.

SPARKISH. Lord, if you won't believe one, you had best try him by your chambermaid there; for chambermaids must needs know chaplains from other men, they are so used to 'em.

LUCY. Let's see; nay, I'll be sworn he has the canonical smirk, and the filthy, clammy palm of a chaplain.

ALITHEA. Well, most reverend doctor, pray let us make an end of this fooling.

HARCOURT. With all my soul, divine, heavenly creature, when you please.

ALITHEA. He speaks like a chaplain indeed.

SPARKISH. Why, was there not 'soul', 'divine', 'heavenly' in what he said.

ALITHEA. Once more, impertinent black coat, cease your persecution, and let us have a conclusion of this ridiculous love.

HARCOURT (aside). I had forgot; I must suit my style to my coat, or I wear it in vain.

ALITHEA. I have no more patience left. Let us make once an end of this troublesome love, I say.

HARCOURT. So be it, seraphic lady, when your honour shall think it meet and convenient to do so.

SPARKISH. Gad, I'm sure none but a chaplain could speak so, I think.

ALITHEA. Let me tell you, sir, this dull trick will not serve your turn. Though you delay our marriage, you shall not hinder it.

HARCOURT. Far be it from me, munificent patroness, to
delay your marriage. I desire nothing more than to marry
you presently, which I might do, if you yourself would; for
my noble, good-natured and thrice generous patron here
would not hinder it.

SPARKISH. No, poor man, not I, faith.

HARCOURT. And now, madam, let me tell you plainly,
nobody else shall marry you. By heavens, I'll die first,
for I'm sure I should die after it.

LUCY (aside). How his love has made him forget his
function, as I have seen it in real parsons!

ALITHEA. That was spoken like a chaplain too! Now you
understand him, I hope.

SPARKISH. Poor man, he takes it heinously to be refused. I
can't blame him, 'tis putting an indignity upon him not to
be suffered. But you'll pardon me, madam, it shan't be,
he shall marry us. Come away, pray, madam.

LUCY (aside). Ha, ha, he! More ado! 'Tis late.

ALITHEA. Invincible stupidity! I tell you he would marry
me as your rival, not as your chaplain.

SPARKISH (pulling her away). Come, come, madam.

LUCY. I pray, madam, do not refuse this reverend divine
the honour and satisfaction of marrying you; for I dare
say he has set his heart upon't, good doctor.

ALITHEA. What can you hope or design by this?

HARCOURT (aside). I could answer her; a reprieve, for a
day only, often revokes a hasty doom. At worst, if she will
not take mercy on me and let me marry her, I have at
least the lover's second pleasure, hindering my rival's
enjoyment, though but for a time.

SPARKISH. Come, madam, 'tis e'en twelve o'clock, and
my mother charged me never to be married out of the
canonical hours; come, come! Lord, here's such a deal
of modesty, I warrant, the first day.

LUCY. Yes, an't please your worship, married women show all their modesty the first day, because married men show all their love the first day.

Exeunt SPARKISH, ALITHEA, HARCOURT *and* LUCY.

Scene Two

The scene changes to a bedchamber, where appear PINCHWIFE *and* MRS PINCHWIFE.

PINCHWIFE. Come, tell me, I say.

MRS PINCHWIFE. Lord! Han't I told it an hundred times over?

PINCHWIFE (*aside*). I would try if, in the repetition of the ungrateful tale, I could find her altering it in the least ·circumstance; for if her story be false, she is so too. – Come, how was't, baggage?

MRS PINCHWIFE. Lord, what pleasure you take to hear it, sure!

PINCHWIFE. No, you take more in telling it, I find. But speak, how was't?

MRS PINCHWIFE. He carried me up into the house next to the Exchange.

PINCHWIFE. So, and you two were only in the room?

MRS PINCHWIFE. Yes, for he sent away a youth, that was there, for some dried fruit and China oranges.

PINCHWIFE. Did he so? Damn him for it – and for –

MRS PINCHWIFE. But presently came up the gentlewoman of the house.

PINCHWIFE. Oh, 'twas well she did! But what did he do whilst the fruit came?

MRS PINCHWIFE. He kissed me an hundred times, and told me he fancied he kissed my fine sister, meaning me, you know, whom he said he loved with all his soul, and bid me be sure to tell her so, and desire her to be at her window by eleven of the clock this morning, and he would walk under it at that time.

PINCHWIFE (*aside*). And he was as good as his word, very punctual; a pox reward him for't.

MRS PINCHWIFE. Well, and he said if you were not within, he would come up to her, meaning me, you know, bud, still.

PINCHWIFE (*aside*). So – he knew her certainly; but for this confession I am obliged to her simplicity. – But what, you stood very still when he kissed you?

MRS PINCHWIFE. Yes, I warrant you; would you have had me discover myself?

PINCHWIFE. But you told me he did some beastliness to you, as you called it. What was't?

MRS PINCHWIFE. Why, he put –

PINCHWIFE. What?

MRS PINCHWIFE. Why, he put the tip of his tongue between my lips, and so mousled me – and I said, I'd bite it.

PINCHWIFE. An eternal canker seize it, for a dog!

MRS PINCHWIFE. Nay, you need not be so angry with him neither, for to say truth, he has the sweetest breath I ever knew.

PINCHWIFE. The devil! – you were satisfied with it then, and would do it again?

MRS PINCHWIFE. Not unless he should force me.

PINCHWIFE. Force you, changeling! I tell you no woman can be forced.

MRS PINCHWIFE. Yes, but she may sure by such a one as he, for he's a proper, goodly strong man; 'tis hard, let me tell you, to resist him.

PINCHWIFE (*aside*). So, 'tis plain she loves him, yet she
  has not love enough to make her conceal it from me.
  But the sight of him will increase her aversion for me,
  and love for him, and that love instruct her how to
  deceive me and satisfy him, all idiot that she is. Love!
  'Twas he gave women first their craft, their art of
  deluding. Out of nature's hands they came plain, open,
  silly, and fit for slaves, as she and heaven intended 'em,
  but damned love – well – I must strangle that little
  monster whilst I can deal with him. – Go, fetch pen, ink,
  and paper out of the next room.

MRS PINCHWIFE. Yes, bud.

  Exit MRS PINCHWIFE.

PINCHWIFE (*aside*). Why should women have more
  invention in love than men? It can only be because they
  have more desires, more soliciting passions, more lust, and
  more of the devil.

  MRS PINCHWIFE *returns*.

  Come, minx, sit down and write.

MRS PINCHWIFE. Ay, dear bud, but I can't do't very well.

PINCHWIFE. I wish you could not at all.

MRS PINCHWIFE. But what should I write for?

PINCHWIFE. I'll have you write a letter to your lover.

MRS PINCHWIFE. O lord, to the fine gentleman a letter!

PINCHWIFE. Yes, to the fine gentleman.

MRS PINCHWIFE. Lord, you do but jeer; sure you jest.

PINCHWIFE. I am not so merry, come, write as I bid you.

MRS PINCHWIFE. What, do you think I am a fool?

PINCHWIFE (*aside*). She's afraid I would not dictate any
  love to him, therefore she's unwilling. – But you had best
  begin.

MRS PINCHWIFE. Indeed, and indeed, but I won't, so
  I won't!

PINCHWIFE. Why?

MRS PINCHWIFE. Because he's in town; you may send for him if you will.

PINCHWIFE. Very well, you would have him brought to you; is it come to this? I say, take the pen and write, or you'll provoke me.

MRS PINCHWIFE. Lord, what d'ye make a fool of me for? Don't I know that letters are never writ but from the country to London and from London into the country? Now he's in town and I am in town too; therefore I can't write to him, you know.

PINCHWIFE (*aside*). So, I am glad it is no worse; she is innocent enough yet. – Yes, you may, when your husband bids you, write letters to people that are in town.

MRS PINCHWIFE. Oh, may I so? Then I'm satisfied.

PINCHWIFE. Come, begin. (*Dictates.*) 'Sir – '

MRS PINCHWIFE. Shan't I say 'Dear Sir'? You know one says always something more than bare 'Sir'.

PINCHWIFE. Write as I bid you, or I will write 'whore' with this penknife in your face.

MRS PINCHWIFE. Nay, good bud. (*She writes.*) 'Sir'.

PINCHWIFE. 'Though I suffered last night your nauseous, loathed kisses and embraces' – Write.

MRS PINCHWIFE. Nay, why should I say so? You know I told you he had a sweet breath.

PINCHWIFE. Write!

MRS PINCHWIFE. Let me but put out 'loathed'.

PINCHWIFE. Write, I say.

MRS PINCHWIFE. Well, then. (*Writes.*)

PINCHWIFE. Let's see what you have writ. (*Takes the paper and reads.*) 'Though I suffered last night your kisses and embraces'. Thou impudent creature! Where is 'nauseous' and 'loathed'?

MRS PINCHWIFE. I can't abide to write such filthy words.

PINCHWIFE. Once more write as I'd have you, and question it not, or I will spoil thy writing with this. (*Holds up the penknife*.) I will stab out those eyes that cause my mischief.

MRS PINCHWIFE. O lord, I will!

PINCHWIFE. So – so – Let's see now! (*Reads*.) 'Though I suffered last night your nauseous, loathed kisses and embraces' – Go on – 'yet I would not have you presume that you shall ever repeat them'. – So.

MRS PINCHWIFE (*she writes*). I have writ it.

PINCHWIFE. On then. – 'I then concealed myself from your knowledge, to avoid your insolencies – '

MRS PINCHWIFE (*she writes*). So –

PINCHWIFE. 'The same reason, now I am out of your hands'

MRS PINCHWIFE (*she writes*). So –

PINCHWIFE. 'Makes me own to you my unfortunate, though innocent frolic, of being in man's clothes'

MRS PINCHWIFE (*she writes*). So –

PINCHWIFE. 'that you may for ever more cease to pursue her, who hates and detests you – '

She writes on.

MRS PINCHWIFE (*sighs*). So-h –

PINCHWIFE. What, do you sigh? – 'detests you – as much as she loves her husband and her honour'.

MRS PINCHWIFE. I vow, husband, he'll ne'er believe I should write such a letter.

PINCHWIFE. What, he'd expect a kinder from you? Come now, your name only.

MRS PINCHWIFE. What, shan't I say 'Your most faithful, humble servant till death'?

PINCHWIFE. No, tormenting fiend! (*Aside.*) Her style, I find, would be very soft. – Come, wrap it up now, whilst I go fetch wax and a candle, and write on the back side 'For Mr Horner'.

Exit PINCHWIFE.

MRS PINCHWIFE. 'For Mr Horner' – So, I am glad he has told me his name. Dear Mr Horner! But why should I send thee such a letter that will vex thee and make thee angry with me? – Well, I will not send it – Ay, but then my husband will kill me – for I see plainly, he won't let me love Mr Horner – but what care I for my husband? – I won't, so I won't send poor Mr Horner such a letter – but then my husband – but oh, what if I writ at bottom, my husband made me write it? – Ay, but then my husband would see't – Can one have no shift? Ah, a London woman would have had a hundred presently. Stay – what if I should write a letter, and wrap it up like this, and write upon't too? Ay, but then my husband would see't – I don't know what to do – But yet y'vads I'll try, so I will – for I will not send this letter to poor Mr Horner, come what will on't. (*She writes and repeats what she hath writ.*) 'Dear Sweet Mr Horner' – So – 'My husband would have me send you a base, rude, unmannerly letter – but I won't – ' so – 'and would have me forbid you loving me – but I won't' – so – 'and would have me say to you, I hate you, poor Mr Horner – but I won't tell a lie for him' – there – 'for I'm sure if you and I were in the country at cards together – ' so – 'I could not help treading on your toe under the table – ' so – 'or rubbing knees with you, and staring in your face 'till you saw me' – very well – 'and then looking down and blushing for an hour together' – so – 'but I must make haste before my husband come; and now he has taught me to write letters, you shall have longer ones from me, who am, dear, dear, poor dear Mr Horner, your most humble friend, and servant to command till death, Margery Pinchwife'. – Stay, I must give him a hint at bottom – so – now wrap it up just like t'other – so – now write 'For Mr Horner' – But, oh now, what shall I do with it? For here comes my husband.

Enter PINCHWIFE.

PINCHWIFE (*aside*). I have been detained by a sparkish coxcomb, who pretended a visit to me; but I fear 'twas to my wife. – What, have you done?

MRS PINCHWIFE. Ay, ay, bud, just now.

PINCHWIFE. Let's see't. What d'ye tremble for? What, you would not have it go?

MRS PINCHWIFE. Here. (*Aside.*) No, I must not give him that; so I had been served if I had given him this.

PINCHWIFE (*he opens and reads the first letter*). Come, where's the wax and seal?

MRS PINCHWIFE (*aside*). Lord, what shall I do now? Nay, then, I have it. – Pray, let me see't. Lord, you think me so arrant a fool I cannot seal a letter? I will do't, so I will.

Snatches the letter from him, changes it for the other, seals it, and delivers it to him.

PINCHWIFE. Nay, I believe you will learn that, and other things too, I which I would not have you.

MRS PINCHWIFE. So; han't I done it curiously? (*Aside.*) I think I have; there's my letter going to Mr Horner, since he'll needs have me send letters to folks.

PINCHWIFE. 'Tis very well; but I warrant, you would not have it go now?

MRS PINCHWIFE. Yes, indeed, but I would, bud, now.

PINCHWIFE. Well you are a good girl then. Come, let me lock you up in your chamber till I come back; and be sure you come not within three strides of the window when I am gone, for I have a spy in the street.

Exit MRS PINCHWIFE. PINCHWIFE *locks the door.*

At least, 'tis fit she think so. If we do not cheat women, they'll cheat us; and fraud may be justly used with secret enemies, of which a wife is the most dangerous; and he that has a handsome one to keep, and a frontier town, must provide against treachery rather than open force. Now I have secured all within I'll deal with the foe without with false intelligence.

Holds up the letter.

Exit PINCHWIFE.

Scene Three

The scene changes to HORNER*'s lodging.*

Enter QUACK *and* HORNER.

QUACK. Well, sir, how fadges the new design? Have you not the luck of all your brother projectors, to deceive only yourself at last?

HORNER. No, good *Domine* doctor, I deceive you, it seems, and others too; for the grave matrons and old rigid husbands think me as unfit for love as they are; but their wives, sisters and daughters know some of 'em better things already!

QUACK. Already!

HORNER. Already, I say. Last night I was drunk with half a dozen of your civil persons, as you call 'em, and people of honour, and so was made free of their society and dressing rooms for ever hereafter; and am already come to the privileges of sleeping upon their pallets, warming smocks, tying shoes and garters, and the like, doctor, already, already, doctor.

QUACK. You have made use of your time, sir.

HORNER. I tell thee, I am now no more interruption to 'em when they sing or talk bawdy than a little squab French page who speaks no English.

QUACK. But do civil persons and women of honour drink, and sing bawdy songs?

HORNER. Oh, amongst friends, amongst friends. For your bigots in honour are just like those in religion; they fear the eye of the world more than the eye of heaven, and think there is no virtue but railing at vice, and no sin but giving scandal. They rail at a poor, little, kept player, and keep themselves some young, modest pulpit comedian to be privy to their sins in their closets, not to tell 'em of them in their chapels.

QUACK. Nay, the truth on't is, priests amongst the women now have quite got the better of us lay confessors, physicians.

HORNER. And they are rather their patients, but –

Enter LADY FIDGET, *looking about her.*

Now we talk of women of honour, here comes one. Step behind the screen there, and but observe if I have not particular privileges with the women of reputation already, doctor, already.

QUACK *steps behind screen.*

LADY FIDGET. Well, Horner, am not I a woman of honour? You see, I'm as good as my word.

HORNER. And you shall see, madam, I'll not be behindhand with you in honour. And I'll be as good as my word too, if you please but to withdraw into the next room.

LADY FIDGET. But first, my dear sir, you must promise to have a care of my dear honour.

HORNER. If you talk a word more of your honour, you'll make me incapable to wrong it. To talk of honour in the mysteries of love is like talking of heaven or the deity in an operation of witchcraft, just when you are employing the devil; it makes the charm impotent.

LADY FIDGET. Nay, fie, let us not be smutty. But you talk of mysteries and bewitching to me; I don't understand you.

HORNER. I tell you, madam, the word 'money' in a mistress's mouth, at such a nick of time, is not a more disheartening sound to a younger brother than that of 'honour' to an eager lover like myself.

LADY FIDGET. But you can't blame a lady of my reputation to be chary.

HORNER. Chary! I have been chary of it already, by the report I have caused of myself.

LADY FIDGET. Ay, but if you should ever let other women know that dear secret, it would come out. Nay, you must have a great care of your conduct, for my acquaintance are so censorious (oh 'tis a wicked censorious world, Mr Horner), I say, are so censorious and detracting that perhaps they'll talk to the prejudice of my honour, though you should not let them know the dear secret.

HORNER. Nay, madam, rather than they shall prejudice your honour, I'll prejudice theirs; and to serve you, I'll lie with 'em all, make the secret their own, and then they'll keep it! I am a Machiavel in love, madam.

LADY FIDGET. Oh, no sir, not that way.

HORNER. Nay, the devil take me, if censorious women are to be silenced any other way!

LADY FIDGET. A secret is better kept, I hope, by a single person than a multitude. Therefore pray do not trust anybody else with it, dear, dear Mr Horner. (*Embracing him.*)

Enter SIR JASPAR FIDGET.

SIR JASPAR. How now!

LADY FIDGET (*aside*). O my husband! – prevented! – and what's almost as bad, found with my arms about another man – that will appear too much – what shall I say? – Sir Jaspar, come hither. I am trying if Mr Horner were ticklish, and he's as ticklish as can be. I love to torment the confounded toad; let you and I tickle him.

SIR JASPAR. No, your ladyship will tickle him better without me, I suppose. But is this your buying china? I thought you had been at the china house?

HORNER (*aside*). China house! That's my cue, I must take it. – A pox! Can't you keep your impertinent wives at home? Some men are troubled with the husbands, but I with the wives. But I'd have you to know, since I cannot be your journeyman by night, I will not be your drudge by day, to squire your wife about and be your man of straw, or scarecrow, only to pies and jays that would be nibbling at your forbidden fruit. I shall shortly be the hackney gentleman-usher of the town.

SIR JASPAR (*aside*). He, he, he! Poor fellow, he's in the right on't, faith; to squire women about for other folks is as ungrateful an employment as to tell money for other folks. He, he, he! Ben't angry, Horner.

LADY FIDGET. No, 'tis I have more reason to be angry, who am left by you to go abroad indecently alone; or, what is more indecent, to pin myself upon such ill-bred people of your acquaintance as this is.

SIR JASPAR. Nay, prithee, what has he done?

LADY FIDGET. Nay, he has done nothing.

SIR JASPAR. But what d'ye take ill, if he has done nothing?

LADY FIDGET. Ha, ha, ha! Faith, I can't but laugh, however. Why, d'ye think the unmannerly toad would not come down to me to the coach? I was fain to come up to fetch him, or go without him, which I was resolved not to do; for he knows china very well, and has himself very good, but will not let me see it lest I should beg some. But I will find it out, and have what I came for yet.

Exit LADY FIDGET *and locks the door, followed by* HORNER *to the door.*

HORNER (*apart to* LADY FIDGET). Lock the door, Madam. – So, she has got into my chamber and locked me out. Oh, the impertinency of womankind! Well, Sir Jaspar, plain dealing is a jewel; if ever you suffer your wife to trouble me again here, she shall carry you home a pair of horns, by my Lord Mayor she shall! Though I cannot furnish you myself, you are sure, yet I'll find a way.

SIR JASPAR (*aside*). Ha, ha, he! At my first coming and finding her arms about him, tickling him it seems, I was half jealous, but now I see my folly. – He, he, he! Poor Horner.

HORNER (*aside*). Nay, though you laugh now, 'twill be my turn ere long.Oh, women, more impertinent, more cunning and more mischievous than their monkeys, and to me almost as ugly – Now is she throwing my things about, and rifling all I have, but I'll get into her the back way, and so rifle her for it.

SIR JASPAR. Ha, ha, ha! Poor angry Horner.

HORNER. Stay here a little, I'll ferret her out to you presently, I warrant.

Exit HORNER *at t'other door.*

SIR JASPAR. Wife! My Lady Fidget! Wife! He is coming into you the back way!

SIR JASPAR calls through the door to his wife; she answers from within.

LADY FIDGET. Let him come, and welcome, which way he will.

SIR JASPAR. He'll catch you, and use you roughly, and be too strong for you.

LADY FIDGET. Don't you trouble yourself, let him if he can.

QUACK (*behind*). This indeed I could not have believed from him, nor any but my own eyes.

Enter MISTRESS SQUEAMISH.

SQUEAMISH. Where's this woman-hater, this toad, this ugly, greasy, dirty sloven?

SIR JASPAR (*aside*). So the women all will have him ugly. Methinks he is a comely person, but his wants make his form contemptible to 'em; and 'tis e'en as my wife said yesterday, talking of him, that a proper handsome eunuch was as ridiculous a thing as a gigantic coward.

SQUEAMISH. Sir Jaspar, your servant. Where is the odious beast?

SIR JASPAR. He's within in his chamber, with my wife; she's playing the wag with him.

SQUEAMISH. Is she so? And he's a clownish beast, he'll give her no quarter, he'll play the wag with her again, let me tell you. Come, let's go help her – What, the door's locked?

SIR JASPAR. Ay, my wife locked it –

SQUEAMISH. Did she so? Let us break it open then.

SIR JASPAR. No, no, he'll do her no hurt.

SQUEAMISH. No. (*Aside.*) But is there no other way to get into 'em? Whither goes this? I will disturb 'em.

Exit SQUEAMISH *at another door.*

Enter OLD LADY SQUEAMISH.

OLD LADY SQUEAMISH. Where is this harlotry, this impudent baggage, this rambling tomrig? O Sir Jaspar, I'm glad to see you here; did you not see my viled grandchild come in hither just now?

SIR JASPAR. Yes.

OLD LADY SQUEAMISH. Ay, but where is she then? Where is she? Lord, Sir Jaspar, I have e'en rattled myself to pieces in pursuit of her. But can you tell what she makes here? They say below, no woman lodges here.

SIR JASPAR. No.

OLD LADY SQUEAMISH. No! What does she here then? Say, if it be not a woman's lodging, what makes she here? But are you sure no woman lodges here?

SIR JASPAR. No, nor no man neither; this is Mr Horner's lodging.

OLD LADY SQUEAMISH. Is it so, are you sure?

SIR JASPAR. Yes, yes.

OLD LADY SQUEAMISH. So, then there's no hurt in't, I hope. But where is he?

SIR JASPAR. He's in the next room with my wife.

OLD LADY SQUEAMISH. Nay, if you trust him with your wife, I may with my Biddy. They say he's a merry, harmless man now, e'en as harmless a man as ever came out of Italy with a good voice, and as pretty harmless company for a lady as a snake without his teeth.

SIR JASPAR. Ay, ay, poor man.

Enter MRS SQUEAMISH.

SQUEAMISH. I can't find 'em. – Oh, are you here, grandmother? I followed, you must know, my Lady Fidget hither. 'Tis the prettiest lodging, and I have been staring on the prettiest pictures.

Enter LADY FIDGET *with a piece of china in her hand, and* HORNER *following.*

LADY FIDGET. And I have been toiling and moiling for the prettiest piece of china, my dear.

HORNER. Nay, she has been too hard for me, do what I could.

SQUEAMISH. O lord, I'll have some china too. Good Mr Horner, don't you think to give other people china, and me none. Come in with me too.

HORNER. Upon my honour, I have none left now.

SQUEAMISH. Nay, nay, I have known you deny your china before now, but you shan't put me off so. Come.

HORNER. This lady had the last there.

LADY FIDGET. Yes indeed, madam, to my certain knowledge he has no more left.

SQUEAMISH. Oh, but it may be he may have some you could not find.

LADY FIDGET. What, d'y think if he had had any left, I would not have had it too? For we women of quality never think we have china enough.

HORNER. Do not take it ill, I cannot make china for you all, but I will have a roll-wagon for you too, another time.

SQUEAMISH. Thank you, dear toad.

LADY FIDGET (*to* HORNER, *aside*). What do you mean by that promise?

HORNER (*apart to* LADY FIDGET). Alas, she has an innocent, literal understanding.

OLD LADY SQUEAMISH. Poor Mr Horner, he has enough to do to please you all, I see.

HORNER. Ay, madam, you see how they use me.

OLD LADY SQUEAMISH. Poor gentleman, I pity you.

HORNER. I thank you, madam. I could never find pity but from such reverend ladies as you are; the young ones will never spare a man.

SQUEAMISH. Come, come, beast, and go dine with us, for we shall want a man at ombre after dinner.

HORNER. That's all their use of me, madam, you see.

SQUEAMISH. Come, sloven, I'll lead you, to be sure of you.

Pulls him by the cravat.

OLD LADY SQUEAMISH. Alas, poor man, how she tugs him! Kiss, kiss her; that's the way to make such nice women quiet.

HORNER. No, madam, that remedy is worse than the torment; they know I dare suffer anything rather than do it.

OLD LADY SQUEAMISH. Prithee kiss her, and I'll give you her picture in little, that you admired so last night; prithee, do!

HORNER. Well, nothing but that could bribe me. I love a woman only in effigy, and good painting, as much as I hate them. I'll do't, for I could adore the devil well painted.

Kisses MRS SQUEAMISH.

SQUEAMISH. Foh, you filthy toad! Nay, now I've done jesting.

OLD LADY SQUEAMISH. Ha, ha, ha! I told you so.

SQUEAMISH. Foh! a kiss of his –

SIR JASPAR. Has no more hurt in't than one of my spaniel's.

SQUEAMISH. No, nor no more good neither.

QUACK *(behind)*. I will now believe anything he tells me.

Enter MR PINCHWIFE.

LADY FIDGET. O lord, here's a man! Sir Jaspar, my mask, my mask! I would not be seen here for the world.

SIR JASPAR. What, not when I am with you?

LADY FIDGET. No, no, my honour – let's be gone.

SQUEAMISH. Oh, grandmother, let us be gone. Make haste, make haste! I know not how he may censure us.

LADY FIDGET. Be found in the lodging of anything like a man! Away!

Exeunt SIR JASPAR, LADY FIDGET, OLD LADY SQUEAMISH, MRS SQUEAMISH.

QUACK *(behind)*. What's here, another cuckold? He looks like one, and none else sure have any business with him.

HORNER. Well, what brings my dear friend hither?

PINCHWIFE. Your impertinency.

HORNER. My impertinency! Why, you gentlemen that have got handsome wives think you have a privilege of saying anything to your friends, and are as brutish as if you were our creditors.

PINCHWIFE. No, sir, I'll ne'er trust you any way.

HORNER. But why not, dear Jack? Why diffide in me thou know'st so well?

PINCHWIFE. Because I do know you so well.

HORNER. Han't I been always thy friend, honest Jack,
always ready to serve thee, in love or battle, before thou
wert married, and am so still?

PINCHWIFE. I believe so; you would be my second now
indeed.

HORNER. Well, then, dear Jack, why so unkind, so grum,
so strange to me? Come, prithee kiss me, dear rogue.
Gad, I was always, I say, and am still as much thy servant
as –

PINCHWIFE. As I am yours, sir. What, you would send a
kiss to my wife, is that it?

HORNER. So, there 'tis – a man can't show his friendship
to a married man, but presently he talks of his wife to
you. Prithee, let thy wife alone, and let thee and I be all
one, as we were wont. What, thou art as shy of my
kindness as a Lombard Street alderman of a courtier's
civility at Locket's.

PINCHWIFE. But you are overkind to me, as kind as if
I were your cuckold already; yet I must confess you ought
to be kind and civil to me, since I am so kind, so civil to
you, as to bring you this. Look you there, sir.

Delivers him a letter.

HORNER. What is't?

PINCHWIFE. Only a love letter, sir.

HORNER. From whom? – How! This is from your wife!
(*Reads.*) Hum – and hum –

PINCHWIFE. Even from my wife, sir. Am I not wondrous
kind and civil to you now too? – (*Aside.*) But you'll not
think her so!

HORNER (*aside*). Ha! Is this a trick of his or hers?

PINCHWIFE. The gentleman's surprised, I find. What, you
expected a kinder letter?

HORNER. No, faith, not I, how could I?

PINCHWIFE. Yes, yes, I'm sure you did; a man so well made as you are, must needs be disappointed if the women declare not their passion at first sight or opportunity.

HORNER (*aside*). But what should this mean? Stay, the postscript. (*Reads aside.*) 'Be sure you love me whatsoever my husband says to the contrary, and let him not see this lest he should come home and pinch me, or kill my squirrel'. – (*Aside.*) It seems he knows not what the letter contains.

PINCHWIFE. Come, ne'er wonder at it so much.

HORNER. Faith, I can't help it.

PINCHWIFE. Now, I think I have deserved your infinite friendship and kindness and have showed myself sufficiently an obliging friend and husband; am I not so, to bring a letter from my wife to her gallant?

HORNER. Ay, the devil take me, art thou the most obliging, kind friend and husband in the world, ha, ha!

PINCHWIFE. Well, you may be merry, sir, but in short I must tell you, sir, my honour will suffer no jesting.

HORNER. What dost thou mean?

PINCHWIFE. Does the letter want a comment? Then know, sir, though I have been so civil a husband as to bring you a letter from my wife, to let you kiss and court her to my face, I will not be a cuckold, sir, I will not.

HORNER. Thou art mad with jealousy. I never saw thy wife in my life, but at the play yesterday, and I know not if it were she or no. I court her, kiss her!

PINCHWIFE. I will not be a cuckold, I say. There will be danger in making me a cuckold.

HORNER. Why, wert thou not well cured of thy last clap?

PINCHWIFE. I wear a sword.

HORNER. It should be taken from thee lest thou should'st do thyself a mischief with it; thou art mad, man.

PINCHWIFE. As mad as I am, and as merry as you are, I must have more reason from you ere we part. I say again, though you kissed and courted last night my wife in man's clothes, as she confesses in her letter –

HORNER (*aside*). Ha!

PINCHWIFE. Both she and I say, you must not design it again, for you have mistaken your woman, as you have done your man.

HORNER (*aside*). Oh –I understand something now. – Was that thy wife? Why would'st thou not tell me 'twas she? Faith, my freedom with her was your fault, not mine.

PINCHWIFE (*aside*). Faith, so 'twas.

HORNER. Fie! I'd never do't to a woman before her husband's face, sure.

PINCHWIFE. But I had rather you should do't to my wife before my face than behind my back, and that you shall never do.

HORNER. No – you will hinder me.

PINCHWIFE. If I would not hinder you, you see by her letter, she would.

HORNER. Well, I must e'en acquiesce then, and be contented with what she writes.

PINCHWIFE. I'll assure you 'twas voluntarily writ; I had no hand in't, you may believe me.

HORNER. I do believe thee, faith.

PINCHWIFE. And believe her too, for she's an innocent creature, has no dissembling in her; and so fare you well, sir.

HORNER. Pray, however, present my humble service to her, and tell her I will obey her letter to a tittle, and fulfil her desires, be what they will, or with what difficulty soever

I do't, and you shall be no more jealous of me, I warrant her and you.

PINCHWIFE. Well, then, fare you well, and play with any man's honour but mine, kiss any man's wife but mine, and welcome.

Exit MR PINCHWIFE.

HORNER. Ha, ha, ha! Doctor.

QUACK. It seems he has not heard the report of you, or does not believe it.

HORNER. Ha, ha! Now, doctor, what think you?

QUACK. Pray let's see the letter – hum – (*Reads the letter.*) 'for – dear – love you'.

HORNER. I wonder how she could contrive it! What say'st thou to't? 'Tis an original.

QUACK. So are your cuckolds, too, originals, for they are like no other common cuckolds, and I will henceforth believe it not impossible for you to cuckold the Grand Signior amidst his guards of eunuchs, that I say!

HORNER. And I say for the letter, 'tis the first love letter that ever was without flames, darts, fates, destinies, lying and dissembling in't.

Enter SPARKISH *pulling in* MR PINCHWIFE.

SPARKISH. Come back, you are a pretty brother-in-law, neither go to church, nor to dinner with your sister bride.

PINCHWIFE. My sister denies her marriage, and you see is gone away from you dissatisfied.

SPARKISH. Pshaw, upon a foolish scruple that our parson was not in lawful orders, and did not say all the Common Prayer; but 'tis her modesty only, I believe. But let women be never so modest the first day, they'll be sure to come to themselves by night, and I shall have enough of her then. In the meantime, Harry Horner, you must dine with me; I keep my wedding at my aunt's in the Piazza.

HORNER. Thy wedding! What stale maid has lived to despair of a husband, or what young one of a gallant?

SPARKISH. Oh, your servant, sir – this gentleman's sister then – no stale maid.

HORNER. I'm sorry for't.

PINCHWIFE (*aside*). How comes he so concerned for her?

SPARKISH. You sorry for't? Why, do you know any ill by her?

HORNER. No, I know none but by thee; 'tis for her sake, not yours, and another man's sake that might have hoped, I thought.

SPARKISH. Another man! Another man! What is his name?

HORNER. Nay, since 'tis past he shall be nameless. (*Aside.*) Poor Harcourt! I am sorry thou hast missed her.

PINCHWIFE (*aside*). He seems to be much troubled at the match.

SPARKISH. Prithee tell me – nay, you shan't go, brother.

PINCHWIFE. I must of necessity, but I'll come to you to dinner.

Exit MR PINCHWIFE.

SPARKISH. But Harry, what, have I a rival in my wife already? But with all my heart, for he may be of use to me hereafter! For though my hunger is now my sauce, and I can fall on heartily without, but the time will come when a rival will be as good sauce for a married man to a wife as an orange to veal.

HORNER. O thou damned rogue, thou hast set my teeth on edge with thy orange!

SPARKISH. Then let's to dinner; there I was with you again. Come.

HORNER. But who dines with thee?

SPARKISH. My friends and relations, my brother Pinchwife, you see, of your acquaintance.

HORNER. And his wife?

SPARKISH. No, gad, he'll ne'er let her come amongst us good fellows. Your stingy country coxcomb keeps his wife from his friends as he does his little firkin of ale for his own drinking, and a gentleman can't get a smack on't; but his servants, when his back is turned, broach it at their pleasures, and dust it away, ha, ha, ha! Gad, I am witty, I think, considering I was married today, by the world. But come –

HORNER. No, I will not dine with you, unless you can fetch her too.

SPARKISH. Pshaw! What pleasure canst thou have with women now, Harry?

HORNER. My eyes are not gone; I love a good prospect yet, and will not dine with you unless she does too. Go fetch her, therefore, but do not tell her husband 'tis for my sake.

SPARKISH. Well, I'll go try what I can do; in the meantime come away to my aunt's lodging, 'tis in the way to Pinchwife's.

HORNER. The poor woman has called for aid, and stretched forth her hand, doctor; I cannot but help her over the pale out of the briars.

Exeunt SPARKISH, HORNER, QUACK.

Scene Four

The scene changes to PINCHWIFE's *house.*

MRS PINCHWIFE *alone leaning on her elbow. A table, pen, ink, and paper.*

MRS PINCHWIFE. Well, 'tis e'en so, I have got the London disease they call love; I am sick of my husband, and for my gallant. I have heard this distemper called a fever, but methinks 'tis liker an ague, for when I think of

my husband, I tremble and am in a cold sweat, and have
inclinations to vomit, but when I think of my gallant, dear
Mr Horner, my hot fit comes and I am all in a fever,
indeed, and as in other fevers my own chamber is tedious
to me, and I would fain be removed to his, and then
methinks I should be well. Ah, poor Mr Horner! Well, I
cannot, will not stay here; therefore I'll make an end of
my letter to him, which shall be a finer letter than my
last, because I have studied it like anything. Oh, sick, sick!

Takes the pen and writes.

Enter MR PINCHWIFE, *who seeing her writing steals softly
behind her, and looking over her shoulder, snatches the paper from
her.*

PINCHWIFE. What, writing more letters?

MRS PINCHWIFE. O lord, bud, why d'ye fright me so?

She offers to run out; he stops her and reads.

PINCHWIFE. How's this! Nay, you shall not stir, madam.
'Dear, dear, dear, Mr Horner – ' Very well – I have
taught you to write letters to good purpose – but let's
see't: 'First, I am to beg your pardon for my boldness
in writing to you, which I'd have you to know I would
not have done had not you said first you loved me so
extremely, which if you do, you will never suffer me to
lie in the arms of another man, whom I loath, nauseate,
and detest' – Now you can write these filthy words! But
what follows? – 'Therefore I hope you will speedily find
some way to free me from this unfortunate match, which
was never, I assure you, of my choice, but I'm afraid
'tis already too far gone. However, if you love me, as I do
you, you will try what you can do, but you must help
me away before tomorrow, or else, alas, I shall be forever
out of your reach, for I can defer no longer our' (*The letter
concludes.*) 'Our'? What is to follow 'our'? Speak, what?
Our journey into the country I suppose? Oh, woman,
damned woman, and love, damned love, their old
tempter! For this is one of his miracles; in a moment he
can make those blind that could see, and those see that

were blind, those dumb that could speak, and those prattle who were dumb before; nay, what is more than all, make these dough-baked, senseless, indocile animals, women, too hard for us, their politic lords and rulers, in a moment. But make an end of your letter and then I'll make an end of you thus, and all my plagues together.

Draws his sword.

MRS PINCHWIFE. O lord, O lord, you are such a passionate man, bud.

Enter SPARKISH.

SPARKISH. How now, what's here to do?

PINCHWIFE. This fool here now!

SPARKISH. What, drawn upon your wife? You should never do that, but at night in the dark, when you can't hurt her! This is my sister-in-law, is it not? (*Pulls aside her handkerchief.*) Ay, faith, e'en our country Margery; one may know her. Come, she and you must go dine with me; dinner's ready, come. But where's my wife? Is she not come home yet? Where is she?

PINCHWIFE. Making you a cuckold; 'tis that they all do, as soon as they can.

SPARKISH. What, the wedding day? No, a wife that designs to make a cully of her husband will be sure to let him win the first stake of love, by the world. But come, they stay dinner for us. Come, I'll lead down our Margery.

PINCHWIFE. No! – Sir, go, we'll follow you.

SPARKISH. I will not wag without you.

PINCHWIFE (*aside*). This coxcomb is a sensible torment to me amidst the greatest in the world.

SPARKISH. Come, come, Madam Margery.

PINCHWIFE. No, I'll lead her my way. What, would you treat your friends with mine, for want of your own wife?

Leads her to t'other door and locks her in and returns.

(*Aside.*) I am contented my rage should take breath.

SPARKISH (*aside*). I told Horner this.

PINCHWIFE. Come now.

SPARKISH. Lord, how shy you are of your wife! But let me
tell you, brother, we men of wit have amongst us a saying
that cuckolding, like the smallpox, comes with a fear, and
you may keep your wife as much as you will out of
danger of infection, but if her constitution incline her to't,
she'll have it sooner or later, by the world, say they.

PINCHWIFE (*aside*). What a thing is a cuckold, that every
fool can make him ridiculous! – Well sir – but let me
advise you, now you are come to be concerned, because
you suspect the danger, not to neglect the means to
prevent it, especially when the greatest share of the
malady will light upon your own head, for –

Hows'e'er the kind wife's belly comes to swell
The husband breeds for her, and first is ill.

Exeunt MR PINCHWIFE *and* SPARKISH.

ACT FIVE

Scene One

MR PINCHWIFE's *house.*

Enter MR PINCHWIFE *and* MRS PINCHWIFE. *A table and candle.*

PINCHWIFE. Come, take the pen and make an end of the letter, just as you intended; if you are false in a tittle, I shall soon perceive it, and punish you with this as you deserve. (*Lays his hand on his sword.*) Write what was to follow – let's see – 'You must make haste and help me away before tomorrow, or else I shall be forever out of your reach, for I can defer no longer our – ' What follows 'our'?

MRS PINCHWIFE. Must all out then, bud?

MRS PINCHWIFE *takes the pen and writes.*

Look you there, then.

PINCHWIFE. Let's see – 'For I can defer no longer our – wedding – Your slighted Alithea'. What's the meaning of this? My sister's name to't? Speak, unriddle!

MRS PINCHWIFE. Yes, indeed, bud.

PINCHWIFE. But why her name to't? Speak – speak I say!

MRS PINCHWIFE. Ay, but you'll tell her then again; if you would not tell her again –

PINCHWIFE. I will not; I am stunned; my head turns round; speak!

MRS PINCHWIFE. Won't you tell her indeed, and indeed?

PINCHWIFE. No, speak, I say.

MRS PINCHWIFE. She'll be angry with me, but I had
  rather she should be angry with me than you, bud; and to
  tell you the truth, 'twas she made me write the letter, and
  taught me what I should write.

PINCHWIFE (*aside*). Ha! I thought the style was somewhat
  better than her own; but how could she come to you to
  teach you, since I had locked you up alone?

MRS PINCHWIFE. Oh, through the keyhole, bud.

PINCHWIFE. But why should she make you write a letter
  for her to him, since she can write herself?

MRS PINCHWIFE. Why, she said because – for I was
  unwilling to do it.

PINCHWIFE. Because what – because?

MRS PINCHWIFE. Because, lest Mr Horner should be
  cruel and refuse her, or vain afterwards, and show the
  letter, she might disown it, the hand not being hers.

PINCHWIFE (*aside*). How's this? Ha! – then I think I shall
  come to myself again. This changeling could not invent
  this lie; but if she could, why should she? She might
  think I should soon discover it – stay – now I think on't
  too, Horner said he was sorry she had married Sparkish,
  and her disowning her marriage to me makes me think
  she has evaded it for Horner's sake. Yet why should
  she take this course? But men in love are fools; women
  may well be so. – But hark you, madam, your sister
  went out in the morning and I have not seen her within
  since.

MRS PINCHWIFE. Alackaday, she has been crying all day
  above, it seems, in a corner.

PINCHWIFE. Where is she? Let me speak with her.

MRS PINCHWIFE (*aside*). O lord, then he'll discover all! –
  Pray hold, bud. What, d'y mean to discover me? She'll
  know I have told you then. Pray bud, let me talk with her
  first.

PINCHWIFE. I must speak with her to know whether
Horner ever made her any promise; and whether she
be married to Sparkish or no.

MRS PINCHWIFE. Pray, dear bud, don't, till I have spoken
with her and told her that I have told you all, for she'll
kill me else.

PINCHWIFE. Go then, and bid her come out to me.

MRS PINCHWIFE. Yes, yes, bud –

PINCHWIFE. Let me see –

MRS PINCHWIFE (aside). I'll go, but she is not within to
come to him. I have just got time to know of Lucy her
maid, who first set me on to work, what lie I shall tell
next, for I am e'en at my wits end!

Exit MRS PINCHWIFE.

PINCHWIFE. Well, I resolve it; Horner shall have her. I'd
rather give him my sister than lend him my wife, and
such an alliance will prevent his pretensions to my wife,
sure. I'll make him of kin to her, and then he won't care
for her.

MRS PINCHWIFE *returns*.

MRS PINCHWIFE. O lord, bud, I told you what anger you
would make with my sister.

PINCHWIFE. Won't she come hither?

MRS PINCHWIFE. No, no, alackaday, she's ashamed to
look you in the face, and she says if you go in to her,
she'll run away downstairs, and shamefully go herself to
Mr Horner, who has promised her marriage, she says,
and she will have no other, so she won't.

PINCHWIFE. Did he so – promise her marriage? Then she
shall have no other. Go tell her so, and if she will come
and discourse with me a little concerning the means, I will
about it immediately. Go!

Exit MRS PINCHWIFE.

His estate is equal to Sparkish's, and his extraction much
better than his as his parts are; but my chief reason is, I'd
rather be of kin to him by the name of brother-in-law
than that of cuckold.

Enter MRS PINCHWIFE.

Well, what says she now?

MRS PINCHWIFE. Why, she says she would only have you
lead her to Horner's lodging – with whom she first will
discourse the matter before she talk with you, which yet
she cannot do; for alack, poor creature, she says she can't
so much as look you in the face, therefore she'll come to
you in a mask; and you must excuse her if she make you
no answer to any question of yours till you have brought
her to Mr Horner; and if you will not chide her, nor
question her she'll come out to you immediately.

PINCHWIFE. Let her come; I will not speak a word to her,
nor require a word from her.

MRS PINCHWIFE. Oh, I forgot; besides, she says, she
cannot look you in the face, though through a mask,
therefore would desire you to put out the candle.

PINCHWIFE. I agree to all; let her make haste – there 'tis
out. (*Puts out the candle.*)

Exit MRS PINCHWIFE.

My case is something better; I'd rather fight with Horner
for not lying with my sister than for lying with my wife,
and of the two I had rather find my sister too forward
than my wife; I expected no other from her free
education, as she calls it, and her passion for the town.
Well – wife and sister are names which make us expect
love and duty, pleasure and comfort, but we find 'em
plagues and torments, and are equally, though differently,
troublesome to their keeper; for we have as much ado to
get people to lie with our sisters as keep 'em from lying
with our wives.

Enter MRS PINCHWIFE *masked, and in hoods and scarves,
and a nightgown and petticoat of* ALITHEA's, *in the dark.*

What, are you come, sister? Let us go then – but first let me lock up my wife. Mrs Margery, where are you?

MRS PINCHWIFE. Here, bud.

PINCHWIFE. Come hither, that I may lock you up. Get you in. (*Locks the door.*) Come, sister, where are you now?

MRS PINCHWIFE *gives him her hand, but when he lets her go, she steals softly on t'other side of him, and is led away by him for his sister Alithea.*

Scene Two

The scene changes to HORNER*'s lodging.*

Enter QUACK *and* HORNER.

QUACK. What, all alone? Not so much as one of your cuckolds here, nor one of their wives! They use to take their turns with you, as if they were to watch you.

HORNER. Yes, it often happens that a cuckold is but his wife's spy, and is more upon family duty when he is with her gallant abroad hindering his pleasure, than when he is at home with her, playing the gallant. But the hardest duty a married woman imposes upon a lover is keeping her husband company always.

QUACK. And his fondness wearies you almost as soon as hers.

HORNER. A pox! Keeping a cuckold company after you have had his wife is as tiresome as the company of a country squire to a witty fellow of the town, when he has got all his money.

QUACK. And as at first a man makes a friend of the husband to get the wife, so at last you are fain to fall out with the wife to be rid of the husband.

HORNER. Ay, most cuckold-makers are true courtiers; when once a poor man has cracked his credit for 'em, they can't abide to come near him.

QUACK. But at first, to draw him in, are so sweet, so kind, so dear, just as you are to Pinchwife. But what becomes of that intrigue with his wife?

HORNER. A pox! He's as surly as an alderman that has been bit, and since he's so coy, his wife's kindness is in vain, for she's a silly innocent.

QUACK. Did she not send you a letter by him?

HORNER. Yes, but that's a riddle I have not yet solved. Allow the poor creature to be willing, she is silly too, and he keeps her up so close –

QUACK. Yes, so close that he makes her but the more willing, and adds but revenge to her love, which two, when met, seldom fail to satisfy each other one way or other.

HORNER. What! Here's the man we are talking of, I think.

Enter MR PINCHWIFE *leading in his wife masked, muffled, and in her sister's gown.*

HORNER. Pshaw!

QUACK. Bringing his wife to you is the next thing to bringing a love letter from her.

HORNER. What means this?

PINCHWIFE. The last time, you know, sir, I brought you a love letter; now you see a mistress, I think you'll say I am a civil man to you!

HORNER. Ay, the devil take me, will I say thou art the civillest man I ever met with, and I have known some. I fancy I understand thee now better than I did the letter. But hark thee, in thy ear –

PINCHWIFE. What?

HORNER. Nothing but the usual question, man; is she sound, on thy word?

PINCHWIFE. What, you take her for a wench, and me for a pimp?

HORNER. Pshaw, wench and pimp, paw words. I know thou art an honest fellow, and hast a great acquaintance amongst the ladies, and perhaps hast made love for me rather than let me make love to thy wife.

PINCHWIFE. Come, sir, in short, I am for no fooling.

HORNER. Nor I neither; therefore prithee let's see her face presently. Make her show, man; art thou sure I don't know her?

PINCHWIFE. I am sure you do know her.

HORNER. A pox, why dost thou bring her to me then?

PINCHWIFE. Because she's a relation of mine −

HORNER. Is she, faith, man? Then thou art still more civil and obliging, dear rogue.

PINCHWIFE. − who desired me to bring her to you.

HORNER. Then she is obliging, dear rogue.

PINCHWIFE. You'll make her welcome, for my sake, I hope.

HORNER. I hope she is handsome enough to make herself welcome. Prithee, let her unmask.

PINCHWIFE. Do you speak to her; she would never be ruled by me.

HORNER. Madam −

MRS PINCHWIFE *whispers to* HORNER.

She says she must speak with me in private. Withdraw, prithee.

PINCHWIFE (*aside*). She's unwilling, it seems, I should know all her undecent conduct in this business. − Well, then, I'll leave you together, and hope when I am gone you'll agree. If not, you and I shan't agree, sir.

HORNER (*aside*). What means the fool? − If she and I agree, 'tis no matter what you and I do.

Whispers to MRS PINCHWIFE *who makes signs with her hand for him to be gone.*

PINCHWIFE. In the meantime I'll fetch a parson, and find out Sparkish and disabuse him. You would have me fetch a parson, would you not? Well, then – Now I think I am rid of her, and shall have no more trouble with her. Our sisters and daughters, like usurers' money, are safest when put out; but our wives, like their writings, never safe but in our closets under lock and key.

Exit MR PINCHWIFE.

Enter BOY.

BOY. Sir Jaspar Fidget, sir, is coming up.

Exit BOY.

HORNER. Here's the trouble of a cuckold, now, we are talking of. A pox on him! Has he not enough to do to hinder his wife's sport, but he must other women's too? – Step in here, madam.

Exit MRS PINCHWIFE.

Enter SIR JASPAR.

SIR JASPAR. My best and dearest friend.

HORNER (*aside to* QUACK). The old style, doctor. – Well, be short, for I am busy. What would your impertinent wife have now?

SIR JASPAR. Well guessed, i'faith, for I do come from her.

HORNER. To invite me to supper? Tell her I can't come. Go.

SIR JASPAR. Nay, now you are out, faith, for my lady and the whole knot of the virtuous gang, as they call themselves, are resolved upon a frolic of coming to you tonight in a masquerade, and are all dressed already.

HORNER. I shan't be at home.

SIR JASPAR (*aside*). Lord, how churlish he is to women! – Nay, prithee don't disappoint 'em, they'll think 'tis my fault, prithee don't. I'll send in the banquet and the fiddles. But make no noise on't, for the poor virtuous rogues would not have it known for the world, that they go a-masquerading, and they would come to no man's ball but yours.

HORNER. Well, well – get you gone, and tell 'em, if they come, 'twill be at the peril of their honour and yours.

SIR JASPAR. He, he, he! We'll trust you for that, farewell.

Exit SIR JASPAR.

HORNER.
Doctor, anon, you too shall be my guest,
But now I'm going to a private feast.

Scene Three

The scene changes to the Piazza of Covent Garden.

Enter SPARKISH *and* PINCHWIFE.

SPARKISH (*with the letter in his hand*). But who could have thought a woman could have been false to me? By the world, I could not have thought it.

PINCHWIFE. You were for giving and taking liberty; she has taken it only, sir, now you find in that letter. You are a frank person, and so is she, you see there.

SPARKISH. Nay, if this be her hand – for I never saw it.

PINCHWIFE. 'Tis no matter whether that be her hand or no; I am sure this hand, at her desire, led her to Mr Horner, with whom I left her just now, to go fetch a parson to 'em, at their desire too, to deprive you of her forever, for it seems yours was but a mock marriage.

SPARKISH. Indeed, she would needs have it that 'twas Harcourt himself in a parson's habit that married us, but I'm sure he told me 'twas his brother Ned.

PINCHWIFE. Oh, there 'tis out, and you were deceived, not she, for you are such a frank person – but I must be gone. You'll find her at Mr Horner's. Go and believe your eyes.

Exit MR PINCHWIFE.

SPARKISH. Nay, I'll to her, and call her as many crocodiles, sirens, harpies, and other heathenish names as a poet would do a mistress who had refused to hear his suit, nay more, his verses on her. But stay, is not that she following a torch at t'other end of the Piazza? And from Horner's certainly – 'tis so.

Enter ALITHEA *following a torch, and* LUCY *behind.*

You are well met, madam, though you don't think so. What, you have made a short visit to Mr Horner, but I suppose you'll return to him presently; by that time the parson can be with him.

ALITHEA. Mr Horner, and the parson, sir!

SPARKISH. Come, madam, no more dissembling, no more jilting, for I am no more a frank person.

ALITHEA. How's this?

LUCY (*aside*). So, 'twill work, I see.

SPARKISH. Could you find out no easy country fool to abuse? None but me, a gentleman of wit and pleasure about the town? But it was your pride to be too hard for a man of parts, unworthy false woman! False as a friend that lends a man money to lose; false as dice, who undo those that trust all they have to 'em.

LUCY (*aside*). He has been a great bubble by his similes, as they say.

ALITHEA. You have been too merry, sir, at your wedding dinner, sure.

SPARKISH. What, d'y mock me too?

ALITHEA. Or you have been deluded.

SPARKISH. By you!

ALITHEA. Let me understand you.

SPARKISH. Have you the confidence – I should call it something else, since you know your guilt – to stand my just reproaches? You did not write an impudent letter to Mr Horner, who I find now has clubbed with you in deluding me with his aversion for women, that I might not, forsooth, suspect him for my rival.

LUCY (*aside*). D'ye think the gentleman can be jealous now, madam?

ALITHEA. I write a letter to Mr Horner!

SPARKISH. Nay, madam, do not deny it; your brother showed it me just now, and told me likewise he left you at Horner's lodging to fetch a parson to marry you to him. And I wish you joy, madam, joy, joy, and to him, too, much joy, and to myself more joy, for not marrying you!

ALITHEA (*aside*). So I find my brother would break off the match, and I can consent to't, since I see this gentleman can be made jealous. – O Lucy, by his rude usage and jealousy, he makes me afraid I am married to him. Art thou sure 'twas Harcourt himself and no parson that married us?

SPARKISH. No, madam, I thank you. I suppose that was a contrivance too of Mr Horner's and yours, to make Harcourt play the parson; but I would, as little as you, have him one now, no, not for the world, for shall I tell you another truth? I never had any passion for you till now, for now I hate you. 'Tis true I might have married your portion, as other men of parts of the town do sometimes, and so your servant. And to show my unconcernedness, I'll come to your wedding and resign you with as much joy as I would a stale wench to a new cully; nay, with as much joy as I would after the first night, if I had been married to you. There's for you, and so your servant, servant.

Exit SPARKISH.

ALITHEA. How was I deceived in a man!

LUCY. You'll believe, then, a fool may be made jealous
now? For that easiness in him, that suffers him to be led
by a wife, will likewise permit him to be persuaded
against her by others.

ALITHEA. But marry Mr Horner! My brother does not
intend it, sure; if I thought he did, I would take thy
advice and Mr Harcourt for my husband. And now
I wish that if there be any over-wise woman of the town,
who, like me, would marry a fool for fortune, liberty, or
title, first, that her husband may love play, and be a cully
to all the town, but her, and suffer none but fortune to be
mistress of his purse; then, if for liberty, that he may send
her into the country under the conduct of some
housewifely mother-in-law; and, if for title, may the world
give 'em none but that of cuckold.

LUCY. And for her greater curse, madam, may he not
deserve it.

ALITHEA. Away, impertinent! – Is not this my old Lady
Lanterlu's?

LUCY. Yes, madam. (*Aside.*) And here I hope we shall find
Mr Harcourt.

Exeunt.

Scene Four

The scene changes again to HORNER's *lodging.*

Enter HORNER, LADY FIDGET, MRS DAINTY FIDGET
and MRS SQUEAMISH.

A table, banquet and bottles.

HORNER (*aside*). A pox! They are come too soon – before
I have sent back my new – mistress. All I have now to do
is to lock her in, that they may not see her –

LADY FIDGET. That we may be sure of our welcome, we have brought our entertainment with us, and are resolved to treat thee, dear toad.

DAINTY. And that we may be merry to purpose, have left Sir Jaspar and my old Lady Squeamish quarrelling at home at backgammon.

SQUEAMISH. Therefore, let us make use of our time, lest they should chance to interrupt us.

LADY FIDGET. Let us sit then.

HORNER. First, that you may be private, let me lock this door and that, and I'll wait upon you presently.

LADY FIDGET. No, sir, shut 'em only and your lips for ever, for we must trust you as much as our women.

HORNER. You know all vanity's killed in me; I have no occasion for talking.

LADY FIDGET. Now, ladies, supposing we had drank each of us our two bottles, let us speak the truth of our hearts.

DAINTY *and* SQUEAMISH. Agreed.

LADY FIDGET. By this brimmer, for truth is nowhere else to be found. (*Aside to* HORNER.) Not in thy heart, false man!

HORNER (*aside to* LADY FIDGET). You have found me a true man, I'm sure!

LADY FIDGET (*aside to* HORNER). Not every way. – But let us sit and be merry.

LADY FIDGET (*sings*).
　　Why should our damned tyrants oblige us to live
　　On the pittance of pleasure which they only give?
　　　　We must not rejoice
　　　　With wine and with noise.
　　In vain we must wake in a dull bed alone,
　　Whilst to our warm rival, the bottle, they're gone.
　　　　Then lay aside charms
　　　　And take up these arms. (*The glasses.*)

'Tis wine only gives 'em their courage and wit,
Because we live sober, to men we submit.
 If for beauties you'd pass
 Take a lick of the glass.
'Twill mend your complexions, and when they are gone,
The best red we have is the red of the grape.
 Then, sisters, lay't on,
 And damn a good shape.

DAINTY. Dear brimmer! Well, in token of our openness and
 plain dealing, let us throw our masks over our heads.

HORNER. So, 'twill come to the glasses anon.

SQUEAMISH. Lovely brimmer! Let me enjoy him first.

LADY FIDGET. No, I never part with a gallant till I've
 tried him. Dear brimmer, that mak'st our husbands short-
 sighted.

DAINTY. And our bashful gallants bold.

SQUEAMISH. And for want of a gallant, the butler lovely
 in our eyes. Drink, eunuch.

LADY FIDGET. Drink thou representative of a husband.
 Damn a husband!

DAINTY. And, as it were a husband, an old keeper.

SQUEAMISH. And an old grandmother.

HORNER. And an English bawd, and a French surgeon.

LADY FIDGET. Ay, we have all reason to curse 'em.

HORNER. For my sake, ladies?

LADY FIDGET. No, for our own, for the first spoils all
 young gallants' industry.

DAINTY. And the other's art makes 'em bold only with
 common women.

SQUEAMISH. And rather run the hazard of the vile
 distemper amongst them than of a denial amongst us.

DAINTY. The filthy toads choose mistresses now as they do
 stuffs, for having been fancied and worn by others.

SQUEAMISH. For being common and cheap.

LADY FIDGET. Whilst women of quality, like the richer stuffs, lie untumbled and unasked for.

HORNER. Ay, neat, and cheap, and new, often they think best.

DAINTY. No, sir, the beasts will be known by a mistress longer than by a suit.

SQUEAMISH. And 'tis not for cheapness neither.

LADY FIDGET. No, for the vain fops will take up druggets and embroider 'em. But I wonder at the depraved appetites of witty men; they use to be out of the common road and hate imitation. Pray tell me, beast, when you were a man, why you rather chose to club with a multitude in a common house for an entertainment than to be the only guest at a good table.

HORNER. Why, faith, ceremony and expectation are unsufferable to those that are sharp bent; people always eat with the best stomach at an ordinary, where every man is snatching for the best bit.

LADY FIDGET. Though he get a cut over the fingers – but I have heard people eat most heartily of another man's meat, that is, what they do not pay for.

HORNER. When they are sure of their welcome and freedom, for ceremony in love and eating is as ridiculous as in fighting; falling on briskly is all should be done on those occasions.

LADY FIDGET. Well then, let me tell you, sir, there is nowhere more freedom than in our houses, and we take freedom from a young person as a sign of good breeding, and a person may be as free as he pleases with us, as frolic, as gamesome, as wild as he will.

HORNER. Han't I heard you all declaim against wild men?

LADY FIDGET. Yes, but for all that, we think wildness in a man as desirable a quality as in a duck or rabbit; a tame man, foh!

HORNER. I know not, but your reputations frightened me, as much as your faces invited me.

LADY FIDGET. Our reputation! Lord, why should you not think that we women make use of our reputation, as you men of yours only to deceive the world with less suspicion? Our virtue is like the statesman's religion, the Quaker's word, the gamester's oath, and the great man's honour – but to cheat those that trust us.

SQUEAMISH. And that demureness, coyness, and modesty that you see in our faces in the boxes at plays is as much a sign of a kind woman as a vizard-mask in the pit.

DAINTY. For, I assure you, women are least masked when they have the velvet vizard on.

LADY FIDGET. You would have found us modest women in our denials only.

SQUEAMISH. Our bashfulness is only the reflection of the men's.

DAINTY. We blush when they are shamefaced.

HORNER. I beg your pardon, ladies; I was deceived in you devilishly. But why that mighty pretence to honour?

LADY FIDGET. We have told you. But sometimes 'twas for the same reason you men pretend business often, to avoid ill company, to enjoy the better and more privately those you love.

HORNER. But why would you ne'er give a friend a wink then?

LADY FIDGET. Faith, your reputation frightened us as much as ours did you, you were so notoriously lewd.

HORNER. And you so seemingly honest.

LADY FIDGET. Was that all that deterred you?

HORNER. And so expensive – you allow freedom, you say?

LADY FIDGET. Ay, ay.

HORNER. That I was afraid of losing my little money, as
well as my little time, both which my other pleasures
required.

LADY FIDGET. Money, foh! You talk like a little fellow
now; do such as we expect money?

HORNER. I beg your pardon, madam. I must confess,
I have heard that great ladies, like great merchants, set
but the higher prices upon what they have, because they
are not in necessity of taking the first offer.

DAINTY. Such as we make sale of our hearts?

SQUEAMISH. We bribed for our love? Foh!

HORNER. With your pardon, ladies, I know, like great men
in offices, you seem to exact flattery and attendance only
from your followers, but you have receivers about you,
and such fees to pay, a man is afraid to pass your grants.
Besides, we must let you win at cards, or we lose your
hearts. And if you make an assignation, 'tis at a
goldsmith's, jeweller's, or china house, where, for your
honour you deposit to him, he must pawn his to the
punctual cit, and so paying for what you take up, pays for
what he takes up.

DAINTY. Would you not have us assured of our gallant's
love?

SQUEAMISH. For love is better known by liberality than by
jealousy.

LADY FIDGET. For one may be dissembled, the other not.
(*Aside.*) But my jealousy can no longer be dissembled, and
they are telling ripe. – Come, here's to our gallants in
waiting, whom we must name, and I'll begin. This is my
false rogue.

Claps him on the back.

SQUEAMISH. How!

HORNER (*aside*). So, all will out now.

SQUEAMISH (*aside to* HORNER). Did you not tell me,
'twas for my sake only you reported yourself no man?

DAINTY (*aside to* HORNER). Oh wretch! Did you not swear to me, 'twas for my love and honour you passed for that thing you do?

HORNER. So, so.

LADY FIDGET. Come, speak ladies; this is my false villain.

SQUEAMISH. And mine too.

DAINTY. And mine.

HORNER. Well, then, you are all three my false rogues too, and there's an end on't.

LADY FIDGET. Well, then, there's no remedy; sister sharers, let us not fall out, but have a care of our honour. Though we get no presents, no jewels of him, we are savers of our honour, the jewel of most value and use, which shines yet to the world unsuspected, though it be counterfeit.

HORNER. Nay, and is e'en as good as if it were true, provided the world think so; for honour, like beauty now, only depends on the opinion of others.

LADY FIDGET. Well, Harry Common, I hope you can be true to three. Swear – but 'tis no purpose to require your oath for you are as often forsworn as you swear to new women.

HORNER. Come, faith, madam, let us e'en pardon one another, for all the difference I find betwixt we men and you women, we forswear ourselves at the beginning of an amour, you as long as it lasts.

Enter SIR JASPAR FIDGET *and* OLD LADY SQUEAMISH.

SIR JASPAR. Oh, my Lady Fidget, was this your cunning to come to Mr Horner without me? But you have been nowhere else, I hope.

LADY FIDGET. No, Sir Jaspar.

OLD LADY SQUEAMISH. And you came straight hither, Biddy?

SQUEAMISH. Yes, indeed, lady grandmother.

SIR JASPAR. 'Tis well, 'tis well; I knew when once they
were thoroughly acquainted with poor Horner, they'd
ne'er be from him. You may let her masquerade it with
my wife and Horner, and I warrant her reputation safe.

Enter BOY.

BOY. Oh, sir, here's the gentleman come whom you bid me
not suffer to come up without giving you notice, with a
lady, too, and other gentlemen.

HORNER. Do you all go in there, whilst I send 'em away,
and boy, do you desire 'em to stay below till I come,
which shall be immediately.

Exeunt SIR JASPAR, LADY SQUEAMISH, LADY
FIDGET, MISTRESS DAINTY *and* SQUEAMISH.

BOY. Yes, sir.

Exit.

Exit HORNER *at t'other door, and returns with* MRS
PINCHWIFE.

HORNER. You would not take my advice to be gone home
before your husband came back; he'll now discover all.
Yet pray, my dearest, be persuaded to go home, and leave
the rest to my management; I'll let you down the back
way.

MRS PINCHWIFE. I don't know the way home, so I don't.

HORNER. My man shall wait upon you.

MRS PINCHWIFE. No, don't you believe that I'll go at all;
what, are you weary of me already?

HORNER. No, my life, 'tis that I may love you long, 'tis to
secure my love, and your reputation with your husband;
he'll never receive you again else.

MRS PINCHWIFE. What care I? D'ye think to frighten me
with that? I don't intend to go to him again; you shall be
my husband now.

HORNER. I cannot be your husband, dearest, since you are married to him.

MRS PINCHWIFE. Oh, would you make me believe that? Don't I see every day at London here, women leave their first husbands, and go and live with other men as their wives? Pish, pshaw! you'd make me angry, but that I love you so mainly.

HORNER. So, they are coming up – in again, in, I hear 'em.

Exit MRS PINCHWIFE.

Well, a silly mistress is like a weak place, soon got, soon lost, a man has scarce time for plunder; she betrays her husband first to her gallant, and then her gallant to her husband.

Enter PINCHWIFE, ALITHEA, HARCOURT, SPARKISH, LUCY *and a* PARSON.

PINCHWIFE. Come, madam, 'tis not the sudden change of your dress, the confidence of your asseverations, and your false witness there, shall persuade me I did not bring you hither just now. Here's my witness, who cannot deny it, since you must be confronted. – Mr Horner, did not I bring this lady to you just now?

HORNER (*aside*). Now must I wrong one woman for another's sake. But that's no new thing with me; for in these cases I am still on the criminal's side, against the innocent.

ALITHEA. Pray speak, sir.

HORNER (*aside*). It must be so – I must be impudent and try my luck; impudence uses to be too hard for truth.

PINCHWIFE. What, you are studying an evasion, or excuse for her? Speak, sir.

HORNER. No, faith, I am something backward only to speak in women's affairs or disputes.

PINCHWIFE. She bids you speak.

ALITHEA. Ay, pray sir do, pray satisfy him.

HORNER. Then truly, you did bring that lady to me just now.

PINCHWIFE. O ho!

ALITHEA. How, sir!

HARCOURT. How, Horner!

ALITHEA. What mean you, sir? I always took you for a man of honour.

HORNER (*aside*). Ay, so much a man of honour that I must save my mistress, I thank you, come what will on't.

SPARKISH. So, if I had had her, she'd have made me believe the moon had been made of Christmas pie.

LUCY (*aside*). Now could I speak, if I durst, and solve the riddle, who am the author of it.

ALITHEA. O unfortunate woman! A combination against my honour, which most concerns me now, because you share in my disgrace, sir, and it is your censure which I must now suffer, that troubles me, not theirs.

HARCOURT. Madam, then have no trouble, you shall now see 'tis possible for me to love too, without being jealous; I will not only believe your innocence myself, but make all the world believe it. (*Apart to* HORNER.) Horner, I must now be concerned for this lady's honour.

HORNER. And I must be concerned for a lady's honour too.

HARCOURT. This lady has her honour, and I will protect it.

HORNER. My lady has not her honour, but has given it me to keep, and I will preserve it.

HARCOURT. I understand you not.

HORNER. I would not have you.

MRS PINCHWIFE (*peeping in behind*). What's the matter with 'em all?

PINCHWIFE. Come, come, Mr Horner, no more disputing.
Here's the parson; I brought him not in vain.

HARCOURT. No, sir, I'll employ him, if this lady please.

PINCHWIFE. How! what d'ye mean?

SPARKISH. Ay, what does he mean?

HORNER. Why, I have resigned your sister to him; he has
my consent.

PINCHWIFE. But he has not mine, sir. A woman's injured
honour, no more than a man's, can be repaired or
satisfied by any but him that first wronged it. And you
shall marry her presently, or –

Lays his hand on his sword. Enter to them MRS PINCHWIFE.

MRS PINCHWIFE. O lord, they'll kill poor Mr Horner!
Besides he shan't marry her whilst I stand by and look
on; I'll not lose my second husband so.

PINCHWIFE. What do I see?

ALITHEA. My sister in my clothes!

SPARKISH. Ha!

MRS PINCHWIFE (*to* PINCHWIFE). Nay, pray now
don't quarrel about finding work for the parson; he shall
marry me to Mr Horner, for now I believe you have
enough of me.

HORNER. Damned, damned loving changeling!

MRS PINCHWIFE. Pray, sister, pardon me for telling so
many lies of you.

HARCOURT. I suppose the riddle is plain now.

LUCY. No, that must be my work. Good sir, hear me.

Kneels to MR PINCHWIFE, *who stands doggedly with his hat
over his eyes.*

PINCHWIFE. I will never hear woman again, but make 'em
all silent, thus –

Offers to draw upon his wife.

HORNER. No, that must not be.

PINCHWIFE. You then shall go first, 'tis all one to me.

Offers to draw on HORNER; *stopped by* HARCOURT.

HARCOURT. Hold!

Enter SIR JASPAR FIDGET, LADY FIDGET,
LADY SQUEAMISH, MRS DAINTY FIDGET *and*
MRS SQUEAMISH.

SIR JASPAR. What's the matter? what's the matter? pray,
what's the matter, sir? I beseech you communicate, sir.

PINCHWIFE. Why, my wife has communicated, sir, as your
wife may have done too, sir, if she knows him, sir.

SIR JASPAR. Pshaw, with him! Ha, ha, he!

PINCHWIFE. D'ye mock me, sir? A cuckold is a kind of a
wild beast, have a care, sir!

SIR JASPAR. No, sure, you mock me, sir – he cuckold you!
It can't be, ha, ha, he! Why, I'll tell you, sir – (*Offers to
whisper.*)

PINCHWIFE. I tell you again, he has whored my wife,
and yours too, if he knows her, and all the women he
comes near; 'tis not his dissembling, his hypocrisy, can
wheedle me.

SIR JASPAR. How, does he dissemble? Is he a hypocrite?
Nay, then – how – wife – sister, is he an hypocrite?

OLD LADY SQUEAMISH. An hypocrite, a dissembler!
Speak, young harlotry, speak, how?

SIR JASPAR. Nay, then – oh, my head too! – Oh thou
libidinous lady!

OLD LADY SQUEAMISH. Oh thou harloting harlotry!
Hast thou done't then?

SIR JASPAR. Speak, good Horner, art thou a dissembler,
a rogue? Hast thou –

HORNER. So –

LUCY (*apart to* HORNER). I'll fetch you off, and her too, if she will but hold her tongue.

HORNER (*apart to* LUCY). Canst thou? I'll give thee –

LUCY (*to* MR PINCHWIFE). Pray, have but patience to hear me, sir, who am the unfortunate cause of all this confusion. Your wife is innocent, I only culpable; for I put her upon telling you all these lies concerning my mistress in order to the breaking off the match concerning my mistress in order to the breaking off the match between Mr Sparkish and her, to make way for Mr Harcourt.

SPARKISH. Did you so, eternal rotten-tooth? Then it seems my mistress was not false to me, I was only deceived by you. Brother that should have been, now, man of conduct, who is a frank person now? To bring your wife to her lover – ha!

LUCY. I assure you, sir, she came not to Mr Horner out of love, for she loves him no more –

MRS PINCHWIFE. Hold, I told lies for you, but you shall tell none for me, for I do love Mr Horner with all my soul and nobody shall say me nay; pray don't you go to make poor Mr Horner believe to the contrary, 'tis spitefully done of you, I'm sure.

HORNER (*aside to* MRS PINCHWIFE). Peace, dear idiot!

MRS PINCHWIFE. Nay, I will not peace.

PINCHWIFE. Not till I make you.

Enter DORILANT *and* QUACK.

DORILANT. Horner, your servant; I am the doctor's guest, he must excuse our intrusion.

QUACK. But what's the matter, gentlemen? For heaven's sake, what's the matter?

HORNER. Oh, 'tis well you are come. 'Tis a censorious world we live in; you may have brought me a reprieve, or else I had died for a crime I never committed, and these innocent ladies had suffered with me. Therefore, pray satisfy these worthy, honourable, jealous gentlemen – that – (*Whispers.*)

QUACK. Oh, I understand you; is that all? – Sir Jaspar, by heavens and upon the word of a physician sir –

Whispers to SIR JASPAR.

SIR JASPAR. Nay, I do believe you truly. – Pardon me, my virtuous lady, and dear of honour.

OLD LADY SQUEAMISH. What, then all's right again?

SIR JASPAR. Ay, ay, and now let us satisfy him too.

They whisper with MR PINCHWIFE.

PINCHWIFE. An eunuch! Pray, no fooling with me.

QUACK. I'll bring half the surgeons in town to swear it.

PINCHWIFE. They! – They'll swear a man that bled to death through his wounds died of an apoplexy.

QUACK. Pray hear me, sir – why, all the town has heard the report of him.

PINCHWIFE. But does all the town believe it?

QUACK. Pray enquire a little, and first of all these.

PINCHWIFE. I'm sure when I left the town he was the lewdest fellow in't.

QUACK. I tell you, sir, he has been in France since; pray ask but these ladies and gentlemen, your friend Mr Dorilant. – Gentlemen and ladies, han't you all heard the late sad report of poor Mr Horner?

ALL LADIES. Ay, ay, ay.

DORILANT. Why, thou jealous fool, dost thou doubt it? He's an arrant French capon.

MRS PINCHWIFE. 'Tis false, sir, you shall not disparage poor Mr Horner, for to my certain knowledge –

LUCY. Oh hold!

SQUEAMISH (*aside to* LUCY). Stop her mouth!

LADY FIDGET (*to* PINCHWIFE). Upon my honour, sir, 'tis as true –

DAINTY. D'ye think we would have been seen in his company?

SQUEAMISH. Trust our unspotted reputations with him!

LADY FIDGET (*aside to* HORNER). This you get, and we too, by trusting your secret to a fool.

HORNER. Peace, madam. (*Aside to* QUACK.) Well, doctor, is not this a good design, that carries a man on unsuspected, and brings him off safe?

PINCHWIFE (*aside*). Well, if this were true, but my wife –

DORILANT *whispers with* MRS PINCHWIFE.

ALITHEA. Come, brother, your wife is yet innocent you see. But have a care of too strong an imagination, lest like an over-concerned, timorous gamester, by fancying an unlucky cast, it should come. Women and fortune are truest still to those that trust 'em.

LUCY. And any wild thing grows but the more fierce and hungry for being kept up, and more dangerous to the keeper.

ALITHEA. There's doctrine for all husbands, Mr Harcourt.

HARCOURT. I edify, madam, so much that I am impatient till I am one.

DORILANT. And I edify so much by example I will never be one.

SPARKISH. And because I will not disparage my parts I'll ne'er be one.

HORNER. And I, alas, can't be one.

PINCHWIFE. But I must be one – against my will, to a country wife, with a country murrain to me.

MRS PINCHWIFE (*aside*). And I must be a country wife still too, I find, for I can't, like a city one, be rid of my musty husband and do what I list.

HORNER. Now, sir, I must pronounce your wife innocent, though I blush whilst I do it, and I am the only man by her now exposed to shame, which I will straight drown in wine, as you shall your suspicion, and the ladies' troubles we'll divert with a ballet. Doctor, where are your maskers?

LUCY. Indeed, she's innocent, sir, I am her witness; and her end of coming out was but to see her sister's wedding, and what she has said to your face of her love to Mr Horner was but the usual innocent revenge on a husband's jealousy – was it not, madam? Speak.

MRS PINCHWIFE (*aside to* LUCY *and* HORNER). Since you'll have me tell more lies – Yes, indeed, bud.

PINCHWIFE.
For my own sake fain I would all believe;
Cuckolds, like lovers, should themselves deceive
But – (*Sighs.*) His honour is least safe, too late I find,
Who trusts it with a foolish wife or friend.

A dance of cuckolds.

HORNER.
Vain fops, but court, and dress, and keep a pother
To pass for women's men with one another;
But he who aims by women to be prized,
First by the men, you see, must be despised!

Epilogue

Spoken by Mrs Knepp

Now, you the vigorous, who dally here
O'er vizard mask in public domineer,
And what you'd do to her if in place where;
Nay, have the confidence to cry 'come out!'
Yet when she says 'Lead on' you are not stout;
But to your well-dressed brother straight turn round
And cry 'Pox on her, Ned, she can't be sound!'
Then slink away, a fresh one to engage,
With so much seeming heat and loving rage,
You'd frighten listening actress on the stage,
Till she at last has seen you huffing come,
And talk of keeping in the tiring-room,
Yet cannot be provoked to lead her home.
Next, you Falstaffs of fifty, who beset
Your buckram maidenheads, which your friends get
And whilst to them you of achievements boast
They share the booty, and laugh at your cost.
In fine, you essenced boys, both old and young,
Who would be thought so eager, brisk, and strong,
Yet do the ladies, not their husbands, wrong;
Whose purses for your manhood make excuse,
And keep your Flanders mares for show, not use;
Encouraged by our woman's man today
A Horner's part may vainly think to play;
And may intrigues so bashfully disown
That they may doubted be by few or none;
May kiss the cards at picquet, ombre, loo,
And so be thought to kiss the lady too;
But, gallants, have a care, faith, what you do.
The world, which to no man his due will give,
You by experience know you can deceive.
And men may still believe you vigorous,
But then we women – there's no coz'ning us!

THE ROVER

Prologue

Written by a person of quality

Wits, like physicians, never can agree,
When of a different society.
And Rabel's drops were never more cried down
By all the learned doctors of the town,
Than a new play, whose author is unknown:
Nor can those doctors with more malice sue
(And powerful purses) the dissenting few
Than those with an insulting pride do rail
At all who are not of their own cabal.

If a young poet hit your humour right,
You judge him then out of revenge and spite;
So amongst men there are ridiculous elves,
Who monkeys hate for being too like themselves.
So that the reason of the grand debate,
Why wit so oft is damned, when good plays take,
Is that you censure as you love or hate.

Thus like a learned conclave poets sit,
Catholic judges both of sense and wit,
And damn or save, as they themselves think fit.
Yet those who to others' faults are so severe,
Are not so perfect, but themselves may err.
Some write correct indeed, but then the whole
(Bating their own dull stuff i' th' play) is stole:
As bees do suck from flowers their honey-dew,
So they rob others, striving to please you.

Some write their characters genteel and fine,
But then they do so toil for every line
That what to you does easy seem, and plain,
Is the hard issue of their labouring brain.
And some th' effects of all their pains we see,

Is but to mimic good extempore.
Others, by long converse about the town,
Have wit enough to write a lewd lampoon,
But their chief skill lies in a bawdy song.
In short, the only wit that's now in fashion
Is but the gleanings of good conversation.
As for the author of this coming play,
I asked him what he thought fit I should say,
In thanks for your good company today:
He called me fool, and said it was well known,
You came not here for our sakes, but your own.
New plays are stuffed with wits, and with debauches,
That crowd and sweat like cits in May Day coaches.

The Persons of the Play

MEN

DON ANTONIO, *the Viceroy's son*

DON PEDRO, *a noble Spaniard, his friend*

BELVILE, *an English Colonel in love with Florinda*

WILLMORE, *the Rover*

FREDERICK, *an English gentleman, and friend to Belvile and Blunt*

BLUNT, *an English country gentleman*

STEPHANO, *servant to Don Pedro*

PHILIPPO, *Lucetta's gallant*

SANCHO, *pimp to Lucetta*

BISKEY *and* SEBASTIAN, *two bravos to Angellica*

DIEGO, *page to Don Antonio*

PAGE *to Hellena*

BOY, *page to Belvile*

BLUNT'S MAN

OFFICERS, SOLDIERS, MASQUERADERS (*men and women*)

WOMEN

FLORINDA, *sister to Don Pedro*

HELLENA, *a gay young woman, designed for a nun, sister to Florinda*

VALERIA, *a kinswoman to Florinda*

ANGELLICA BIANCA, *a famous courtesan*

MORETTA, *her woman*

CALLIS, *governess to Florinda and Hellena*

LUCETTA, *a jilting wench*

Scene: Naples, in carnival time.

ACT ONE

A chamber. Enter FLORINDA *and* HELLENA.

FLORINDA. What an impertinent thing is a young girl bred in a nunnery! How full of questions! Prithee no more, Hellena; I have told thee more than thou understand'st already.

HELLENA. The more's my grief; I would fain know as much as you, which makes me so inquisitive; nor is't enough I know you're a lover, unless you tell me too, who 'tis you sigh for.

FLORINDA. When you're a lover, I'll think you fit for a secret of that nature.

HELLENA. 'Tis true, I never was a lover yet – but I begin to have a shrewd guess, what 'tis to be so, and fancy it very pretty to sigh, and sing, and blush and wish, and dream and wish, and long and wish to see the man; and when I do, look pale and tremble, just as you did when my brother brought home the fine English Colonel to see you – what do you call him, Don Belvile?

FLORINDA. Fie, Hellena.

HELLENA. That blush betrays you – I am sure 'tis so – or is it Don Antonio the viceroy's son? – or perhaps the rich old Don Vincentio, whom my father designs you for a husband? – Why do you blush again?

FLORINDA. With indignation; and how near soever my father thinks I am to marrying that hated object, I shall let him see I understand better what's due to my beauty, birth, and fortune, and more to my soul, than to obey those unjust commands.

HELLENA. Now hang me if I don't love thee for that dear disobedience. I love mischief strangely, as most of our sex do, who are come to love nothing else – but tell me, dear Florinda, don't you love that fine *Anglese?* For I vow, next to loving him myself, 'twill please me most that you do so, for he is so gay and so handsome.

FLORINDA. Hellena, a maid designed for a nun ought not to be so curious in a discourse of love.

HELLENA. And dost thou think that ever I'll be a nun? Or at least till I'm so old, I'm fit for nothing else. Faith, no, sister; and that which makes me long to know whether you love Belvile, is because I hope he has some mad companion or other, that will spoil my devotion. Nay, I'm resolved to provide myself this carnival, if there be e'er a handsome proper fellow of my humour above ground, though I ask first.

FLORINDA. Prithee be not so wild.

HELLENA. Now you have provided yourself of a man, you take no care for poor me. Prithee tell me, what dost thou see about me that is unfit for love? Have I not a world of youth? A humour gay? A beauty passable? A vigour desirable? Well shaped? Clean limbed? Sweet breathed? And sense enough to know how all these ought to be employed to the best advantage? Yes, I do and will. Therefore lay aside your hopes of my fortune, by my being a devotee, and tell me how you came acquainted with this Belvile; for I perceive you knew him before he came to Naples.

FLORINDA. Yes, I knew him at the siege of Pamplona: he was then a colonel of French horse, who when the town was ransacked, nobly treated my brother and myself, preserving us from all insolences; and I must own (besides great obligations) I have I know not what, that pleads kindly for him about my heart, and will suffer no other to enter. – But see, my brother.

Enter DON PEDRO, STEPHANO, *with a masquing habit, and* CALLIS.

PEDRO. Good morrow, sister. Pray, when saw you your
lover Don Vincentio?

FLORINDA. I know not, sir. – Callis, when was he here?
For I consider it so little, I know not when it was.

PEDRO. I have a command from my father here to tell you,
you ought not to despise him, a man of so vast a fortune,
and such a passion for you. – Stephano, my things.

Puts on his masquing habit.

FLORINDA. A passion for me! 'Tis more than e'er I saw, or
he had a desire should be known. I hate Vincentio, sir,
and I would not have a man so dear to me as my brother
follow the ill customs of our country, and make a slave of
his sister. – And sir, my father's will, I'm sure, you may
divert.

PEDRO. I know not how dear I am to you, but I wish only
to be ranked in your esteem, equal with the English
Colonel Belvile. – Why do you frown and blush? Is there
any guilt belongs to the name of that cavalier?

FLORINDA. I'll not deny I value Belvile: when I was
exposed to such dangers as the licensed lust of common
soldiers threatened, when rage and conquest flew through
the city – then Belvile, this criminal for my sake, threw
himself into all dangers to save my honour; and will you
not allow him my esteem?

PEDRO. Yes, pay him what you will in honour – but you
must consider Don Vincentio's fortune, and the jointure
he'll make you.

FLORINDA. Let him consider my youth, beauty and
fortune; which ought not to be thrown away on his age
and jointure.

PEDRO. 'Tis true, he's not so young and fine a gentleman
as that Belvile – but what jewels will that cavalier present
you with? Those of his eyes and heart?

HELLENA. And are not those better than any Don
Vincentio has brought from the Indies?

PEDRO. Why how now! Has your nunnery-breeding taught
   you to understand the value of hearts and eyes?

HELLENA. Better than to believe Vincentio's deserve value
   from any woman. He may perhaps increase her bags, but
   not her family.

PEDRO. This is fine – go up to your devotion, you are not
   designed for the conversation of lovers.

HELLENA (*aside*). Nor saints, yet awhile, I hope. [*To*
   PEDRO.] – Is't not enough you make a nun of me, but
   you must cast my sister away too, exposing her to a worse
   confinement than a religious life?

PEDRO. The girl's mad. Is it a confinement to be carried
   into the country, to an ancient villa belonging to the
   family of the Vincentios these five hundred years, and
   have no other prospect than that pleasing one of seeing
   all her own that meets her eyes – a fine air, large fields
   and gardens, where she may walk and gather flowers?

HELLENA. When? By moon-light? For I am sure she dares
   not encounter with the heat of the sun; that were a task
   only for Don Vincentio and his Indian breeding, who
   loves it in the dog-days. – And if these be her daily
   divertissements, what are those of the night? To lie in a
   wide moth-eaten bed-chamber with furniture in fashion in
   the reign of King Sancho the First; the bed, that which
   his forefathers lived and died in.

PEDRO. Very well.

HELLENA. This apartment (new furbished and fitted out for
   the young wife) he (out of freedom) makes his dressing
   room; and being a frugal and a jealous coxcomb, instead
   of a valet to uncase his feeble carcass, he desires you to
   do that office – signs of favour, I'll assure you, and such
   as you must not hope for, unless your woman be out of
   the way.

PEDRO. Have you done yet?

HELLENA. That honour being past, the giant stretches
   himself, yawns and sighs a belch or two, loud as a musket,

throws himself into bed, and expects you in his foul sheets, and e'er you can get yourself undressed, calls you with a snore or two. – And are not these fine blessings to a young lady?

PEDRO. Have you done yet?

HELLENA. And this man you must kiss, nay, you must kiss none but him too – and nuzzle through his beard to find his lips – and this you must submit to for threescore years, and all for a jointure.

PEDRO. For all your character of Don Vincentio, she is as like to marry him as she was before.

HELLENA. Marry Don Vincentio! Hang me, such a wedlock would be worse than adultery with another man. I had rather see her in the *Hostel de Dieu,* to waste her youth there in vows and be a handmaid to lazars and cripples, than to lose it in such a marriage.

PEDRO. You have considered, sister, that Belvile has no fortune to bring to you, banished his country, despised at home, and pitied abroad?

HELLENA. What then? The Viceroy's son is better than that old Sir Fisty. Don Vincentio! Don Indian! He thinks he's trading to Gambo still, and would barter himself (that bell and bauble) for your youth and fortune.

PEDRO. Callis, take her hence, and lock her up all this carnival, and at Lent she shall begin her everlasting penance in a monastery.

HELLENA. I care not. I had rather be a nun, than be obliged to marry as you would have me, if I were designed for't.

PEDRO. Do not fear the blessing of that choice – you shall be a nun.

HELLENA (*aside*). Shall I so? You may chance to be mistaken in my way of devotion – a nun! Yes, I am like to make a fine nun! I have an excellent humour for a grate. No, I'll have a saint of my own to pray to shortly, if I like any that dares venture on me.

PEDRO. Callis, make it your business to watch this wild cat. As for you, Florinda, I've only tried you all this while, and urged my father's will; but mine is, that you would love Antonio, he is brave and young, and all that can complete the happiness of a gallant maid. – This absence of my father will give us opportunity to free you from Vincentio, by marrying here, which you must do tomorrow.

FLORINDA. Tomorrow!

PEDRO. Tomorrow, or 'twill be too late – 'tis not my friendship to Antonio which makes me urge this, but love to thee and hatred to Vincentio – therefore resolve upon tomorrow.

FLORINDA. Sir, I shall strive to do, as shall become your sister.

PEDRO. I'll both believe and trust you – adieu.

Exeunt PEDRO *and* STEPHANO.

HELLENA. As becomes his sister! That is to be as resolved your way, as he is his.

HELLENA *goes to* CALLIS.

FLORINDA. I ne'er till now perceived my ruin near,
I've no defence against Antonio's love,
For he has all the advantages of nature,
The moving arguments of youth and fortune.

HELLENA. But hark you, Callis, you will not be so cruel to lock me up indeed: will you?

CALLIS. I must obey the commands I hate – besides, do you consider what a life you are going to lead?

HELLENA. Yes, Callis, that of a nun: and till then I'll be indebted a world of prayers to you, if you'll let me now see, what I never did, the divertissements of a carnival.

CALLIS. What, go in masquerade? 'Twill be a fine farewell to the world, I take it — pray what would you do there?

HELLENA. That which all the world does, as I am told – be as mad as the rest, and take all innocent freedoms. –

Sister, you'll go too, will you not? Come prithee be not
sad – we'll outwit twenty brothers, if you'll be ruled by
me. – Come put off this dull humour with your clothes,
and assume one as gay, and as fantastic as the dress my
cousin Valeria and I have provided, and let's ramble.

FLORINDA. Callis, will you give us leave to go?

CALLIS (*aside*). I have a youthful itch of going myself. [*To*
FLORINDA.] – Madam, if I thought your brother might
not know it, and I might wait on you; for by my troth I'll
not trust young girls alone.

FLORINDA. Thou see'st my brother's gone already, and
thou shalt attend and watch us.

Enter STEPHANO.

STEPHANO. Madam, the habits are come, and your cousin
Valeria is dressed, and stays for you.

FLORINDA. 'Tis well – I'll write a note, and if I chance to
see Belvile, and want an opportunity to speak to him, that
shall let him know what I've resolved in favour of him.

HELLENA. Come, let's in and dress us.

Exeunt.

Scene Two

A long street. Enter BELVILE, *melancholy,* BLUNT *and*
FREDERICK.

FREDERICK. Why, what the devil ails the Colonel, in a
time when all the world is gay, to look like mere Lent
thus? Hadst thou been long enough in Naples to have
been in love, I should have sworn some such judgement
had befallen thee.

BELVILE. No, I have made no new amours since I came to
Naples.

FREDERICK. You have left none behind you in Paris?

BELVILE. Neither.

FREDERICK. I cannot divine the cause then; unless the old cause, the want of money.

BLUNT. And another old cause, the want of a wench – would not that revive you?

BELVILE. You are mistaken, Ned.

BLUNT. Nay, 'sheartlikins, then thou'rt past cure.

FREDERICK. I have found it out; thou hast renewed thy acquaintance with the lady that cost thee so many sighs at the siege of Pamplona – pox on't, what d'ye call her – her brother's a noble Spaniard – nephew to the dead general – Florinda – ay, Florinda – and will nothing serve thy turn but that damned virtuous woman, whom on my conscience thou lov'st in spite too, because thou seest little or no possibility of gaining her?

BELVILE. Thou art mistaken; I have int'rest enough in that lovely virgin's heart to make me proud and vain, were it not abated by the severity of her brother Pedro, who perceiving my happiness –

FREDERICK. Has civilly forbid thee the house?

BELVILE. 'Tis so, to make way for a powerful rival, the Viceroy's son, who has the advantage of me in being a man of fortune, a Spaniard, and her brother's friend; which gives him liberty to make his court, whilst I have recourse only to letters, and distant looks from her window, which are as soft and kind as those which Heaven sends down on penitents.

BLUNT. Hey day! 'Sheartlikins, simile! By this light the man is quite spoiled.

FREDERICK. What the devil are we made of, that we cannot be thus concerned for a wench?

BLUNT. 'Sheartlikins, our Cupids are like the cooks of the camp – they can roast or boil a woman, but they have none of the fine tricks to set 'em off, no hogoes to make the sauce pleasant, and the stomach sharp.

FREDERICK. I dare swear I have had a hundred as young, kind and handsome as this Florinda; and dogs eat me, if they were not as troublesome to me i' th' morning as they were welcome o'er night.

BLUNT. And yet, I warrant, he would not touch another woman, if he might have her for nothing.

BELVILE. That's thy joy, a cheap whore.

BLUNT. Why, 'sheartlikins, I love a frank soul. – When did you ever hear of an honest woman that took a man's money? I warrant 'em good ones. – But gentlemen, you may be free; you have been kept so poor with parliaments and protectors, that the little stock you have is not worth preserving – but I thank my stars, I had more grace than to forfeit my estate by cavaliering.

BELVILE. Methinks only following the court should be sufficient to entitle 'em to that.

BLUNT. 'Sheartlikins, they know I follow it to do it no good, unless they pick a hole in my coat for lending you money now and then; which is a greater crime to my conscience, gentlemen, than to the Commonwealth.

Enter WILLMORE.

WILLMORE. Ha! Dear Belvile! Noble colonel!

BELVILE. Willmore! Welcome ashore, my dear rover! – What happy wind blew us this good fortune?

WILLMORE. Let me salute my dear Fred, and then command me. – How is't, honest lad?

FREDERICK. Faith, sir, the old compliment, infinitely the better to see my dear mad Willmore again. – Prithee why camest thou ashore? And where's the Prince?

WILLMORE. He's well, and reigns still lord of the watery element. – I must aboard again within a day or two, and my business ashore was only to enjoy myself a little this carnival.

BELVILE. Pray know our new friend, sir; he's but bashful, a raw traveller, but honest, stout, and one of us.

Embraces BLUNT.

WILLMORE. That you esteem him, gives him an int'rest here.

BLUNT. Your servant, sir.

WILLMORE. But well, faith, I'm glad to meet you again in a warm climate, where the kind sun has its god-like power still over the wine and women. − Love and mirth are my business in Naples; and if I mistake not the place, here's an excellent market for chapmen of my humour.

BELVILE. See, here be those kind merchants of love you look for.

Enter several MEN *in masquing habits, some playing on musical instruments, others dancing after;* WOMEN *dressed like courtesans, with papers pinned on their breasts, and baskets of flowers in their hands.*

BLUNT. 'Sheartlikins, what have we here!

FREDERICK. Now the game begins.

WILLMORE. Fine pretty creatures! May a stranger have leave to look and love? − What's here? *(Reads the papers.)* − 'Roses for every month!'

BLUNT. Roses for every month! What means that?

BELVILE. They are, or would have you think they're courtesans, who here in Naples are to be hired by the month.

WILLMORE. Kind and obliging to inform us. − [*To a* WOMAN.] Pray where do these roses grow? I would fain plant some of 'em in a bed of mine.

WOMAN. Beware such roses, sir.

WILLMORE. A pox of fear: I'll be baked with thee between a pair of sheets, and that's thy proper still; so I might but strew such roses over me and under me. − Fair one, would you would give me leave to gather at your bush this idle month, I would go near to make somebody smell of it all the year after.

BELVILE. And thou hast need of such a remedy, for thou stink'st of tar and ropes' ends, like a dock or pest-house.

The WOMAN *puts herself into the hands of a* MAN *and exit.*

WILLMORE. Nay, nay, you shall not leave me so.

BELVILE. By all means use no violence here.

WILLMORE. Death! Just as I was going to be damnably in love, to have her led off! I could pluck that rose out of his hand, and even kiss the bed, the bush grew in.

FREDERICK. No friend to love like a long voyage at sea.

BLUNT. Except a nunnery, Fred.

WILLMORE. Death! But will they not be kind, quickly be kind? Thou know'st I'm no tame sigher, but a rampant lion of the forest.

Advances, from the farther end of the scenes, two men dressed all over with horns of several sorts, making grimaces at one another, with papers pinned on their backs.

BELVILE. Oh the fantastical rogues, how they're dressed! 'Tis a satire against the whole sex.

WILLMORE. Is this a fruit that grows in this warm country?

BELVILE. Yes: 'tis pretty to see these Italians start, swell, and stab at the word cuckold, and yet stumble at horns on every threshold.

WILLMORE. See what's on their back. (*Reads.*) 'Flowers of every night.' – Ah rogue! And more sweet than roses of ev'ry month! This is a gardener of Adam's own breeding.

They dance.

BELVILE. What think you of those grave people? – Is a wake in Essex half so mad or extravagant?

WILLMORE. I like their sober grave way, 'tis a kind of legal authorised fornication, where the men are not chid for't, nor the women despised, as amongst our dull English. Even the monsieurs want that part of good manners.

BELVILE. But here in Italy, a monsieur is the humblest best-bred gentleman. – Duels are so baffled by bravos that an age shows not one, but between a Frenchman and a hang-man, who is as much too hard for him on the Piazza, as they are for a Dutchman on the New Bridge. – But see, another crew.

Enter FLORINDA, HELLENA, *and* VALERIA, *dressed like gipsies;* CALLIS *and* STEPHANO, LUCETTA, PHILIPPO *and* SANCHO *in masquerade.*

HELLENA. Sister, there's your Englishman, and with him a handsome proper fellow. I'll to him, and instead of telling him his fortune, try my own.

WILLMORE. Gipsies, on my life. – Sure these will prattle if a man cross their hands. (*Goes to* HELLENA.) – Dear, pretty (and I hope) young devil, will you tell an amorous stranger what luck he's like to have?

HELLENA. Have a care how you venture with me, sir, lest I pick your pocket, which will more vex your English humour, than an Italian fortune will please you.

WILLMORE. How the devil cam'st thou to know my country and humour?

HELLENA. The first I guess by a certain forward impudence, which does not displease me at this time; and the loss of your money will vex you, because I hope you have but very little to lose.

WILLMORE. Egad, child, thou'rt i' th' right; it is so little I dare not offer it thee for a kindness. – But cannot you divine what other things of more value I have about me, that I would more willingly part with?

HELLENA. Indeed no, that's the business of a witch, and I am but a gipsy yet. – Yet without looking in your hand, I have a parlous guess, 'tis some foolish heart you mean, an inconstant English heart, as little worth stealing as your purse.

WILLMORE. Nay, then thou dost deal with the devil, that's certain. – Thou hast guessed as right as if thou hadst

been one of that number it has languished for. I find
you'll be better acquainted with it; nor can you take it in
a better time, for I am come from sea, child; and Venus
not being propitious to me in her own element, I have a
world of love in store. – Would you would be
good-natured and take some on't off my hands.

HELLENA. Why – I could be inclined that way – but for a
foolish vow I am going to make – to die a maid.

WILLMORE. Then thou art damned without redemption;
and as I am a good Christian, I ought in charity to divert
so wicked a design; therefore prithee, dear creature, let
me know quickly when and where I shall begin to set a
helping hand to so good a work.

HELLENA. If you should prevail with my tender heart (as
I begin to fear you will, for you have horrible loving eyes)
there will be difficulty in't, that you'll hardly undergo for
my sake.

WILLMORE. Faith, child, I have been bred in dangers, and
wear a sword that has been employed in a worse cause
than for a handsome kind woman. – Name the danger –
let it be any thing but a long siege, and I'll undertake it.

HELLENA. Can you storm?

WILLMORE. Oh, most furiously.

HELLENA. What think you of a nunnery wall? For he that
wins me must gain that first.

WILLMORE. A nun! Oh, how I love thee for't! There's no
sinner like a young saint. – Nay, now there's no denying
me; the old law had no curse (to a woman) like dying a
maid: witness Jephthah's daughter.

HELLENA. A very good text this, if well handled; and I
perceive, Father Captain, you would impose no severe
penance on her who were inclined to console herself
before she took orders.

WILLMORE. If she be young and handsome.

HELLENA. Ay, there's it – but if she be not –

WILLMORE. By this hand, child, I have an implicit faith, and dare venture on thee with all faults. – Besides, 'tis more meritorious to leave the world when thou hast tasted and proved the pleasure on't; then 'twill be a virtue in thee, which now will be pure ignorance.

HELLENA. I perceive, good Father Captain, you design only to make me fit for Heaven – but if on the contrary you should quite divert me from it, and bring me back to the world again, I should have a new man to seek, I find; and what a grief that will be – for when I begin, I fancy I shall love like anything: I never tried yet.

WILLMORE. Egad, and that's kind. – Prithee, dear creature, give me credit for a heart, for faith, I'm a very honest fellow. – Oh, I long to come first to the banquet of love; and such a swinging appetite I bring. Oh, I'm impatient. Thy lodging, sweetheart, thy lodging, or I'm a dead man.

HELLENA. Why must we be either guilty of fornication or murder if we converse with you men? – And is there no difference between leave to love me, and leave to lie with me?

WILLMORE. Faith, child, they were made to go together.

LUCETTA (*pointing to* BLUNT). Are you sure this is the man?

They withdraw.

SANCHO. When did I mistake your game?

LUCETTA. This is a stranger, I know by his gazing; if he be brisk he'll venture to follow me; and then, if I understand my trade, he's mine. He's English too, and they say that's a sort of good-natured loving people, and have generally so kind an opinion of themselves, that a woman with any wit may flatter 'em into any sort of fool she pleases.

She often passes by BLUNT *and gazes on him; he struts, and cocks, and walks, and gazes on her.*

BLUNT. 'Tis so – she is taken – I have beauties which my false glass at home did not discover.

FLORINDA. This woman watches me so, I shall get no opportunity to discover myself to him, and so miss the intent of my coming. (*Looking in* [BELVILE's] *hand.*) – But as I was saying, sir – by this line you should be a lover.

BELVILE. I thought how right you guessed, all men are in love, or pretend to be so. – Come, let me go; I'm weary of this fooling.

Walks away.

FLORINDA. I will not till you have confessed whether the passion that you have vowed Florinda be true or false.

She holds him; he strives to get from her.

BELVILE (*turns quick towards her*). Florinda!

FLORINDA. Softly.

BELVILE. Thou hast named one will fix me here for ever.

FLORINDA. She'll be disappointed then, who expects you this night at the garden gate, and if you fail not – as let me see the other hand – you will go near to do, she vows to die or make you happy.

Looks on CALLIS, *who observes 'em.*

BELVILE. What canst thou mean?

FLORINDA. That which I say. – Farewell.

Offers to go.

BELVILE. Oh charming sybil, stay, complete that joy, which, as it is, will turn into distraction! – Where must I be? At the garden gate? I know it – at night, you say – I'll sooner forfeit Heaven than disobey.

Enter DON PEDRO *and other maskers, and pass over the stage.*

CALLIS. Madam, your brother's here.

FLORINDA. Take this to instruct you farther.

Gives [BELVILE] *a letter, and goes off.*

FREDERICK. Have a care, sir, what you promise; this may
be a trap laid by her brother to ruin you.

BELVILE. Do not disturb my happiness with doubts.

Opens the letter.

WILLMORE [*to* HELLENA]. My dear pretty creature, a
thousand blessings on thee; still in this habit, you say, and
after dinner at this place.

HELLENA. Yes, if you will swear to keep your heart, and
not bestow it between this and that.

WILLMORE. By all the little gods of love I swear, I'll leave
it with you; and if you run away with it, those deities of
justice will revenge me.

Exeunt all the women [*except* LUCETTA].

FREDERICK. Do you know the hand?

BELVILE. 'Tis Florinda's. All blessings fall upon the virtuous
maid.

FREDERICK. Nay, no idolatry, a sober sacrifice I'll allow
you.

BELVILE. Oh friends, the welcom'st news, the softest letter!
– Nay, you shall all see it; and could you now be serious,
I might be made the happiest man the sun shines on!

WILLMORE. The reason of this mighty joy?

BELVILE. See how kindly she invites me to deliver her from
the threatened violence of her brother – will you not assist
me?

WILLMORE. I know not what thou mean'st, but I'll make
one at any mischief where a woman's concerned. – But
she'll be grateful to us for the favour, will she not?

BELVILE. How mean you?

WILLMORE. How should I mean? Thou know'st there's but
one way for a woman to oblige me.

BELVILE. Do not profane – the maid is nicely virtuous.

WILLMORE. Who, pox, then she's fit for nothing but a husband. Let her e'en go, Colonel.

FREDERICK. Peace, she's the Colonel's mistress, sir.

WILLMORE. Let her be the devil; if she be thy mistress, I'll serve her – name the way.

BELVILE. Read here this postscript.

Gives him a letter.

WILLMORE (*reads*). 'At ten at night at the garden gate – of which, if I cannot get the key, I will contrive a way over the wall – come attended with a friend or two.' Kind heart, if we three cannot weave a string to let her down a garden wall, 'twere pity but the hangman wove one for us all.

FREDERICK. Let her alone for that; your woman's wit, your fair kind woman, will out-trick a broker or a Jew, and contrive like a Jesuit in chains. – But see, Ned Blunt is stol'n out after the lure of a damsel.

Exeunt BLUNT and LUCETTA.

BELVILE. So he'll scarce find his way home again unless we get him cried by the bellman in the market-place. And 'twould sound prettily – a lost English boy of thirty.

FREDERICK. I hope 'tis some common crafty sinner, one that will fit him. It may be she'll sell him for Peru, the rogue's sturdy and would work well in a mine. At least I hope she'll dress him for our mirth; cheat him of all, then have him well-favour'dly banged, and turned out naked at midnight.

WILLMORE. Prithee what humour is he of, that you wish him so well?

BELVILE. Why, of an English elder brother's humour, educated in a nursery, with a maid to tend him till fifteen, and lies with his grandmother till he's of age; one that knows no pleasure beyond riding to the next fair, or going up to London with his right worshipful father in parliament-time; wearing gay clothes, or making honourable love to his lady mother's laundry-maid; gets drunk at a hunting-match, and ten to one then gives some proofs of his prowess. – A pox upon him, he's our banker, and has all our cash about him; and if he fail, we are all broke.

FREDERICK. Oh let him alone for that matter, he's of a damned stingy quality, that will secure our stock. I know not in what danger it were indeed if the jilt should pretend she's in love with him, for 'tis a kind believing coxcomb; otherwise if he part with more than a piece of eight – geld him: for which offer he may chance to be beaten if she be a whore of the first rank.

BELVILE. Nay the rogue will not be easily beaten, he's stout enough. Perhaps if they talk beyond his capacity, he may chance to exercise his courage upon some of them; else I'm sure they'll find it as difficult to beat as to please him.

WILLMORE. 'Tis a lucky devil to light upon so kind a wench!

FREDERICK. Thou hadst a great deal of talk with thy little gipsy, couldst thou do no good upon her? For mine was hard-hearted.

WILLMORE. Hang her, she was some damned honest person of quality, I'm sure, she was so very free and witty. If her face be but answerable to her wit and humour, I would be bound to constancy this month to gain her. In the mean time, have you made no kind acquaintance since you came to town? – You do not use to be honest so long, gentlemen.

FREDERICK. Faith, love has kept us honest, we have been all fired with a beauty newly come to town, the famous Paduana Angellica Bianca.

WILLMORE. What, the mistress of the dead Spanish General?

BELVILE. Yes, she's now the only adored beauty of all the youth in Naples, who put on all their charms to appear lovely in her sight, their coaches, liveries, and themselves, all gay, as on a monarch's birthday, to attract the eyes of this fair charmer, while she has the pleasure to behold all languish for her that see her.

FREDERICK. 'Tis pretty to see with how much love the men regard her, and how much envy the women.

WILLMORE. What gallant has she?

BELVILE. None, she's exposed to sale, and four days in the week she's yours – for so much a month.

WILLMORE. The very thought of it quenches all manner of fire in me – yet prithee let's see her.

BELVILE. Let's first to dinner, and after that we'll pass the day as you please – but at night ye must all be at my devotion.

WILLMORE. I will not fail you.

[*Exeunt.*]

ACT TWO

Scene One

The long street. Enter BELVILE *and* FREDERICK *in masking habits, and* WILLMORE *in his own clothes, with a vizard in his hand.*

WILLMORE. But why thus disguised and muzzled?

BELVILE. Because whatever extravagances we commit in these faces, our own may not be obliged to answer 'em.

WILLMORE. I should have changed my eternal buff too; but no matter, my little gipsy would not have found me out then: for if she should change hers, it is impossible I should know her, unless I should hear her prattle. A pox on't, I cannot get her out of my head. Pray Heaven, if ever I do see her again, she prove damnably ugly, that I may fortify myself against her tongue.

BELVILE. Have a care of love, for o' my conscience she was not of a quality to give thee any hopes.

WILLMORE. Pox on 'em, why do they draw a man in then? She has played with my heart so, that 'twill never lie still till I have met with some kind wench, that will play the game out with me. – Oh for my arms full of soft, white, kind – woman! Such as I fancy Angellica.

BELVILE. This is her house, if you were but in stock to get admittance; they have not dined yet; I perceive the picture is not out.

Enter BLUNT.

WILLMORE. I long to see the shadow of the fair substance, a man may gaze on that for nothing.

BLUNT. Colonel, thy hand – and thine, Fred. I have been an ass, a deluded fool, a very coxcomb from my birth till this hour, and heartily repent my little faith.

BELVILE. What the devil's the matter with thee, Ned?

[BLUNT]. Oh, such a mistress, Fred, such a girl!

WILLMORE. Ha! Where?

FREDERICK. Ay, where?

[BLUNT]. So fond, so amorous, so toying, and so fine! And all for sheer love, ye rogue! Oh, how she looked and kissed! And soothed my heart from my bosom! I cannot think I was awake, and yet methinks I see and feel her charms still. – Fred – try if she have not left the taste of her balmy kisses upon my lips –

Kisses him.

BELVILE. Ha! Ha! Ha!

WILLMORE. Death man, where is she?

[BLUNT]. What a dog was I to stay in dull England so long. – How have I laughed at the Colonel when he sighed for love! But now the little archer has revenged him, and by this one dart I can guess at all his joys, which then I took for fancies, mere dreams and fables. Well, I'm resolved to sell all in Essex, and plant here forever.

BELVILE. What a blessing 'tis, thou hast a mistress thou dar'st boast of; for I know thy humour is rather to have a proclaimed clap than a secret amour.

WILLMORE. Dost know her name?

BLUNT. Her name? No, 'sheartlikins: what care I for names? She's fair, young, brisk and kind, even to ravishment: and what a pox care I for knowing her by any other title?

WILLMORE. Didst give her anything?

BLUNT. Give her! – Ha, ha, ha! Why, she's a person of quality. – That's a good one, give her! 'Sheartlikins, dost

think such creatures are to be bought? Or are we
provided for such a purchase? Give her, quoth ye? Why,
she presented me with this bracelet, for the toy of a
diamond I used to wear. No, gentlemen, Ned Blunt is not
every body. – She expects me again to-night.

WILLMORE. Egad, that's well; we'll all go.

BLUNT. Not a soul: no, gentlemen, you are wits; I am a
dull country rogue, I.

FREDERICK. Well, sir, for all your person of quality, I shall
be very glad to understand your purse be secure; 'tis our
whole estate at present, which we are loath to hazard in
one bottom: come sir, unlade.

BLUNT. Take the necessary trifle, useless now to me, that
am beloved by such a gentlewoman. – 'Sheartlikins,
money! Here, take mine too.

FREDERICK. No, keep that to be cozened, that we may
laugh.

WILLMORE. Cozened! – Death! Would I could meet with
one that would cozen me of all the love I could spare
tonight.

FREDERICK. Pox 'tis some common whore upon my life.

BLUNT. A whore! Yes, with such clothes, such jewels, such a
house, such furniture, and so attended! A whore!

BELVILE. Why yes, sir, they are whores, though they'll
neither entertain you with drinking, swearing, or bawdry;
are whores in all those gay clothes and right jewels; are
whores with those great houses richly furnished with velvet
beds, store of plate, handsome attendance, and fine
coaches, are whores, and arrant ones.

WILLMORE. Pox on't, where do these fine whores live?

BELVILE. Where no rogues in office ycleped constables dare
give 'em laws, nor the wine-inspired bullies of the town
break their windows; yet they are whores, though this
Essex calf believe 'em persons of quality.

BLUNT. 'Sheartlikins, y'are all fools, there are things about this Essex calf that shall take with the ladies, beyond all your wit and parts. – This shape and size, gentlemen, are not to be despised; my waist too, tolerably long, with other inviting signs, that shall be nameless.

WILLMORE. Egad I believe he may have met with some person of quality that may be kind to him.

BELVILE. Dost thou perceive any such tempting things about him that should make a fine woman, and of quality, pick him out from all mankind, to throw away her youth and beauty upon, nay, and her dear heart, too? – No, no, Angellica has raised the price too high.

WILLMORE. May she languish for mankind till she die, and be damned for that one sin alone.

Enter two BRAVOS *and hang up a great picture of Angellica's against the balcony, and two little ones at each side of the door.*

BELVILE. See there the fair sign to the inn, where a man may lodge that's fool enough to give her price.

WILLMORE *gazes on the picture.*

BLUNT. 'Sheartlikins, gentlemen, what's this?

BELVILE. A famous courtesan that's to be sold.

BLUNT. How! To be sold! Nay then I have nothing to say to her. – Sold! What impudence is practised in this country? – With what order and decency whoring's established here by virtue of the Inquisition. – Come, let's be gone, I'm sure we're no chapmen for this commodity.

FREDERICK. Thou art none, I'm sure, unless thou couldst have her in thy bed at a price of a coach in the street.

WILLMORE. How wondrous fair she is – a thousand crowns a month – by Heaven, as many kingdoms were too little. A plague of this poverty – of which I ne'er complain, but when it hinders my approach to beauty, which virtue ne'er could purchase.

Turns from the picture.

BLUNT. What's this? (*Reads.*) 'A thousand crowns a month!'
– 'Sheartlikins, here's a sum! Sure 'tis a mistake. [*To a*
BRAVO.] Hark you, friend, does she take or give so
much by the month?

FREDERICK. A thousand crowns! Why, 'tis a portion for
the Infanta.

BLUNT. Hark ye, friends, won't she trust?

BRAVO. This is a trade, sir, that cannot live by credit.

Enter DON PEDRO *in masquerade, followed by*
STEPHANO.

BELVILE. See, here's more company; let's walk off a while.

Exeunt English. PEDRO *reads. Enter* ANGELLICA *and*
MORETTA *in the balcony, and draw a silk curtain.*

PEDRO. Fetch me a thousand crowns, I never wished to
buy this beauty at an easier rate.

Passes off.

ANGELLICA. Prithee what said those fellows to thee?

BRAVO. Madam, the first were admirers of beauty only, but
no purchasers; they were merry with your price and
picture, laughed at the sum, and so passed off.

ANGELLICA. No matter, I'm not displeased with their
rallying; their wonder feeds my vanity, and he that wishes
but to buy, gives me more pride than he that gives my
price can make my pleasure.

BRAVO. Madam, the last I knew through all his disguises to
be Don Pedro, nephew to the general, and who was with
him in Pamplona.

ANGELLICA. Don Pedro! My old gallant's nephew! When
his uncle died, he left him a vast sum of money; it is he
who was so in love with me at Padua, and who used to
make the general so jealous.

MORETTA. Is this he that used to prance before our
window, and take such care to show himself an amorous

ass? If I am not mistaken, he is the likeliest man to give your price.

ANGELLICA. The man is brave and generous, but of an humour so uneasy and inconstant that the victory over his heart is as soon lost as won; a slave that can add little to the triumph of the conqueror: but inconstancy's the sin of all mankind, therefore I'm resolved that nothing but gold shall charm my heart.

MORETTA. I'm glad on't; 'tis only interest that women of our profession ought to consider, though I wonder what has kept you from that general disease of our sex so long, I mean that of being in love.

ANGELLICA. A kind, but sullen star, under which I had the happiness to be born; yet I have had no time for love; the bravest and noblest of mankind have purchased my favours at so dear a rate, as if no coin but gold were current with our trade. – But here's Don Pedro again; fetch me my lute – for 'tis for him or Don Antonio the Viceroy's son, that I have spread my nets.

Enter at one door DON PEDRO [*and*] STEPHANO; DON ANTONIO *and* DIEGO *at the other door, with people following him in masquerade, antickly attired, some with music: they both go up to the picture.*

ANTONIO. A thousand crowns! Had not the painter flattered her, I should not think it dear.

PEDRO. Flattered her? By Heaven he cannot. I have seen the original, nor is there one charm here more than adorns her face and eyes; all this soft and sweet, with a certain languishing air, that no artist can represent.

ANTONIO. What I heard of her beauty before had fired my soul, but this confirmation of it has blown it to a flame.

PEDRO. Ha!

PAGE. Sir, I have known you throw away a thousand crowns on a worse face, and though y'are near your marriage, you may venture a little love here; Florinda will not miss it.

PEDRO (*aside*). Ha! Florinda! Sure 'tis Antonio.

ANTONIO. Florinda! Name not those distant joys, there's not one thought of her will check my passion here.

PEDRO (*aside*). Florinda scorned! And all my hopes defeated of the possession of Angellica!

A noise of a lute above. ANTONIO *gazes up.*

Her injuries, by Heaven, he shall not boast of!

Song to a lute above.

SONG.

[I]

When Damon first began to love,
He languished in a soft desire,
And knew not how the gods to move,
To lessen or increase his fire.
For Caelia in her charming eyes
Wore all love's sweets, and all his cruelties.

II

But as beneath a shade he lay,
Weaving of flowers for Caelia's hair,
She chanced to lead her flock that way,
And saw the am'rous shepherd there.
She gazed around upon the place,
And saw the grove (resembling night)
To all the joys of love invite,
Whilst guilty smiles and blushes dressed her face.
At this the bashful youth all transport grew,
And with kind force he taught the virgin how
To yield what all his sighs could never do.

ANTONIO. By Heaven, she's charming fair!

ANGELLICA *throws open the curtains and bows to* ANTONIO, *who pulls off his vizard, and bows and blows up kisses.* PEDRO *unseen looks in his face.*

PEDRO (*aside*). 'Tis he, the false Antonio!

ANTONIO (*to the* BRAVO). Friend, where must I pay my
off'ring of love? My thousand crowns I mean.

PEDRO. That off'ring I have designed to make,
And yours will come too late.

ANTONIO. Prithee be gone, I shall grow angry else,
And then thou art not safe.

PEDRO. My anger may be fatal, sir, as yours;
And he that enters here may prove this truth.

ANTONIO. I know not who thou art, but I am sure thou'rt
worth my killing, for aiming at Angellica.

They draw and fight. Enter WILLMORE *and* BLUNT, *who
draw and part 'em.*

BLUNT. 'Sheartlikins, here's fine doings.

WILLMORE. Tilting for the wench, I'm sure – nay, gad, if
that would win her I have as good a sword as the best of
ye. – Put up – put up, and take another time and place,
for this is designed for lovers only.

They all put up.

PEDRO. We are prevented; dare you meet me tomorrow on
the Molo?

For I've a title to a better quarrel,
That of Florinda, in whose credulous heart
Thou'st made an int'rest, and destroyed my hopes.

ANTONIO. Dare!
I'll meet thee there as early as the day.

PEDRO. We will come thus disguised, that whosoever
chance to get the better, he may escape unknown.

ANTONIO. It shall be so.

Exeunt PEDRO *and* STEPHANO.

Who should this rival be? Unless the English Colonel, of
whom I've often heard Don Pedro speak; it must be he,
and time he were removed. who lays a claim to all my
happiness.

WILLMORE having gazed all this while on the picture, pulls down a little one.

WILLMORE. This posture's loose and negligent,
The sight on't would beget a warm desire
In souls, whom impotence and age had chilled.
– This must along with me.

BRAVO. What means this rudeness, sir? – Restore the picture.

ANTONIO. Ha! Rudeness committed to the fair Angellica! – Restore the picture, sir.

WILLMORE. Indeed I will not, sir.

ANTONIO. By Heaven but you shall.

WILLMORE. Nay, do not show your sword; if you do, by this dear beauty – I will show mine too.

ANTONIO. What right can you pretend to't?

WILLMORE. That of possession which I will maintain – you perhaps have a thousand crowns to give for the original.

ANTONIO. No matter, sir, you shall restore the picture.

ANGELLICA *and* MORETTA *above.*

ANGELLICA. Oh, Moretta! What's the matter?

ANTONIO [*to* WILLMORE]. Or leave your life behind.

WILLMORE. Death! You lie – I will do neither.

They fight, the Spaniards join with ANTONIO, BLUNT *laying on like mad.*

ANGELLICA. Hold, I command you, if for me you fight.

They leave off and bow.

WILLMORE. How heavenly fair she is! – Ah plague of her price.

ANGELLICA. You sir in buff, you that appear a soldier, that first began this insolence –

WILLMORE. 'Tis true, I did so, if you call it insolence for a man to preserve himself; I saw your charming picture,

and was wounded; quite through my soul each pointed
beauty ran; and wanting a thousand crowns to procure
my remedy, I laid this little picture to my bosom – which
if you cannot allow me, I'll resign.

ANGELLICA. No, you may keep the trifle.

ANTONIO. You shall first ask me leave, and this.

[*They*] *fight again as before. Enter* BELVILE *and*
FREDERICK *who join with the English.*

ANGELLICA. Hold! Will you ruin me! – Biskey, Sebastian,
part 'em!

The SPANIARDS *are beaten off.*

MORETTA. Oh madam, we're undone, a pox upon that
rude fellow, he's set on to ruin us: we shall never see good
days till all these fighting poor rogues are sent to the
galleys.

Enter BELVILE, BLUNT, FREDERICK *and*
WILLMORE *with his shirt bloody.*

BLUNT. 'Sheartlikins, beat me at this sport, and I'll ne'er
wear sword more.

BELVILE (*to* WILLMORE). The devil's in thee for a mad
fellow, thou art always one at an unlucky adventure. –
Come, let's be gone whilst we're safe, and remember these
are Spaniards, a sort of people that know how to revenge
an affront.

FREDERICK. You bleed; I hope you are not wounded.

WILLMORE. Not much. – A plague on your Dons, if they
fight no better they'll ne'er recover Flanders. – What the
devil was't to them that I took down the picture?

BLUNT. Took it! 'Sheartlikins, we'll have the great one too;
'tis ours by conquest. – Prithee help me up and I'll pull it
down –

ANGELLICA. Stay, sir, and ere you affront me farther, let
me know how you durst commit this outrage – to you I
speak, sir, for you appear a gentleman.

WILLMORE. To me, madam? – Gentlemen, your servant.

BELVILE *stays him.*

BELVILE. Is the devil in thee? Dost know the danger of ent'ring the house of an incensed courtesan?

WILLMORE. I thank you for your care – but there are other matters in hand, there are, though we have no great temptation. – Death! Let me go.

FREDERICK. Yes, to your lodging, if you will, but not in here. – Damn these gay harlots. – By this hand I'll have as sound and handsome a whore for a patacoon. – Death, man, she'll murder thee.

WILLMORE. Oh, fear me not, shall I not venture where a beauty calls? A lovely charming beauty? For fear of danger! When by Heaven there's none so great as to long for her, whilst I want money to purchase her.

FREDERICK. Therefore 'tis loss of time, unless you had the thousand crowns to pay.

WILLMORE. It may be she may give a favour, at least I shall have the pleasure of saluting her when I enter, and when I depart.

BELVILE. Pox, she'll as soon lie with thee, as kiss thee, and sooner stab than do either – you shall not go.

ANGELLICA. Fear not, sir, all I have to wound with, is my eyes.

BLUNT. Let him go, 'sheartlikins, I believe the gentlewoman means well.

BELVILE. Well, take thy fortune, we'll expect you in the next street. – Farewell fool – farewell – ·

WILLMORE. B'ye, Colonel –

Goes in.

FREDERICK. The rogue's stark mad for a wench.

Exeunt.

Scene Two

A fine chamber.

Enter WILLMORE, ANGELLICA, *and* MORETTA.

ANGELLICA. Insolent sir, how durst you pull down my
   picture?

WILLMORE. Rather, how durst you set it up, to tempt
   poor am'rous mortals with so much excellence? Which I
   find you have but too well consulted by the unmerciful
   price you set upon't. – Is all this heaven of beauty shown
   to move despair in those that cannot buy? And can you
   think th'effects of that despair should be less extravagant
   than I have shown?

ANGELLICA. I sent for you to ask my pardon, sir, not to
   aggravate your crime. – I thought I should have seen you
   at my feet imploring it.

WILLMORE. You are deceived. I came to rail at you, and
   rail such truths, too, as shall let you see the vanity of that
   pride, which taught you how to set such price on sin. For
   such it is, whilst that which is love's due is meanly
   bartered for.

ANGELLICA. Ha, ha, ha, alas, good captain, what pity 'tis
   your edifying doctrine will do no good upon me. –
   Moretta, fetch the gentleman a glass, and let him survey
   himself, to see what charms he has, (*Aside, in a soft tone.*) –
   and guess my business.

MORETTA. He knows himself of old, I believe those
   breeches and he have been acquainted ever since he was
   beaten at Worcester.

ANGELLICA. Nay, do not abuse the poor creature –

MORETTA. Good weather-beaten Corporal, will you march
   off? We have no need of your doctrine, though you have
   of our charity; but at present we have no scraps; we can
   afford no kindness for God's sake; in fine, sirrah, the price
   is too high i'th' mouth for you, therefore troop, I say.

WILLMORE [*giving money to* MORETTA]. Here, good fore-
woman of the shop, serve me, and I'll be gone.

MORETTA. Keep it to pay your laundress, your linen stinks
of the gun-room; for here's no selling by retail.

WILLMORE. Thou hast sold plenty of thy stale ware at a
cheap rate.

MORETTA. Ay, the more silly kind heart I, but this is an
age wherein beauty is at higher rates. In fine, you know
the price of this.

WILLMORE. I grant you 'tis here set down a thousand
crowns a month. – Pray, how much may come to my
share for a pistole? Bawd, take your black-lead and sum it
up, that I may have a pistole's worth of this vain gay
thing, and I'll trouble you no more.

MORETTA. Pox on him, he'll fret me to death.
Abominable fellow, I tell thee, we only sell by the whole
piece.

WILLMORE. 'Tis very hard, the whole cargo or nothing. –
Faith, madam, my stock will not reach it, I cannot be
your chapman. –Yet I have countrymen in town,
merchants of love, like me; I'll see if they'll put in for a
share, we cannot lose much by it, and what we have no
use for, we'll sell upon the Friday's mart, at 'Who gives
more?' I am studying, madam, how to purchase you,
though at present I am unprovided of money.

ANGELLICA. Sure, this from any other man would anger
me – nor shall he know the conquest he has made. [*To*
WILLMORE.] – Poor angry man, how I despise this
railing.

WILLMORE. Yes, I am poor – but I'm a gentleman,
And one that scorns this baseness which you practise.
Poor as I am, I would not sell my self.
No, not to gain your charming high-prized person.
Though I admire you strangely for your beauty,
Yet I condemn your mind.
– And yet I would at any rate enjoy you;

At your own rate – but cannot. – See here
The only sum I can command on earth;
I know not where to eat when this is gone:
Yet such a slave I am to love and beauty,
This last reserve I'll sacrifice to enjoy you.
– Nay, do not frown; I know you're to be bought,
And would be bought by me, by me,
For a mean trifling sum, if I could pay it down.
Which happy knowledge I will still repeat,
And lay it to my heart: it has a virtue in't,
And soon will cure those wounds your eyes have made.
– And yet – there's something so divinely powerful there –
Nay, I will gaze – to let you see my strength.

Holds her, looks on her, and pauses and sighs.

By Heaven, bright creature, I would not for the world
Thy fame were half so fair as is thy face.

Turns her away from him.

ANGELLICA (*aside*). His words go through me to the very
   soul.
   [*To him.*] – If you have nothing else to say to me.

WILLMORE. Yes, you shall hear how infamous you are –
   For which I do not hate thee:
   But that secures my heart, and all the flames it feels
   Are but so many lusts,
   I know it by their sudden bold intrusion.
   The fire's impatient and betrays, 'tis false –
   For had it been the purer flame of love,
   I should have pined and languished at your feet,
   Ere found the impudence to have discovered it.
   I now dare stand your scorn, and your denial.

MORETTA. Sure she's bewitched, that she can stand thus
   tamely, and hear his saucy railing. Sirrah, will you be
   gone?

ANGELLICA (*to* MORETTA). How dare you take this
   liberty! Withdraw. – Pray tell me, sir, are not you guilty of
   the same mercenary crime? When a lady is proposed to
   you for a wife, you never ask how fair, discreet, or

virtuous she is; but what's her fortune – which, if but
small, you cry, 'She will not do my business' – and basely
leave her, though she languish for you. – Say, is not this
as poor?

WILLMORE. It is a barbarous custom, which I will scorn to
defend in our sex, and do despise in yours.

ANGELLICA. Thou'rt a brave fellow! Put up thy gold,
    and know,
That were thy fortune large, as is thy soul,
Thou shouldst not buy my love,
Couldst thou forget those mean effects of vanity
Which set me out to sale; and, as a lover,
Prize my yielding joys.
Canst thou believe they'll be entirely thine,
Without considering they were mercenary?

WILLMORE (*aside*). I cannot tell; I must bethink me first –
    ha,
death, I'm going to believe her.

ANGELLICA. Prithee, confirm that faith – or if thou canst
not – flatter me a little, 'twill please me from thy mouth.

WILLMORE (*aside*). Curse on thy charming tongue! Dost
    thou return
My feigned contempt with so much subtlety?
[*To her.*] Thou'st found the easiest way into my heart,
Though I yet know that all thou say'st is false.

Turns from her in rage.

ANGELLICA. By all that's good 'tis real,
    I never loved before, though oft a mistress.
    – Shall my first vows be slighted?

WILLMORE (*aside*). What can she mean?

ANGELLICA (*in an angry tone*). I find you cannot credit me.

WILLMORE. I know you take me for an arrant ass,
    An ass that may be soothed into belief,
    And then be used at pleasure.
    – But, madam I have been so often cheated

By perjured, soft, deluding hypocrites,
That I've no faith left for the cozening sex,
Especially for women of your trade.

ANGELLICA. The low esteem you have of me, perhaps
May bring my heart again:
For I have pride that yet surmounts my love.

She turns with pride, he holds her.

WILLMORE. Throw off this pride, this enemy to bliss,
And show the power of love: 'tis with those arms
I can be only vanquished, made a slave.

ANGELLICA. Is all my mighty expectation vanished?
– No, I will not hear thee talk – thou hast a charm
In every word, that draws my heart away.
And all the thousand trophies I designed
Thou hast undone. – Why art thou soft?
Thy looks are bravely rough, and meant for war.
Could'st thou not storm on still?
I then, perhaps, had been as free as thou.

WILLMORE (*aside*). Death! How she throws her fire about
my soul!
[*To her.*] Take heed, fair creature, how you raise my
hopes,
Which once assumed pretend to all dominion.
There's not a joy thou hast in store
I shall not then command:
For which I'll pay thee back my soul, my life,
Come, let's begin th'account this happy minute.

ANGELLICA. And will you pay me then the price I ask?

WILLMORE. Oh, why dost thou draw me from an awful
worship,
By showing thou art no divinity?
Conceal the fiend, and show me all the angel;
Keep me but ignorant, and I'll be devout,
And pay my vows forever at this shrine.

Kneels and kisses her hand.

ANGELLICA. The pay I mean is but thy love for mine.
  – Can you give that?

WILLMORE. Entirely – come, let's withdraw: where I'll
  renew my vows – and breathe 'em with such ardour, thou
  shalt not doubt my zeal.

ANGELLICA. Thou hast a power too strong to be resisted.

Exeunt WILLMORE *and* ANGELLICA.

MORETTA. Now my curse go with you. – Is all our project
  fallen to this? To love the only enemy to our trade? Nay,
  to love such a shameroon, a very beggar; nay, a pirate-
  beggar, whose business is to rifle and be gone, a
  no-purchase, no-pay tatterdemalion, and English picaroon;
  a rogue that fights for daily drink, and takes a pride in
  being loyally lousy. – Oh, I could curse now, if I durst. –
  This is the fate of most whores.

Trophies, which from believing fops we win,
Are spoils to those who cozen us again.

[*Exit.*]

ACT THREE

Scene One

A street. Enter FLORINDA, VALERIA, HELLENA, *in antic different dresses from what they were in before,* CALLIS *attending.*

FLORINDA. I wonder what should make my brother in so ill a humour: I hope he has not found out our ramble this morning.

HELLENA. No, if he had, we should have heard on't at both ears, and have been mewed up this afternoon; which I would not for the world should have happened. – Hey ho! I'm as sad as a lover's lute.

VALERIA. Well, methinks we have learnt this trade of gipsies as readily as if we had been bred upon the road to Loretto: and yet I did so fumble, when I told the stranger his fortune, that I was afraid I should have told my own and yours by mistake. – But, methinks Hellena has been very serious ever since.

FLORINDA. I would give my garters she were in love, to be revenged upon her for abusing me. – How is't, Hellena?

HELLENA. Ah! – Would I had never seen my mad monsieur – and yet for all your laughing, I am not in love – and yet this small acquaintance, o' my conscience, will never out of my head.

VALERIA. Ha, ha, ha – I laugh to think how thou art fitted with a lover, a fellow that, I warrant, loves every new face he sees.

HELLENA. Hum – he has not kept his word with me here – and may be taken up – that thought is not very pleasant to me. – What the deuce should this be now that I feel?

VALERIA. What is't like?

HELLENA. Nay, the Lord knows – but if I should be hanged I cannot choose but be angry and afraid, when I think that mad fellow should be in love with anybody but me. – What to think of myself, I know not. – Would I could meet with some true damned gipsy that I might know my fortune.

VALERIA. Know it! Why there's nothing so easy. Thou wilt love this wandering inconstant till thou find'st thy self hanged about his neck, and then be as mad to get free again.

FLORINDA. Yes, Valeria; we shall see her bestride his baggage-horse and follow him to the campaign.

HELLENA. So, so; now you are provided for, there's no care taken of poor me. – But since you have set my heart awishing, I am resolved to know for what. I will not die of the pip, so I will not.

FLORINDA. Art thou mad to talk so? Who will like thee well enough to have thee, that hears what a mad wench thou art?

HELLENA. Like me! I don't intend every he that likes me shall have me, but he that I like: I should have stayed in the nunnery still, if I had liked my Lady Abbess as well as she liked me. No, I came thence, not (as my wise brother imagines) to take an eternal farewell of the world, but to love and to be beloved; and I will be beloved, or I'll get one of your men, so I will.

VALERIA. Am I put into the number of lovers?

HELLENA. You? Why coz, I know thou'rt too good natured to leave us in any design: thou wouldst venture a cast, though thou camest off a loser, especially with such a gamester. – I observe your man, and your willing ear incline that way; and if you are not a lover, 'tis an art soon learnt – that I find. (*Sighs.*)

FLORINDA. I wonder how you learnt to love so easily.
I had a thousand charms to meet my eyes and ears, e'er

I could yield, and 'twas the knowledge of Belvile's merit,
not the surprising person, took my soul. – Thou art too
rash, to give a heart at first sight.

HELLENA. Hang your considering lover; I never thought
beyond the fancy that 'twas a very pretty, idle, silly kind
of pleasure to pass one's time with: to write little, soft,
nonsensical billets, and with great difficulty and danger
receive answers, in which I shall have my beauty praised,
my wit admired (though little or none) and have the
vanity and power to know I am desirable; then I have the
more inclination that way, because I am to be a nun, and
so shall not be suspected to have any such earthly
thoughts about me. – But when I walk thus – and sigh
thus – they'll think my mind's upon my monastery, and
cry, 'How happy 'tis she's so resolved!' – But not a word
of man.

FLORINDA. What a mad creature's this?

HELLENA. I'll warrant, if my brother hears either of you
sigh, he cries (gravely) 'I fear you have the indiscretion to
be in love, but take heed of the honour of our house and
your own unspotted fame'; and so he conjures on till he
has laid the soft-winged god in your hearts, or broke the
bird's nest. – But see here comes your lover: but where's
my inconstant? Let's step aside, and we may learn
something.

[*They*] *go aside. Enter* BELVILE, FREDERICK *and*
BLUNT.

BELVILE. What means this? The picture's taken in.

BLUNT. It may be the wench is good-natured and will be
kind gratis. Your friend's a proper handsome fellow.

BELVILE. I rather think she has cut his throat and is fled:
I am mad he should throw himself into dangers. – Pox
on't, I shall want him, too, at night. Let's knock and ask
for him.

HELLENA. My heart goes a-pit a-pat, for fear 'tis my man
they talk of.

[BELVILE *and* BLUNT] *knock;* MORETTA *above.*

MORETTA. What would you have?

BELVILE. Tell the stranger that entered here about two hours ago, that his friends stay here for him.

MORETTA. A curse upon him for Moretta, would he were at the devil – but he's coming to you.

[*Enter* WILLMORE.]

HELLENA. Aye, aye, 'tis he. Oh, how this vexes me.

BELVILE. And how, and how, dear lad, has fortune smiled? Are we to break her windows, or raise up altars to her, ha?

WILLMORE. Does not my fortune sit triumphant on my brow? Dost not see the little wanton god there, all gay and smiling? Have I not an air about my face and eyes that distinguish me from the crowd of common lovers? By Heaven, Cupid's quiver has not half so many darts as her eyes. – Oh, such a *bona roba*, to sleep in her arms is lying in fresco, all perfumed air about me.

HELLENA (*aside*). Here's fine encouragement for me to fool on.

WILLMORE. Hark'ee, where didst thou purchase that rich Canary we drank to-day? Tell me, that I may adore the spigot, and sacrifice to the butt: the juice was divine into which I must dip my rosary, and then bless all things that I would have bold or fortunate!

BELVILE. Well, sir, let's go take a bottle and hear the story of your success.

FREDERICK. Would not French wine do better?

WILLMORE. Damn the hungry balderdash; cheerful sack has a generous virtue in't, inspiring a successful confidence, gives eloquence to the tongue, and vigour to the soul, and has in a few hours completed all my hopes and wishes. There's nothing left to raise a new desire in me. – Come, let's be gay and wanton – and gentlemen, study, study what you want, for here are friends – that will supply, gentlemen [*He shows coins.*] Hark! What a charming sound they make! – 'Tis he and she gold whilst here, and shall beget new pleasures every moment.

BLUNT. But hark'ee, sir, you are not married, are you?

WILLMORE. All the honey of matrimony, but none of the sting, friend.

BLUNT. 'Sheartlikins, thou'rt a fortunate rogue.

WILLMORE. I am so, sir, let these inform you. – Ha, how sweetly they chime! Pox of poverty, it makes a man a slave, makes wit and honour sneak, my soul grew lean and rusty for want of credit.

BLUNT. 'Sheartlikins, this I like well; it looks like my lucky bargain! Oh, how I long for the approach of my squire, that is to conduct me to her house again. Why! Here's two provided for.

FREDERICK. By this light, y'are happy men.

BLUNT. Fortune is pleased to smile on us, gentlemen – to smile on us.

Enter SANCHO *and pulls down* BLUNT *by the sleeve. They go aside.*

SANCHO. Sir, my lady expects you – she has removed all that might oppose your will and pleasure – and is impatient till you come.

BLUNT. Sir, I'll attend you. – Oh, the happiest rogue! I'll take no leave, lest they either dog me, or stay me.

Exit with SANCHO.

BELVILE. But then the little gipsy is forgot?

WILLMORE. A mischief on thee for putting her into my thoughts; I had quite forgot her else, and this night's debauch had drunk her quite down.

HELLENA. Had it so, good Captain?

Claps him on the back.

WILLMORE (*aside*). Ha! I hope she did not hear me.

HELLENA. What, afraid of such a champion?

WILLMORE. Oh! You're a fine lady of your word, are you
not? To make a man languish a whole day –

HELLENA. In tedious search of me.

WILLMORE. Egad, child, thou'rt in the right, hadst thou
seen what a melancholy dog I have been ever since I was
a lover, how I have walked the streets like a Capuchin,
with my hands in my sleeves – faith, sweetheart, thou
wouldst pity me.

HELLENA [*aside*]. Now, if I should be hanged I can't be
angry with him, he dissembles so heartily. – Alas, good
Captain, what pains you have taken. – Now were I
ungrateful not to reward so true a servant.

WILLMORE. Poor soul! That's kindly said, I see thou
bearest a conscience – come then for a beginning, show
me thy dear face.

HELLENA. I'm afraid, my small acquaintance, you have
been staying that swinging stomach you boasted of this
morning; I then remember my little collation would have
gone down with you, without the sauce of a handsome
face – is your stomach so queasy now?

WILLMORE. Faith, long fasting, child, spoils a man's
appetite – yet, if you durst treat, I could so lay about me
still.

HELLENA. And would you fall to, before a priest says
grace?

WILLMORE. Oh, fie, fie, what an old, out-of-fashioned
thing hast thou named? Thou couldst not dash me more
out of countenance, shouldst thou show me an ugly face.

Whilst he is seemingly courting HELLENA, *enter*
ANGELLICA, MORETTA, BISKEY, *and* SEBASTIAN,
all in masquerade: ANGELLICA *sees* WILLMORE *and stares.*

ANGELLICA. Heavens, 'tis he! And passionately fond to see
another woman!

MORETTA. What could you less expect from such a swaggerer?

ANGELLICA. Expect? As much as I paid him – a heart entire
Which I had pride enough to think, when'er I gave,
It would have raised the man above the vulgar,
Made him all soul, and that all soft and constant.

HELLENA. You see, Captain, how willing I am to be friends with you, till time and ill luck make us lovers; and ask you the question first, rather than put your modesty to the blush, by asking me: for alas, I know you captains are such strict men, and such severe observers of your vows to chastity, that 'twill be hard to prevail with your tender conscience to marry a young willing maid.

WILLMORE. Do not abuse me, for fear I should take thee at thy word, and marry thee indeed, which I'm sure will be revenge sufficient.

HELLENA. O' my conscience, that will be our destiny, because we are both of one humour; I am as inconstant as you, for I have considered, captain, that a handsome woman has a great deal to do whilst her face is good, for then is our harvest-time to gather friends; and should I in these days of my youth, catch a fit of foolish constancy, I were undone; 'tis loitering by day-light in our great journey. Therefore I declare, I'll allow but one year for love, one year for indifference, and one year for hate – and then – go hang yourself – for I protest myself the gay, the kind, and the inconstant – the devil's in't if this won't please you.

WILLMORE. Oh, most damnably! – I have a heart with a hole quite through it too, no prison, mine, to keep a mistress in.

ANGELLICA (*aside*). Perjured man! How I believe thee now.

HELLENA. Well, I see our business as well as humours are alike, yours to cozen as many maids as will trust you, and I as many men as have faith. – See if I have not as desperate a lying look, as you can have for the heart of you.

Pulls off her vizard; he starts.

How do you like it, captain?

WILLMORE. Like it! By Heaven, I never saw so much
beauty! Oh the charms of those sprightly black eyes, that
strangely fair face, full of smiles and dimples! Those soft,
round, melting cherry lips and small even white teeth! –
Not to be expressed, but silently adored! – Oh, one look
more, and strike me dumb, or I shall repeat nothing else
till I'm mad.

He seems to court her to pull off her vizard: she refuses.

ANGELLICA. I can endure no more – nor is it fit to
interrupt him; for if I do, my jealousy has so destroyed
my reason, I shall undo him – therefore I'll retire. And
you Sebastian (*To one of her* BRAVOS.) follow that woman,
and learn who 'tis; while you (*To the other* BRAVO.) tell
the fugitive, I would speak to him instantly.

Exit. This while FLORINDA [*vizarded*] *is talking to*
BELVILE, *who stands sullenly.* FREDERICK *courting*
VALERIA.

VALERIA. Prithee, dear stranger, be not so sullen, for
though you have lost your love, you see my friend frankly
offers you hers, to play with in the mean time.

BELVILE. Faith, madam, I am sorry I can't play at her game.

FREDERICK. Pray leave your intercession and mind your
own affair, they'll better agree apart; he's a modest sigher
in company, but alone no woman 'scapes him.

FLORINDA. Sure, he does but rally – yet if it should be
true – I'll tempt him farther. [*To* BELVILE.] Believe me,
noble stranger, I'm no common mistress. And for a little
proof on't – wear this jewel – nay, take it, sir, 'tis right,
and bills of exchange may sometimes miscarry.

BELVILE. Madam, why am I chose out of all mankind to
be the object of your bounty?

VALERIA. There's another civil question asked.

FREDERICK. Pox of's modesty, it spoils his own markets,
and hinders mine.

FLORINDA. Sir, from my window I have often seen you; and women of my quality have so few opportunities for love, that we ought to lose none.

FREDERICK. Ay, this is something! Here's a woman! – When shall I be blessed with so much kindness from your fair mouth? (*Aside to* BELVILE.) – Take the jewel, fool.

BELVILE. You tempt me strangely, madam, every way.

FLORINDA (*aside*). So, if I find him false, my whole repose is gone.

BELVILE. And but for a vow I've made to a very fair lady, this goodness had subdued me.

FREDERICK [*to* BELVILE]. Pox on't be kind, in pity to me be kind, for I am to thrive here but as you treat her friend.

HELLENA [*to* WILLMORE]. Tell me what you did in yonder house, and I'll unmask.

WILLMORE. Yonder house – oh – I went to – a – to – why, there's a friend of mine lives there.

HELLENA. What a she, or a he friend?

WILLMORE. A man upon honour! A man. – A she friend! No, no, madam, you have done my business, I thank you.

HELLENA. And was't your man friend that had more darts in's eyes than Cupid carries in's whole budget of arrows?

WILLMORE. So –

HELLENA. 'Ah such a *bona roba:* to be in her arms is lying in fresco, all perfumed air about me.' – Was this your man friend too?

WILLMORE. So –

HELLENA. That gave you the he, and the she-gold, that begets young pleasures?

WILLMORE. Well, well, madam, then you see there are ladies in the world, that will not be cruel – there are, madam, there are –

HELLENA. And there be men too as fine, wild, inconstant fellows as yourself, there be, Captain, there be, if you go to that now – therefore I'm resolved –

WILLMORE. Oh!

HELLENA. To see your face no more –

WILLMORE. Oh!

HELLENA. Till tomorrow.

WILLMORE. Egad you frighted me.

HELLENA. Nor then neither, unless you'll swear never to see that lady more.

WILLMORE. See her! – Why! Never to think of womankind again?

HELLENA. Kneel, and swear.

[WILLMORE] *kneels; she gives him her hand.*

WILLMORE. I do, never to think – to see – to love – nor lie with any but thy self.

HELLENA. Kiss the book.

WILLMORE. Oh, most religiously.

Kisses her hand.

HELLENA. Now, what a wicked creature am I, to damn a proper fellow.

CALLIS (*to* FLORINDA). Madam, I'll stay no longer; 'tis e'en dark.

FLORINDA [*to* BELVILE]. However, sir, I'll leave this with you – that when I'm gone, you may repent the opportunity you have lost by your modesty.

Gives him the jewel, which is her picture, and exits. He gazes after her.

WILLMORE [*to* HELLENA]. 'Twill be an age till tomorrow – and till then I will most impatiently expect you. – Adieu, my dear, pretty angel.

Exeunt all the women.

BELVILE. Ha! Florinda's picture! 'Twas she herself − what a dull dog was I? I would have given the world for one minute's discourse with her −

FREDERICK. This comes of your modesty. − Ah pox o' your vow, 'twas ten to one but we had lost the jewel by't.

BELVILE. Willmore! The blessed'st opportunity lost! − Florinda, friends, Florinda!

WILLMORE. Ah rogue! Such black eyes, such a face, such a mouth, such teeth − and so much wit!

BELVILE. All, all, and a thousand charms besides.

WILLMORE. Why, dost thou know her?

BELVILE. Know her! Ay, ay, and a pox take me with all my heart for being modest.

WILLMORE. But hark ye, friend of mine, are you my rival? And have I been only beating the bush all this while?

BELVILE. I understand thee not − I'm mad − see here −

Shows the picture [of FLORINDA].

WILLMORE. Ha! Whose picture's this? − 'Tis a fine wench!

FREDERICK. The Colonel's mistress, sir.

WILLMORE. Oh, oh, here − I thought it had been another prize − come, come, a bottle will set thee right again.

Gives the picture back.

BELVILE. I am content to try, and by that time 'twill be late enough for our design.

WILLMORE. Agreed.

Love does all day the soul's great empire keep,
But wine at night lulls the soft god asleep.

Exeunt.

Scene Two

Lucetta's house. Enter BLUNT *and* LUCETTA *with a light.*

LUCETTA. Now we are safe and free, no fears of the
coming home of my old jealous husband, which made me
a little thoughtful when you came in first – but now love
is all the business of my soul.

BLUNT (*aside*). I am transported. – Pox on't, that I had but
some fine things to say to her, such as lovers use – I was
a fool not to learn of Fred a little by heart before I came.
– Something I must say. [*To her.*] 'Sheartlikins, sweet soul!
I am not used to compliment, but I'm an honest
gentleman, and thy humble servant.

LUCETTA. I have nothing to pay for so great a favour, but
such a love as cannot but be great, since at first sight of
that sweet face and shape it made me your absolute
captive.

BLUNT (*aside*). Kind heart, how prettily she talks! Egad I'll
show her husband a Spanish trick; send him out of the
world, and marry her: she's damnably in love with me,
and will ne'er mind settlements, and so there's that saved.

LUCETTA. Well, sir, I'll go and undress me, and be with
you instantly.

BLUNT. Make haste then, for 'dsheartlikins, dear soul, thou
canst not guess at the pain of a longing lover when his
joys are drawn within the compass of a few minutes.

LUCETTA. You speak my sense, and I'll make haste to
prove it.

Exit.

BLUNT. 'Tis a rare girl, and this one night's enjoyment with
her will be worth all the days I ever passed in Essex. –
Would she would go with me into England, though to say
truth, there's plenty of whores already. – But a pox on
'em they are such mercenary prodigal whores, that they
want such a one as this, that's free and generous, to give

'em good examples. – Why, what a house she has! How rich and fine!

Enter SANCHO.

SANCHO. Sir, my lady has sent me to conduct you to her chamber.

BLUNT. Sir, I shall be proud to follow. – Here's one of her servants too: 'sheartlikins, by this garb and gravity he might be a Justice of Peace in Essex, and is but a pimp here.

Exeunt.

Scene Three

The scene changes to a chamber with an alcove bed in it, a table, etc., LUCETTA *in bed. Enter* SANCHO *and* BLUNT, *who takes the candle of* SANCHO *at the door.*

SANCHO. Sir, my commission reaches no farther.

BLUNT. Sir, I'll excuse your compliment. –

[*Exit* SANCHO.]

What, in bed, my sweet mistress?

LUCETTA. You see, I still out-do you in kindness.

BLUNT. And thou shalt see what haste I'll make to quit scores – oh, the luckiest rogue!

Undresses himself.

LUCETTA. Should you be false or cruel now!

BLUNT. False, 'sheartlikins, what dost thou take me for a Jew? An insensible heathen. – A pox of thy old jealous husband: an' he were dead – egad, sweet soul, it should be none of my fault if I did not marry thee.

LUCETTA. It never should be mine.

BLUNT. Good soul, I'm the fortunatest dog!

LUCETTA. Are you not undressed yet?

BLUNT. As much as my impatience will permit.

Goes towards the bed in his shirt, drawers.

LUCETTA. Hold, sir, put out the light, it may betray us else.

BLUNT. Any thing, I need no other light but that of thine eyes! – (*Aside.*) 'Sheartlikins, there I think I had it.

Puts out the candle; the bed descends; he gropes about to find it.

Why – why – where am I got? What, not yet? – Where are you, sweetest? – Ah, the rogue's silent now – a pretty love-trick, this – how she'll laugh at me anon! – You need not, my dear rogue! You need not! I'm all on fire already – come, come, now call me in pity. – Sure, I'm enchanted! I have been round the chamber, and can find neither woman, nor bed. – I locked the door, I'm sure she cannot go that way; or if she could, the bed could not. – Enough, enough, my pretty wanton, do not carry the jest too far.

Lights on a trap, and is let down.

Ha, betrayed! Dogs! Rogues! Pimps! Help! Help!

Enter LUCETTA, PHILIPPO, *and* SANCHO *with a light.*

PHILIPPO. Ha, ha, ha! He's dispatched finely.

LUCETTA. Now, sir, had I been coy, we had missed of this booty.

PHILIPPO. Nay when I saw 'twas a substantial fool, I was mollified; but when you dote upon a serenading coxcomb, upon a face, fine clothes, and a lute, it makes me rage.

LUCETTA. You know I was never guilty of that folly, my dear Philippo, but with your self – but come, let's see what we have got by this.

PHILIPPO. A rich coat! – Sword and hat! – These breeches too – are well-lined! – See here a gold watch! – A purse – Ha! Gold! – At least two hundred pistoles! A bunch of

diamond rings; and one with the family arms! – A gold
box, with a medal of his king! And his lady mother's
picture! – These were sacred relics, believe me! – See, the
waistband of his breeches have a mine of gold! – Old
Queen Bess's! We have a quarrel to her ever since
eighty-eight, and may therefore justify the theft, the
Inquisition might have committed it.

LUCETTA. See, a bracelet of bowed gold, these, his sisters
tied about his arm at parting – but well – for all this, I
fear his being a stranger may make a noise, and hinder
our trade with them hereafter.

PHILIPPO. That's our security; he is not only a stranger to
us, but to the country, too – the common shore into
which he is descended, thou know'st, conducts him into
another street, which this light will hinder him from ever
finding again – he knows neither your name, nor that of
the street where your house is, nay, nor the way to his
own lodgings.

LUCETTA. And art not thou an unmerciful rogue, not to
afford him one night for all this? – I should not have
been such a Jew.

PHILIPPO. Blame me not, Lucetta, to keep as much of thee
as I can to my self – come, that thought makes me
wanton – let's to bed – Sancho, lock up these.

This is the fleece which fools do bear,
Designed for witty men to shear.

Exeunt.

Scene Four

The scene changes, and discovers BLUNT *creeping out of a common
shore, his face, etc., all dirty.*

BLUNT (*climbing up*). Oh Lord! I am got out at last and
(which is a miracle) without a clue – and now to damning
and cursing – but if that would ease me, where shall I

begin? With my fortune, my self, or the quean that
cozened me? – What a dog was I to believe in woman!
Oh coxcomb – ignorant conceited coxcomb! To fancy she
could be enamoured with my person, at first sight
enamoured. – Oh, I'm a cursed puppy, 'tis plain, 'fool'
was writ upon my forehead, she perceived it – saw the
Essex calf there – for what allurements could there be in
this countenance, which I can endure because I'm
acquainted with it. – Oh, dull silly dog! To be thus
soothed into a cozening! Had I been drunk, I might
fondly have credited the young quean! But as I was in my
right wits, to be thus cheated, confirms it: I am a dull
believing English country fop. – But my comrades! Death
and the devil, there's the worst of all– then a ballad will
be sung to-morrow on the Prado, to a lousy tune of the
Enchanted Squire and the Annihilated Damsel. – But
Fred, that rogue, and the Colonel, will abuse me beyond
all Christian patience. – Had she left me my clothes, I
have a bill of exchange at home would have saved my
credit – but now all hope is taken from me. – Well, I'll
home (if I can find the way) with this consolation, that I
am not the first kind believing coxcomb; but there are,
gallants, many such good natures amongst ye.

And though you've better arts to hide your follies,
Adsheartlikins, y'are all as arrant cullies.

[*Exit.*]

Scene Five

The garden, in the night. Enter FLORINDA *in an undress, with a
key and a little box.*

FLORINDA. Well, thus far I'm in my way to happiness; I
    have got my self free from Callis; my brother too, I find
    by yonder light, is got into his cabinet, and thinks not of
    me. I have by good fortune got the key of the garden
    back-door. – I'll open it, to prevent Belvile's knocking – a
    little noise will now alarm my brother. Now am I as

fearful as a young thief. (*Unlocks the door.*) – Hark – what
noise is that? Oh, 'twas the wind that played amongst the
boughs. – Belvile stays long, methinks – it's time – stay –
for fear of a surprise, I'll hide these jewels in yonder
jessamin.

She goes to lay down the box. Enter WILLMORE *drunk.*

WILLMORE. What the devil is become of these fellows,
Belvile and Frederick? They promised to stay at the next
corner for me, but who the devil knows the corner of a
full moon? – Now – whereabouts am I? – hah – what
have we here? A garden! – A very convenient place to
sleep in – hah – what has God sent us here? A female –
by this light, a woman; I'm a dog if it be not a very
wench. –

FLORINDA. He's come! – Hah – who's there?

WILLMORE. Sweet soul, let me salute thy shoe-string!

FLORINDA. 'Tis not my Belvile. – Good Heavens, I know
him not. – Who are you, and from whence come you?

WILLMORE. Prithee – prithee, child – not so many hard
questions – let it suffice I am here, child. – Come, come
kiss me.

FLORINDA. Good gods! What luck is mine?

WILLMORE. Only good luck, child, parlous good luck. –
Come hither – 'tis a delicate, shining wench – by this
hand, she's perfumed, and smells like any nosegay. –
Prithee, dear soul, let's not play the fool and lose time –
precious time – for as Gad shall save me, I'm as honest a
fellow as breathes, though I'm a little disguised at present.
– Come, I say – why, thou may'st be free with me, I'll be
very secret. I'll not boast who 'twas obliged me, not I –
for hang me if I know thy name.

FLORINDA. Heavens! What a filthy beast is this?

WILLMORE. I am so, and thou ought'st the sooner to lie
with me for that reason. – For look you, child, there will
be no sin in't, because 'twas neither designed nor

premeditated; 'tis pure accident on both sides – that's a
certain thing now. – Indeed, should I make love to you,
and you vow fidelity – and swear and lie till you believed
and yielded – that were to make it wilful fornication, the
crying sin of the nation. – Thou art, therefore (as thou art
a good Christian) obliged in conscience to deny me
nothing. Now – come, be kind without any more idle
prating.

FLORINDA. Oh, I am ruined – wicked man, unhand me.

WILLMORE. Wicked! Egad, child, a judge, were he young
and vigorous, and saw those eyes of thine, would know
'twas they gave the first blow – the first provocation. –
Come, prithee let's lose no time, I say – this is a fine,
convenient place.

FLORINDA. Sir, let me go, I conjure you, or I'll call out.

WILLMORE. Ay, ay, you were best to call witness to see
how finely you treat me – do –

FLORINDA. I'll cry murder, rape, or any thing if you do
not instantly let me go!

WILLMORE. A rape! Come, come, you lie, you baggage,
you lie. What, I'll warrant you would fain have the world
believe now that you are not so forward as I. No, not you
– why at this time of night was your cobweb-door set
open, dear spider – but to catch flies? – Ha, come – or
I shall be damnably angry. – Why, what a coil is here –

FLORINDA. Sir, can you think –

WILLMORE. That you would do't for nothing? Oh, oh, I
find what you would be at – look here, here's a pistole for
you – here's a work indeed – here – take it, I say –

FLORINDA. For Heaven's sake, sir, as you're a gentleman –

WILLMORE. So – now, now– she would be wheedling me
for more – what, you will not take it then – you are
resolved you will not? – Come, come take it or I'll put it
up again; for, look ye, I never give more. – Why, how
now, mistress, are you so high i'th' mouth, a pistole won't

down with you? Hah – why, what a work's here – in good time – come, no struggling to be gone. – But an y'are good at a dumb wrestle, I'm for ye. – Look ye, I'm for ye –

She struggles with him. Enter BELVILE *and* FREDERICK.

BELVILE. The door is open, a pox of this mad fellow, I'm angry that we've lost him, I durst have sworn he had followed us.

FREDERICK. But you were so hasty, Colonel, to be gone.

FLORINDA. Help, help! – Murder! – Help – oh, I am ruined!

BELVILE. Ha, sure, that's Florinda's voice. (*Comes up to them.*) A man! Villain, let go that lady.

A noise. WILLMORE *turns and draws,* FREDERICK *interposes.*

FLORINDA. Belvile! Heavens! My brother, too, is coming, and 'twill be impossible to escape. – Belvile, I conjure you to walk under my chamber-window, from whence I'll give you some instructions what to do. – This rude man has undone us.

Exit.

WILLMORE. Belvile!

Enter PEDRO, STEPHANO, *and other* SERVANTS, *with lights.*

PEDRO. I'm betray'd; run, Stephano, and see if Florinda be safe.

Exit STEPHANO. *They fight and* PEDRO's *party beats 'em out. Going out, meets* STEPHANO.

So, whoe'er they be, all is not well, I'll to Florinda's chamber.

STEPHANO. You need not, sir, the poor lady's fast asleep and thinks no harm: I would not awake her, sir, for fear of frighting her with your danger.

PEDRO. I'm glad she's there. – Rascals, how came the
garden-door open?

STEPHANO. That question comes too late, sir: some of my
fellow-servants masquerading I'll warrant.

PEDRO. Masquerading! A lewd custom to debauch our
youth – there's something more in this than I imagine.

Exeunt.

Scene Six

Scene changes to the street. Enter BELVILE *in rage,* FREDERICK
holding him, and WILLMORE *melancholy.*

WILLMORE. Why, how the devil should I know Florinda?

BELVILE. Ah plague of your ignorance! If it had not been
Florinda, must you be a beast? – A brute, a senseless
swine?

WILLMORE. Well, sir, you see I am endued with patience
– I can bear – though egad y'are very free with me
methinks – I was in good hopes the quarrel would have
been on my side, for so uncivilly interrupting me.

BELVILE. Peace, brute, whilst thou'rt safe – oh, I'm distracted.

WILLMORE. Nay, nay, I'm an unlucky dog, that's certain.

BELVILE. Ah, curse upon the star that ruled my birth, or
whatsoever other influence that makes me still so
wretched.

WILLMORE. Thou break'st my heart with these complaints;
there is no star in fault, no influence but sack, the cursed
sack I drunk.

FREDERICK. Why, how the devil came you so drunk?

WILLMORE. Why, how the devil came you so sober?

BELVILE. A curse upon his thin skull; he was always beforehand that way.

FREDERICK. Prithee, dear Colonel, forgive him, he's sorry for his fault.

BELVILE. He's always so after he has done a mischief – a plague on all such brutes

WILLMORE. By this light I took her for an arrant harlot.

BELVILE. Damn your debauched opinion; tell me, sot, hadst thou so much sense and light about thee to distinguish her woman, and couldst not see something about her face and person, to strike an awful reverence into thy soul?

WILLMORE. Faith no, I considered her as mere a woman as I could wish.

BELVILE. 'Sdeath I have no patience – draw, or I'll kill you.

WILLMORE. Let that alone till to-morrow, and if I set not all right again, use your pleasure.

BELVILE. To-morrow, damn it.
The spiteful light will lead me to no happiness.
To-morrow is Antonio's, and perhaps
Guides him to my undoing. – Oh that I could meet
This rival, this powerful fortunate!

WILLMORE. What then?

BELVILE. Let thy own reason, or my rage, instruct thee.

WILLMORE. I shall be finely informed then, no doubt;
hear me, Colonel – hear me – show me the man and I'll do his business.

BELVILE. I know him no more than thou, or if I did, I should not need thy aid.

WILLMORE. This you say is Angellica's house, I promised the kind baggage to lie with her to-night.

Offers to go in. Enter ANTONIO *and his page.* ANTONIO *knocks on the hilt of his sword.*

ANTONIO. You paid the thousand crowns I directed?

PAGE. To the lady's old woman, sir, I did.

WILLMORE. Who the devil have we here?

BELVILE. I'll now plant myself under Florinda's window, and if I find no comfort there, I'll die.

Exeunt BELVILE *and* FREDERICK. *Enter* MORETTA.

MORETTA. Page!

PAGE. Here's my lord.

WILLMORE. How is this, a picaroon going to board my frigate! Here's one chase-gun for you.

Drawing his sword, jostles ANTONIO *who turns and draws. They fight,* ANTONIO *falls.*

MORETTA. Oh, bless us, we're all undone!

Runs in, and shuts the door.

PAGE. Help, murder!

BELVILE *returns at the noise of fighting.*

BELVILE. Ha, the mad rogue's engaged in some unlucky adventure again.

Enter two or three MASQUERADERS.

MASQUERADER. Ha, a man killed!

WILLMORE. How! A man killed! Then I'll go home to sleep.

Puts up, and reels out. Exeunt MASQUERADERS *another way.*

BELVILE. Who should it be? Pray Heaven the rogue is safe, for all my quarrel to him.

As BELVILE *is groping about, enter an* OFFICER *and six* SOLDIERS.

SOLDIER. Who's there?

OFFICER. So, here's one dispatched – secure the murderer.

BELVILE. Do not mistake my charity for murder: I came to his assistance.

SOLDIERS *seize on* BELVILE.

OFFICER. That shall be tried, sir. St Jago, swords drawn in the carnival time!

Goes to ANTONIO.

ANTONIO. Thy hand prithee.

OFFICER. Ha, Don Antonio! Look well to the villain there. – How is it, sir?

ANTONIO. I'm hurt.

BELVILE. Has my humanity made me a criminal?

OFFICER. Away with him.

BELVILE. What a cursed chance is this!

Exeunt SOLDIERS *with* BELVILE.

ANTONIO (*to the* OFFICER). This is the man that has set upon me twice – carry him to my apartment till you have further orders from me.

Exit ANTONIO, *led.*

ACT FOUR

Scene One

A fine room. BELVILE *discover[ed] as by dark alone.*

BELVILE. When shall I be weary of railing on fortune, who
is resolved never to turn with smiles upon me? – Two
such defeats in one night – none but the devil and that
mad rogue could have contrived to have plagued me with
– I am here a prisoner – but where? – Heaven knows –
and if there be murder done, I can soon decide the fate
of a stranger in a nation without mercy. – Yet this is
nothing to the torture my soul bows with, when I think of
losing my fair, my dear Florinda. – Hark – my door
opens – a light – a man – and seems of quality – armed
too. – Now shall I die like a dog without defence.

Enter ANTONIO *in a night-gown, with a light; his arm in a
scarf, and a sword under his arm: he sets the candle on the table.*

ANTONIO. Sir, I come to know what injuries I have done
you, that could provoke you to so mean an action, as to
attack me basely, without allowing time for my defence.

BELVILE. Sir, for a man in my circumstances to plead innocence, would look like fear – but view me well, and you
will find no marks of coward on me, nor anything that
betrays that brutality you accuse me with.

ANTONIO. In vain, sir, you impose upon my sense.
You are not only he who drew on me last night,
But yesterday before the same house, that of Angellica.
Yet there is something in your face and mien
That makes me wish I were mistaken.

BELVILE. I own I fought today in the defence of a friend of
mine, with whom you (if you're the same) and your party,
were first engaged.

Perhaps you think this crime enough to kill me,
But if you do, I cannot fear you'll do it basely.

ANTONIO. No, sir, I'll make you fit for a defence with this.

Gives him the sword.

BELVILE. This gallantry surprises me – nor know I how to
use this present, sir, against a man so brave.

ANTONIO. You shall not need;
For know, I come to snatch you from a danger
That is decreed against you;
Perhaps your life, or long imprisonment:
And 'twas with so much courage you offended,
I cannot see you punished.

BELVILE. How shall I pay this generosity?

ANTONIO. It had been safer to have killed another
Than have attempted me.
To show your danger, sir, I'll let you know my quality:
And 'tis the Viceroy's son whom you have wounded.

BELVILE (*aside*). The Viceroy's son!
Death and confusion! Was this plague reserved
To complete all the rest? (*Aside.*) Obliged by him!
The man of all the world I would destroy.

ANTONIO. You seem disordered, sir.

BELVILE. Yes, trust me, sir, I am, and 'tis with pain
That man receives such bounties,
Who wants the power to pay 'em back again.

ANTONIO. To gallant spirits 'tis indeed uneasy;
– But you may quickly overpay me, sir.

BELVILE (*aside*). Then I am well – kind Heaven! But set
us even,
That I may fight with him, and keep my honour safe.
[*To* ANTONIO.] Oh, I'm impatient, sir, to be discounting
The mighty debt I owe you; command me quickly –

ANTONIO. I have a quarrel with a rival, sir,
About the maid we love.

BELVILE (*aside*). Death, 'tis Florinda he means –
  That thought destroys my reason, and I shall kill him –

ANTONIO. My rival, sir,
  Is one has all the virtues man can boast of.

BELVILE (*aside*). Death! Who should this be?

ANTONIO. He challenged me to meet him on the Molo,
  As soon as day appear'd; but last night's quarrel
  Has made my arm unfit to guide a sword.

BELVILE. I apprehend you, sir, you'd have me kill the man
  That lays a claim to the maid you speak of.
  – I'll do't – I'll fly to do't!

ANTONIO. Sir, do you know her?

BELVILE. – No, sir, but 'tis enough she is admired by you.

ANTONIO. Sir, I shall rob you of the glory on't,
  For you must fight under my name and dress.

BELVILE. That opinion must be strangely obliging that
  makes
  You think I can personate the brave Antonio,
  Whom I can but strive to imitate.

ANTONIO. You say too much to my advantage.
  Come, sir, the day appears that calls you forth.
  Within, sir, is the habit.

Exit ANTONIO.

BELVILE. Fantastic fortune, thou deceitful light,
  That cheats the wearied traveller by night,
  Though on a precipice each step you tread,
  I am resolved to follow where you lead.

Exit.

Scene Two

The Molo. Enter FLORINDA *and* CALLIS *in masks, with*
STEPHANO.

FLORINDA (*aside*). I'm dying with my fears; Belvile's not
coming, as I expected, under my window, makes me
believe that all those fears are true. [*To* STEPHANO.] –
Canst thou not tell with whom my brother fights?

STEPHANO. No, madam, they were both in masquerade,
I was by when they challenged one another, and they had
decided the quarrel then, but were prevented by some
cavaliers; which made 'em put it off till now – but I am
sure 'tis about you they fight.

FLORINDA (*aside*). Nay then 'tis with Belvile, for what other
lover have I that dares fight for me, except Antonio? And
he is too much in favour with my brother. – If it be he,
for whom shall I direct my prayers to Heaven?

STEPHANO. Madam, I must leave you; for if my master
see me, I shall be hanged for being your conductor. – I
escaped narrowly for the excuse I made for you last night
i' th' garden.

FLORINDA. And I'll reward thee for't – prithee no more.

Exit STEPHANO. *Enter* DON PEDRO *in his masking habit.*

PEDRO. Antonio's late to-day, the place will fill, and we
may be prevented.

Walks about.

FLORINDA (*aside*). Antonio? Sure I heard amiss.

PEDRO. But who will not excuse a happy lover.
When soft, fair arms confine the yielding neck,
And the kind whisper languishingly breathes,
Must you be gone so soon?
Sure I had dwelt for ever on her bosom.
– But stay, he's here.

Enter BELVILE *dressed in Antonio's clothes.*

FLORINDA (*aside*). 'Tis not Belvile, half my fears are vanished.

PEDRO. Antonio! –

BELVILE (*aside*). This must be he. [*To* PEDRO.] You're early, sir, – I do not use to be out-done this way.

PEDRO. The wretched, sir, are watchful, and 'tis enough You've the advantage of me in Angellica.

BELVILE (*aside*). Angellica!
    Or I've mistook my man! Or else Antonio,
    Can he forget his interest in Florinda,
    And fight for common prize?

PEDRO. Come, sir, you know our terms.

BELVILE (*aside*). By Heaven, not I!
    [*To* PEDRO.] – No talking, I am ready, sir.

    Offers to fight. FLORINDA *runs in.*

FLORINDA (*to* BELVILE). Oh, hold! Whoe'er you be,
        I do conjure you hold!
    If you strike here – I die –

PEDRO. Florinda!

BELVILE. Florinda imploring for my rival!

PEDRO. Away, this kindness is unseasonable.

    Puts her by. They fight; she runs in just as BELVILE *disarms* PEDRO.

FLORINDA. Who are you, sir, that dares deny my prayers?

BELVILE.
    Thy prayers destroy him; if thou wouldst preserve him,
    Do that thou'rt unacquainted with, and curse him.

    She holds [BELVILE].

FLORINDA. By all you hold most dear, by her you love,
    I do conjure you, touch him not.

BELVILE. By her I love!
    See – I obey – and at your feet resign
    The useless trophy of my victory.

Lays his sword at her feet.

PEDRO. Antonio, you've done enough to prove you love
Florinda.

BELVILE. Love Florinda!
Does Heaven love adoration, pray'r, or penitence?
Love her! Here sir, – your sword again.

Snatches up the sword, and gives it to him.

Upon this truth I'll fight my life away.

PEDRO. No, you've redeemed my sister, and my friendship.

He gives him FLORINDA *and pulls off his vizard to show his
face, and puts it on again.*

BELVILE. Don Pedro!

PEDRO. Can you resign your claims to other women,
And give your heart entirely to Florinda?

BELVILE. Entire, as dying saints' confessions are.
I can delay my happiness no longer.
This minute, let me make Florinda mine.

PEDRO. This minute let it be – no time so proper,
This night my father will arrive from Rome,
And possibly may hinder what we purpose.

FLORINDA. Oh Heavens! This minute!

Enter masqueraders and pass over [the stage].

BELVILE [*aside*]. Oh, do not ruin me!

PEDRO. The place begins to fill; and that we may not be
observed, do you walk off to St Peter's Church, where I
will meet you, and conclude your happiness.

BELVILE. I'll meet you there – (*Aside.*) if there be no more
saints' churches in Naples.

FLORINDA. Oh, stay, sir, and recall your hasty doom:
Alas, I have not prepared my heart
To entertain so strange a guest.

PEDRO. Away, this silly modesty is assumed too late.

BELVILE. Heaven, madam! What do you do?

FLORINDA. Do! Despise the man that lays a tyrant's claim.
To what he ought to conquer by submission.

BELVILE. You do not know me – move a little this way.

Draws her aside.

FLORINDA. Yes, you may force me even to the altar,
But not the holy man that offers there
Shall force me to be thine.

PEDRO *talks to* CALLIS *this while.*

BELVILE. Oh, do not lose so blest an opportunity!
See – 'tis your Belvile – not Antonio,
Whom your mistaken scorn and anger ruins.

Pulls off his vizard.

FLORINDA. Belvile!
Where was my soul it could not meet thy voice,
And take this knowledge in?

As they are talking, enter WILLMORE, *finely dressed, and*
FREDERICK.

WILLMORE. No intelligence! No news of Belvile yet – well,
I am the most unlucky rascal in nature – ha! – Am I
deceived – or is it he – look, Fred – 'tis he – my dear
Belvile.

Runs and embraces him. BELVILE's *vizard falls out on's hand.*

BELVILE. Hell and confusion seize thee!

PEDRO. Ha! Belvile! I beg your pardon, sir.

Takes FLORINDA *from him.*

BELVILE. Nay, touch her not. She's mine by conquest, sir;
I won her by my sword.

WILLMORE. Didst thou so – and egad, child, we'll keep
her by the sword.

Draws on PEDRO, BELVILE *goes between* [*them*].

BELVILE. Stand off.
  Thou'rt so profanely lewd, so cursed by Heaven,
  All quarrels thou espousest must be fatal.

WILLMORE. Nay, an you be so hot, my valour's coy,
  And shall be courted when you want it next.

Puts up his sword.

BELVILE (*to* PEDRO). You know I ought to claim a
    victor's right.
  But you're the brother to divine Florinda
  To whom I'm such a slave – to purchase her,
  I durst not hurt the man she holds so dear.

PEDRO. 'Twas by Antonio's, not by Belvile's sword
  This question should have been decided, sir.
  I must confess much to your bravery's due,
  Both now, and when I met you last in arms.
  But I am nicely punctual in my word,
  As men of honour ought, and beg your pardon.
  – For this mistake, another time shall clear.

Aside to FLORINDA *as they are going out.*

  – This was some plot between you and Belvile:
  But I'll prevent you.

[*Exit* PEDRO *and* FLORINDA.]

BELVILE *looks after her and begins to walk up and down in
rage.*

WILLMORE. Do not be modest now, and lose the woman:
  but if we shall fetch her back, so –

BELVILE. Do not speak to me.

WILLMORE. Not speak to you! – Egad, I'll speak to you,
  and will be answered too!

BELVILE. Will you, sir!

WILLMORE. I know I've done some mischief, but I'm so
  dull a puppy, that I'm the son of a whore, if I know how,
  or where – prithee inform my understanding. –

BELVILE. Leave me I say, and leave me instantly.

WILLMORE. I will not leave you in this humour, nor till I know my crime.

BELVILE. Death, I'll tell you, sir –

Draws and runs at WILLMORE, *he runs out;* BELVILE *after him,* FREDERICK *interposes [but remains].*

Enter ANGELLICA, MORETTA, *and* SEBASTIAN.

ANGELLICA. Ha – Sebastian – is that not Willmore? Haste, haste, and bring him back.

[*Exit* SEBASTIAN.]

FREDERICK. The Colonel's mad – I never saw him thus before; I'll after 'em, lest he do some mischief, for I am sure Willmore will not draw on him.

Exit.

ANGELLICA. I am all rage! My first desires defeated
For one, for aught he knows, that has no
Other merit than her quality,
Her being Don Pedro's sister. – He loves her:
I know 'tis so – dull, dull, insensible –
He will not see me now, though oft invited;
And broke his word last night – false, perjured man!
– He that but yesterday fought for my favours,
And would have made his life a sacrifice
To've gained one night with me,
Must now be hired and courted to my arms.

MORETTA. I told you what would come on't, but
Moretta's an old doting fool. – Why did you give him five
hundred crowns, but to set himself out for other lovers?
You should have kept him poor, if you had meant to have
had any good from him.

ANGELLICA.
Oh, name not such mean trifles. Had I given him all
My youth has earned from sin,
I had not lost a thought nor sigh upon't.
But I have given him my eternal rest,

My whole repose, my future joys, my heart;
My virgin heart. Moretta! Oh 'tis gone!

MORETTA. Curse on him, here he comes;
How fine she has made him, too.

Enter WILLMORE *and* SEBASTIAN. ANGELLICA *turns and walks away.*

WILLMORE. How now, turned shadow!
Fly when I pursue, and follow when I fly!

Sings.

Stay, gentle shadow of my dove,
    And tell me ere I go,
Whether the substance may not prove
    A fleeting thing like you.

As she turns, she looks on him.

There's a soft, kind look remaining yet.

ANGELLICA. Well, sir, you may be gay: all happiness, all
joys pursue you still, Fortune's your slave and gives you
every hour choice of new hearts and beauties, till you are
cloyed with the repeated bliss, which others vainly
languish for. – But know, false man, that I shall be
revenged.

Turns away in rage.

WILLMORE. So, 'gad, there are of those faint-hearted
lovers, whom such a sharp lesson next their hearts would
make as impotent as fourscore – pox o' this whining – my
business is to laugh and love – a pox on't; I hate your
sullen lover, a man shall lose as much time to put you in
humour now, as would serve to gain a new woman.

ANGELLICA. I scorn to cool that fire I cannot raise,
Or do the drudgery of your virtuous mistress.

WILLMORE. A virtuous mistress! Death, what a thing thou
hast found out for me! Why what the devil should I do
with a virtuous woman? – A sort of ill-natured creatures,
that take a pride to torment a lover. Virtue is but an

infirmity in woman, a disease that renders even the handsome ungrateful; whilst the ill-favoured, for want of solicitations and address, only fancy themselves so. – I have lain with a woman of quality, who has all the while been railing at whores.

ANGELLICA. I will not answer for your mistress's virtue,
Though she be young enough to know no guilt:
And I could wish you would persuade my heart,
'Twas the two hundred thousand crowns you courted.

WILLMORE. Two hundred thousand crowns! What story's this? – What trick? – What woman? – Ha.

ANGELLICA. How strange you make it! Have you forgot the creature you entertained on the Piazza last night?

WILLMORE (*aside*). Ha, my gipsy worth two hundred thousand crowns! – Oh, how I long to be with her – pox, I knew she was of quality.

ANGELLICA. False man, I see my ruin in thy face.
How many vows you breathed upon my bosom,
Never to be unjust – have you forgot so soon?

WILLMORE (*aside*). Faith no, I was just coming to repeat 'em – but here's a humour indeed – would make a man a saint. – Would she would be angry enough to leave me, and command me not to wait on her.

Enter HELLENA, *dressed in man's clothes.*

HELLENA [*aside*]. This must be Angellica, I know it by her mumping matron here. – Ay, ay, 'tis she: my mad Captain's with her too, for all his swearing – how this unconstant humour makes me love him. [*To* MORETTA.] Pray, good grave gentlewoman, is not this Angellica?

MORETTA. My too young sir, it is. [*Aside.*] I hope 'tis one from Don Antonio.

Goes to ANGELLICA.

HELLENA (*aside*). Well, something I'll do to vex him for this.

ANGELLICA. I will not speak with him; am I in humour to receive a lover?

WILLMORE. Not speak with him! Why I'll be gone – and wait your idler minutes. – Can I show less obedience to the thing I love so fondly?

Offers to go.

ANGELLICA. A fine excuse this – stay –

WILLMORE. And hinder your advantage: should I repay your bounties so ungratefully?

ANGELLICA [*to* HELLENA]. Come hither, boy, –
    [*To* WILLMORE.] – that I may let you see
    How much above the advantages you name
    I prize one minute's joy with you.

WILLMORE (*impatient to be gone*). Oh, you destroy me with this endearment. – (*Aside.*) Death, how shall I get away? (*To* ANGELLICA.) Madam, 'twill not be fit I should be seen with you – besides, it will not be convenient – and I've a friend – that's dangerously sick.

ANGELLICA. I see you're impatient – yet you shall stay.

WILLMORE (*aside and walks about impatiently*). And miss my assignation with my gipsy.

    MORETTA *brings* HELLENA, *who addresses herself to* ANGELLICA.

HELLENA. Madam,
    You'll hardly pardon my intrusion,
    When you shall know my business;
    And I'm too young to tell my tale with art:
    But there must be a wondrous store of goodness
    Where so much beauty dwells.

ANGELLICA. A pretty advocate, whoever sent thee. –
    Prithee proceed. – (*To* WILLMORE *who is stealing off.*)
    Nay, sir, you shall not go.

WILLMORE (*aside*). Then I shall lose my dear gipsy for ever.
    – Pox on't, she stays me out of spite.

[HELLENA.] I am related to a lady, madam,
   Young, rich, and nobly born, but has the fate
   To be in love with a young English gentleman.
   Strangely she loves him, at first sight she loved him,
   But did adore him when she heard him speak;
   For he, she said, had charms in every word,
   That failed not to surprise, to wound, and conquer –

WILLMORE (*aside*). Ha, egad I hope this concerns me.

ANGELLICA. 'Tis my false man he means – would he were
   gone.
   This praise will raise his pride, and ruin me –
   (*To* WILLMORE.) Well, since you are so impatient to be
   gone,
   I will release you, sir.

WILLMORE (*aside*). Nay, then I'm sure 'twas me he spoke
   of, this cannot be the effects of kindness in her.

   (*To* ANGELLICA.) – No, madam, I've considered better
   on't,
   And will not give you cause of jealousy.

ANGELLICA. But, sir, I've – business, that –

WILLMORE. This shall not do, I know 'tis but to try me.

ANGELLICA. Well, to your story, boy, (*Aside.*) though 'twill
   undo me.

HELLENA. With this addition to his other beauties,
   He won her unresisting, tender heart,
   He vowed and sighed, and swore he loved her dearly;
   And she believed the cunning flatterer,
   And thought herself the happiest maid alive:
   To-day was the appointed time by both,
   To consummate their bliss;
   The virgin, altar, and the priest were dressed,
   And while she languished for th' expected bridegroom,
   She heard, he paid his broken vows to you.

WILLMORE (*aside*). So, this is some dear rogue that's in
   love with me, and this way lets me know it; or if it be not
   me, she means some one whose place I may supply.

ANGELLICA. Now I perceive
  The cause of thy impatience to be gone,
  And all the business of this glorious dress.

WILLMORE. Damn the young prater, I know not what he
  means.

HELLENA. Madam,
  In your fair eyes I read too much concern.
  To tell my farther business.

ANGELLICA. Prithee, sweet youth, talk on, thou may'st
    perhaps
  Raise here a storm that may undo my passion,
  And then I'll grant thee any thing.

HELLENA. Madam, 'tis to entreat you (oh, unreasonable!)
  You would not see this stranger;
  For if you do, she vows you are undone,
  Though nature never made a man so excellent;
  And sure, he'ad been a god, but for inconstancy.

WILLMORE (*aside*). Ah, rogue, how finely he's instructed!
  'Tis plain some woman that has seen me *en passant*.

ANGELLICA. Oh, I shall burst with jealousy! Do you know
  the man you speak of? –

HELLENA. Yes, madam, he used to be in buff and scarlet.

ANGELLICA (*to* WILLMORE). Thou, false as Hell, what
  canst thou say to this?

WILLMORE. By Heaven –

ANGELLICA. Hold, do not damn thyself –

HELLENA. Nor hope to be believed.

  He walks about, they follow.

ANGELLICA. Oh, perjured man!
  Is't thus you pay my generous passion back?

HELLENA. Why would you, sir, abuse my lady's faith?

ANGELLICA. And use me so unhumanely?

HELLENA. A maid so young, so innocent −

WILLMORE. Ah, young devil!

ANGELLICA. Dost thou not know thy life is in my power?

HELLENA. Or think my lady cannot be revenged?

WILLMORE (*aside*). So, so, the storm comes finely on.

ANGELLICA. Now thou art silent, guilt has struck thee
    dumb.
  Oh, hadst thou still been so, I'd lived in safety.

She turns away and weeps.

WILLMORE (*aside to* HELLENA). Sweetheart, the lady's
  name and house − quickly: I'm impatient to be with her. −

Looks towards ANGELLICA *to watch her turning; and as she
comes towards them, he meets her.*

HELLENA (*aside*). So now is he for another woman.

WILLMORE. The impudent'st young thing in nature!
  I cannot persuade him out of his error, madam.

ANGELLICA. I know he's in the right − yet thou'st a tongue
  That would persuade him to deny his faith.

In rage walks away.

WILLMORE (*said softly to* HELLENA). Her name, her
  name, dear boy −

HELLENA. Have you forgot it, sir?

WILLMORE (*aside*). Oh, I perceive he's not to know I am a
  stranger to his lady. (*To* HELLENA.) − Yes, yes, I do
  know − but I have forgot the −

ANGELLICA *turns.*

  − By Heaven, such early confidence I never saw.

ANGELLICA. Did I not charge you with this mistress, sir?
  Which you denied, though I beheld your perjury.
  This little generosity of thine has rendered back my heart.

Walks away.

WILLMORE [*to* HELLENA].
> So, you have made sweet work here, my little mischief;
> Look your lady be kind and good natured now, or
> I shall have but a cursed bargain on't.

ANGELLICA *turns towards them.*

> (*To* ANGELLICA.) The rogue's bred up to mischief;
> Art thou so great a fool to credit him?

ANGELLICA. Yes, I do; and you in vain impose upon me.
> [*To* HELLENA.] – Come hither, boy. – Is not this he you
> spake of?

HELLENA. I think – it is; I cannot swear, but I vow he has
> just such another lying lover's look.

HELLENA *looks in his face, he gazes on her.*

WILLMORE (*aside*). Ha! Do not I know that face? –
> By Heaven, my little gipsy! What a dull dog was I?
> Had I but looked that way, I'd known her.
> Are all my hopes of a new woman banished?
> – Egad, if I do not fit thee for this, hang me.
> [*To* ANGELLICA.] – Madam, I have found out the plot.

HELLENA [*aside*].
> Oh lord, what does he say? Am I discovered now?

WILLMORE. Do you see this young spark here?

HELLENA [*aside*]. He'll tell her who I am.

WILLMORE. Who do you think this is?

HELLENA [*aside*]. Ay, ay, he does know me. [*To*
> WILLMORE.] Nay, dear Captain, I am undone if you
> discover me.

WILLMORE. Nay, nay, no cogging; she shall know what a
> precious mistress I have.

HELLENA. Will you be such a devil?

WILLMORE. Nay, nay, I'll teach you to spoil sport you will
> not make. – [*To* ANGELLICA.] This small ambassador
> comes not from a person of quality, as you imagine, and

he says; but from a very arrant gipsy, the talkingst, pratingst, cantingst little animal thou ever saw'st.

ANGELLICA. What news you tell me! That's the thing I mean.

HELLENA (*aside*). Would I were well off the place. – If ever I go a-captain-hunting again. –

WILLMORE. Mean that thing? That gipsy thing? Thou may'st as well be jealous of thy monkey, or parrot as of her: a German motion were worth a dozen of her, and a dream were a better enjoyment, a creature of a constitution fitter for Heaven than man.

HELLENA (*aside*). Though I'm sure he lies, yet this vexes me.

ANGELLICA. You are mistaken, she's a Spanish woman. Made up of no such dull materials.

WILLMORE. Materials! Egad, and she be made of any that will either dispense, or admit of love, I'll be bound to continence.

HELLENA (*aside to him*). Unreasonable man, do you think so?

[WILLMORE] (*to* HELLENA). You may return, my little brazen head, and tell your lady, that till she be handsome enough to be beloved, or I dull enough to be religious, there will be small hopes of me.

ANGELLICA. Did you not promise then to marry her?

WILLMORE. Not I, by Heaven.

ANGELLICA. You cannot undeceive my fears and torments. till you have vowed you will not marry her.

HELLENA (*aside*). If he swears that, he'll be revenged on me indeed for all my rogueries.

ANGELLICA. I know what arguments you'll bring against me, fortune and honour.

WILLMORE. Honour! I tell you, I hate it in your sex; and those that fancy themselves possessed of that foppery, are the most impertinently troublesome of all woman-kind,

and will transgress nine commandments to keep one: and
to satisfy your jealousy I swear –

HELLENA (*aside to him*). Oh, no swearing, dear Captain –

WILLMORE. If it were possible I should ever be inclined to
marry, it should be some kind young sinner, one that has
generosity enough to give a favour handsomely to one
that can ask it discreetly, one that has wit enough to
manage an intrigue of love – oh, how civil such a wench
is, to a man that does her the honour to marry her.

ANGELLICA. By Heaven, there's no faith in any thing he
says.

Enter SEBASTIAN.

SEBASTIAN. Madam, Don Antonio –

ANGELLICA. Come hither.

HELLENA [*aside*]. Ha, Antonio! He may be coming hither,
and he'll certainly discover me, I'll therefore retire without
a ceremony.

Exit HELLENA.

ANGELLICA. I'll see him, get my coach ready.

SEBASTIAN. It waits you, madam.

WILLMORE [*aside*]. This is lucky. [*To* ANGELLICA.]
What, madam, now I may be gone and leave you to the
enjoyment of my rival?

ANGELLICA. Dull man, that canst not see how ill, how
poor,
That false dissimulation looks – be gone,
And never let me see thy cozening face again,
Lest I relapse and kill thee.

WILLMORE. Yes, you can spare me now – farewell till
you're in better humour – I'm glad of this release – now
for my gipsy:

For though to worse we change, yet still we find
New joys, new charms, in a new miss that's kind.

Exit.

ANGELLICA. He's gone, and in this ague of my soul
   The shivering fit returns;
   Oh with what willing haste he took his leave,
   As if the longed-for minute were arrived
   Of some blessed assignation.
   In vain I have consulted all my charms,
   In vain this beauty prized, in vain believed
   My eyes could kindle any lasting fires.
   I had forgot my name, my infamy,
   And the reproach that honour lays on those
   That dare pretend a sober passion here.
   Nice reputation, though it leave behind
   More virtues than inhabit where that dwells,
   Yet that once gone, those virtues shine no more.
   – Then since I am not fit to be beloved,
   I am resolved to think on a revenge
   On him that soothed me thus to my undoing.

Exeunt.

Scene Three

A street.

Enter FLORINDA *and* VALERIA *in habits different from what they have been seen in.*

FLORINDA. We're happily escaped, and yet I tremble still.

VALERIA. A lover and fear! Why, I am but half an one, and yet I have courage for any attempt. Would Hellena were here. I would fain have had her as deep in this mischief as we, she'll fare but ill else I doubt.

FLORINDA. She pretended a visit to the Augustine nuns, but I believe some other design carried her out, pray Heavens, we light on her. – Prithee what didst do with Callis?

VALERIA. When I saw no reason would do good on her, I followed her into the wardrobe, and as she was looking

for something in a great chest, I toppled her in by the
heels, snatched the key of the apartment where you were
confined, locked her in, and left her bawling for help.

FLORINDA. 'Tis well you resolve to follow my fortunes, for
thou darest never appear at home again after such an
action.

VALERIA. That's according as the young stranger and I
shall agree. – But to our business – I delivered your letter,
your note to Belvile, when I got out under pretence of
going to mass, I found him at his lodging, and believe me
it came seasonably; for never was man in so desperate a
condition. I told him of your resolution of making your
escape to-day, if your brother would be absent long
enough to permit you; if not, to die rather than be
Antonio's.

FLORINDA. Thou should'st have told him I was confined
to my chamber upon my brother's suspicion, that the
business on the Molo was a plot laid between him and I.

VALERIA. I said all this, and told him your brother was
now gone to his devotion, and he resolves to visit every
church till he find him; and not only undeceive him in
that, but caress him so as shall delay his return home.

FLORINDA. Oh, Heavens! He's here, and Belvile with him
too.

They put on their vizards.

Enter DON PEDRO, BELVILE, WILLMORE; BELVILE
and DON PEDRO *seeming in serious discourse.*

VALERIA. Walk boldly by them, and I'll come at distance,
lest he suspect us.

She walks by them and looks back on them.

WILLMORE. Ha! A woman! And of an excellent mien!

PEDRO. She throws a kind look back on you.

WILLMORE. Death, 'tis a likely wench, and that kind look
shall not be cast away – I'll follow her.

BELVILE. Prithee do not.

WILLMORE. Do not! By Heavens to the Antipodes, with such an invitation.

[VALERIA] *goes out and* WILLMORE *follows her.*

BELVILE. 'Tis a mad fellow for a wench.

Enter FREDERICK.

FREDERICK. Oh Colonel, such news.

BELVILE. Prithee what?

FREDERICK. News that will make you laugh in spite of fortune.

BELVILE. What, Blunt has had some damned trick put upon him? Cheated, banged, or clapped?

FREDERICK. Cheated sir, rarely cheated of all but his shirt and drawers; the unconscionable whore too turned him out before consummation, so that traversing the streets at midnight, the watch found him in this *fresco*, and conducted him home; by Heaven 'tis such a sight, and yet I durst as well been hanged as laughed at him, or pity him; he beats all that do but ask him a question, and is in such an humour –

PEDRO. Who is't has met with this ill usage, sir?

BELVILE. A friend of ours, whom you must see for mirth's sake. (*Aside.*) I'll employ him to give Florinda time for an escape.

PEDRO. What is he?

BELVILE. A young countryman of ours, one that has been educated at so plentiful a rate, he yet ne'er knew the want of money, and 'twill be a great jest to see how simply he'll look without it. For my part I'll lend him none, and the rogue know not how to put on a borrowing face, and ask first. I'll let him see how good 'tis to play our parts whilst I play his. – Prithee, Fred, do you go home and keep him in that posture till we come.

Exeunt [BELVILE, DON PEDRO, *and* FREDERICK].

Enter FLORINDA *from the farther end of the scene, looking behind her.*

FLORINDA. I am followed still. – Hah – my brother too advancing this way, good Heavens defend me from being seen by him.

She goes off.

Enter WILLMORE, *and after him* VALERIA, *at a little distance.*

WILLMORE. Ah! There she sails, she looks back as she were willing to be boarded, I'll warrant her prize.

He goes out, VALERIA *following.*

Enter HELLENA, *just as he goes out, with a* PAGE.

HELLENA. Hah, is not that my Captain that has a woman in chase? – 'Tis not Angellica. [*To* PAGE.] Boy, follow those people at a distance, and bring me an account where they go in. (*Exit* PAGE.) I'll find his haunts and plague him everywhere. – Ha – my brother!

BELVILE, WILLMORE, PEDRO *cross the stage;* HELLENA *runs off.*

Scene Four

Scene changes to another street.

Enter FLORINDA.

FLORINDA. What shall I do, my brother now pursues me. Will no kind power protect me from his tyranny? – Hah, here's a door open, I'll venture in, since nothing can be worse than to fall into his hands, my life and honour are at stake, and my necessity has no choice.

She goes in.

Enter VALERIA, *and* HELLENA'S PAGE *peeping after*
FLORINDA.

PAGE. Here she went in, I shall remember this house.

Exit BOY.

VALERIA. This is Belvile's lodging; she's gone in as readily
as if she knew it. – Hah – here's that mad fellow again, I
dare not venture in – I'll watch my opportunity.

Goes aside.

Enter WILLMORE, *gazing about him.*

WILLMORE. I have lost her hereabouts. – Pox on't she
must not scape me so.

Goes out.

Scene Five

Scene changes to BLUNT*'s chamber, discovers him sitting on a couch
in his shirt and drawers, reading.*

BLUNT. So, now my mind's a little at peace, since I have
resolved revenge. – A pox on this tailor though, for not
bringing home the clothes I bespoke; and a pox of all
poor cavaliers, a man can never keep a spare suit for 'em;
and I shall have these rogues come in and find me naked;
and then I'm undone; but I'm resolved to arm my self –
the rascals shall not insult over me too much. (*Puts on an
old rusty sword and buff belt.*) – Now, how like a morris-
dancer I am equipped – a fine lady-like whore to cheat
me thus, without affording me a kindness for my money,
a pox light on her, I shall never be reconciled to the sex
more, she has made me as faithless as a physician, as
uncharitable as a churchman, and as ill-natured as a poet.
Oh how I'll use all womankind hereafter! What would
I give to have one of 'em within my reach now! Any
mortal thing in petticoats, kind fortune, send me; and I'll
forgive thy last night's malice. – Here's a cursed book, too

(*A Warning to All Young Travellers*) that can instruct me how to prevent such mischief now 'tis too late! Well, 'tis a rare convenient thing to read a little now and then, as well as hawk and hunt.

Sits down again and reads.

Enter to him FLORINDA.

FLORINDA. This house is haunted sure, 'tis well furnished and no living thing inhabits it − hah − a man! Heavens, how he's attired! Sure 'tis some rope-dancer, or fencing master; I tremble now for fear, and yet I must venture now to speak to him. [*To* BLUNT.] Sir, if I may not interrupt your meditations −

He starts up and gazes.

BLUNT. Hah − what's here? Are my wishes granted? And is not that a she creature? 'Adsheartlikins 'tis! What wretched thing art thou − hah!

FLORINDA. Charitable sir, you've told your self already what I am; a very wretched maid, forced by a strange unlucky accident, to seek a safety here, and must be ruined, if you do not grant it.

BLUNT. Ruined! Is there any ruin so inevitable as that which now threatens thee? Dost thou know, miserable woman, into what den of mischiefs thou art fallen? What abyss of confusion? − Hah − dost not see something in my looks that frights thy guilty soul, and makes thee wish to change that shape of woman for any humble animal, or devil? For those were safer for thee, and less mischievous.

FLORINDA. Alas, what mean you, sir? I must confess, your looks have something in 'em makes me fear; but I beseech you, as you seem a gentleman, pity a harmless virgin, that takes your house for sanctuary.

BLUNT. Talk on, talk on, and weep too, till my faith return. Do, flatter me out of my senses again − a harmless virgin with a pox, as much one as t'other, adsheartlikins. Why, what the devil can I not be safe in my house for you? Not in my chamber? Nay, even being naked too cannot secure me. This is an impudence greater than has invaded me yet. – Come, no resistance.

Pulls her rudely.

FLORINDA. Dare you be so cruel?

BLUNT. Cruel, adsheartlikins as a galley slave, or a Spanish whore: cruel, yes, I will kiss and beat thee all over; kiss, and see thee all over; thou shalt lie with me too, not that I care for the enjoyment, but to let thee see I have ta'en deliberated malice to thee, and will be revenged on one whore for the sins of another; I will smile and deceive thee, flatter thee, and beat thee, kiss and swear, and lie to thee, embrace thee and rob thee, as she did me, fawn on thee, and strip thee stark naked; then hang thee out at my window by the heels, with a paper of scurvy verses fastened to thy breast, in praise of damnable women. – Come, come along!

FLORINDA. Alas, sir, must I be sacrificed for the crimes of the most infamous of my sex! I never understood the sins you name.

BLUNT. Do, persuade the fool you love him, or that one of you can be just or honest; tell me I was not an easy coxcomb, or any strange impossible tale: it will be believed sooner than thy false showers or protestations. A generation of damned hypocrites, to flatter my very clothes from my back! Dissembling witches! Are these the returns you make an honest gentleman that trusts, believes, and loves you? – But if I be not even with you – come along, or I shall –

Pulls her again.

Enter FREDERICK.

FREDERICK. Hah, what's here to do?

BLUNT. Adsheartlikins, Fred I am glad thou art come, to be a witness of my dire revenge.

FREDERICK. What's this, a person of quality too, who is upon the ramble to supply the defects of some grave impotent husband?

BLUNT. No, this has another pretence; some very unfortunate accident brought her hither, to save a life pursued by I know not who, or why, and forced to take sanctuary here at Fools' Haven. Adsheartlikins to me of all mankind for protection? Is the ass to be cajoled again, think ye? No, young one, no prayers or tears shall mitigate my rage; therefore prepare for both my pleasures of enjoyment and revenge, for I am resolved to make up my loss here on thy body, I'll take it out in kindness and in beating.

FREDERICK. Now, mistress of mine, what do you think of this?

FLORINDA. I think he will not – dares not be so barbarous.

FREDERICK. Have a care, Blunt, she fetched a deep sigh, she is enamoured with thy shirt and drawers; she'll strip thee even of that. There are, of her calling such unconscionable baggages, and such dexterous thieves, they'll flay a man, and he shall ne'er miss his skin, till he feels the cold. There was a countryman of ours robbed of a row of teeth whilst he was a-sleeping, which the jilt made him buy again when he waked. – [*To* FLORINDA.] You see, lady, how little reason we have to trust you.

BLUNT. 'Dsheartlikins, why, this is most abominable.

FLORINDA. Some such devils there may be, but by all that's holy I am none such, I entered here to save a life in danger.

BLUNT. For no goodness I'll warrant her.

FREDERICK. Faith, damsel, you had e'en confessed the plain truth, for we are fellows not to be caught twice in the same trap. Look on that wreck, a tight vessel when he set out of haven, well-trimmed and laden, and see how a female picaroon of this island of rogues has shattered him, and canst thou hope for any mercy?

BLUNT. No, no, gentlewoman, come along, adsheartlikins we must be better acquainted. – [*To* FREDERICK.] We'll both lie with her, and then let me alone to bang her.

FREDERICK. I'm ready to serve you in matters of revenge,
that has a double pleasure in't.

BLUNT. Well said. You hear, little one, how you are
condemned by public vote to the bed within, there's no
resisting your destiny, sweetheart.

Pulls her.

FLORINDA. Stay, sir, I have seen you with Belvile, an
English cavalier, for his sake use me kindly; you know
him, sir.

BLUNT. Belvile! Why, yes, sweeting, we do know Belvile,
and wish he were with us now, he's a cormorant at whore
and bacon, he'd have a limb or two of thee, my virgin
pullet: but 'tis no matter. we'll leave him the bones to
pick.

FLORINDA. Sir, if you have any esteem for that Belvile, I
conjure you to treat me with more gentleness; he'll thank
you for the justice.

FREDERICK. Hark ye, Blunt, I doubt we are mistaken in
this matter.

FLORINDA. Sir, if you find me not worth Belvile's care, use
me as you please; and that you may think I merit better
treatment than you threaten – pray take this present –

Gives him a ring: he looks on it.

BLUNT. Hum – a diamond! Why, 'tis a wonderful virtue
now that lies in this ring, a mollifying virtue;
adsheartlikins there's more persuasive rhetoric in't, than all
her sex can utter.

FREDERICK. I begin to suspect something; and 'twould
anger us vilely to be trussed up for a rape upon a maid of
quality, when we only believe we ruffle a harlot.

BLUNT. Thou art a credulous fellow, but adsheartlikins I
have no faith yet; why, my saint prattled as parlously as
this does, she gave me a bracelet too, a devil on her: but
I sent my man to sell it today for necessaries, and it
proved as counterfeit as her vows of love.

FREDERICK. However, let it reprieve her till we see
    Belvile.

BLUNT. That's hard, yet I will grant it.

Enter a SERVANT.

SERVANT. Oh, sir, the Colonel is just come in with his new
    friend and a Spaniard of quality, and talks of having you
    to dinner with 'em.

BLUNT. 'Dsheartlikins, I'm undone – I would not see 'em
    for the world: hark ye, Fred, lock up the wench in your
    chamber.

FREDERICK. Fear nothing, madam, whate'er he threatens,
    you are safe whilst in my hands.

Exeunt FREDERICK *and* FLORINDA.

BLUNT. And, sirrah – upon your life, say – I am not at
    home – or that I am asleep – or – or anything – away –
    I'll prevent their coming this way.

Locks the door and exeunt.

ACT FIVE

Blunt's chamber.

After a great knocking at his chamber door, enter BLUNT *softly, crossing the stage in his shirt and drawers, as before.*

[VOICES] (*call within*). Ned, Ned Blunt, Ned Blunt.

BLUNT. The rogues are up in arms. 'dsheartlikins, this villainous Frederick has betrayed me, they have heard of my blessed fortune.

[VOICES] (*and knocking within*). Ned Blunt, Ned, Ned –

BELVILE [*within*]. Why, he's dead, sir, without dispute dead, he has not been seen to-day; let's break open the door – here – boy –

BLUNT. Ha, break open the door! 'Dsheartlikins that mad fellow will be as good as his word.

BELVILE [*within*]. Boy, bring something to force the door.

A great noise within at the door again.

BLUNT. So, now must I speak in my own defence, I'll try what rhetoric will do – hold – hold, what do you mean, gentlemen, what do you mean?

BELVILE (*within*). Oh rogue, art alive? Prithee open the door, and convince us.

BLUNT. Yes, I am alive, gentlemen – but at present a little busy.

BELVILE (*within*). How! Blunt grown a man of business! Come, come, open, and let's see this miracle.

BLUNT. No, no, no, no, gentlemen, 'tis no great business – but – I am – at – my devotion – 'dsheartlikins, will you not allow a man time to pray?

BELVILE (*within*). Turned religious! A greater wonder than
the first, therefore open quickly, or we shall unhinge, we
shall.

BLUNT. This won't do. Why, hark ye, Colonel; to tell you
the plain truth, I am about a necessary affair of life. – I
have a wench with me – you apprehend me? [*Aside.*] The
devil's in't if they be so uncivil as to disturb me now.

WILLMORE [*within*]. How, a wench! Nay, then we must
enter and partake; no resistance – unless it be your lady
of quality, and then we'll keep our distance.

BLUNT [*aside*]. So, the business is out.

WILLMORE [*within*]. Come, come, lend's more hands to the
door – now heave all together – (*Breaks open the door.*) so,
well done, my boys –

Enter BELVILE, WILLMORE, FREDERICK, PEDRO
and Belvile's PAGE: BLUNT *looks simply, they all laugh at
him, he lays his hand on his sword, and comes up to*
WILLMORE.

BLUNT. Hark ye, sir, laugh out your laugh quickly, d'ye
hear, and be gone, I shall spoil your sport else;
'dsheartlikins, sir, I shall – the jest has been carried on too
long – (*Aside.*) A plague upon my tailor –

WILLMORE. 'Sdeath, how the whore has dressed him!
Faith sir, I'm sorry.

BLUNT. Are you so, sir? Keep't to yourself then, sir, I
advise you, d'ye hear? For I can as little endure your pity
as his mirth.

Lays his hand on's sword.

BELVILE. Indeed, Willmore, thou wert a little too rough
with Ned Blunt's mistress. Call a person of quality whore,
and one so young, so handsome, and so eloquent! – Ha,
ha, ha.

BLUNT. Hark ye, sir, you know me, and know I can be
angry; have a care – for 'dsheartlikins I can fight too – I
can, sir – do you mark me – no more.

BELVILE. Why so peevish, good Ned? Some
disappointments, I'll warrant – what, did the jealous count
her husband return just in the nick?

BLUNT. Or the devil, sir – (*They laugh.*) D'ye laugh? Look ye
settle me a good sober countenance, and that quickly too,
or you shall know Ned Blunt is not –

BELVILE. Not everybody, we know that.

BLUNT. Not an ass, to be laughed at, sir.

WILLMORE. Unconscionable sinner, to bring a lover so
near his happiness, a vigorous passionate lover, and then
not only cheat him of his moveables, but his very desires,
too.

BELVILE. Ah, sir, a mistress is a trifle with Blunt; he'll have
a dozen the next time he looks abroad; his eyes have
charms not to be resisted: there needs no more than to
expose that taking person to the view of the fair, and he
leads 'em all in triumph.

PEDRO. Sir, though I'm a stranger to you, I am ashamed
at the rudeness of my nation; and could you learn who
did it, would assist you to make an example of 'em.

BLUNT. Why, ay, there's one speaks sense now, and
handsomely; and let me tell you gentlemen, I should not
have showed myself like a jack-pudding, thus to have
made you mirth, but that I have revenge within my
power; for know, I have got into my possession a female,
who had better have fallen under any curse, than the ruin
I design her: 'dsheartlikins, she assaulted me here in my
own lodgings, and had doubtless committed a rape upon
me, had not this sword defended me.

FREDERICK. I know not that, but o' my conscience thou
had ravished her, had she not redeemed herself with a
ring – let's see it, Blunt.

BLUNT *shows the ring.*

BELVILE [*aside*]. Hah! – The ring I gave Florinda when we
exchanged our vows. – Hark ye, Blunt –

Goes to whisper to him.

WILLMORE. No whispering, good Colonel, there's a
woman in the case, no whispering.

BELVILE [*to* BLUNT]. Hark ye, fool, be advised, and
conceal both the ring and the story, for your reputation's
sake; do not let people know what despised cullies we
English are: to be cheated and abused by one whore, and
another rather bribe thee than be kind to thee, is an
infamy to our nation.

WILLMORE. Come, come, where's the wench? We'll see
her, let her be what she will, we'll see her.

PEDRO. Ay, ay, let us see her. I can soon discover whether
she be of quality, or for your diversion.

BLUNT. She's in Fred's custody.

WILLMORE. Come, come, the key. (*To* FREDERICK, *who
gives him the key; they are going.*)

BELVILE. Death! What shall I do? – Stay, gentlemen. – Yet
if I hinder 'em, I shall discover all – hold, let's go one at
once – give me the key.

WILLMORE. Nay, hold there, Colonel, I'll go first.

FREDERICK. Nay, no dispute, Ned and I have the
propriety of her.

WILLMORE. Damn propriety – then we'll draw cuts.

BELVILE *goes to whisper* WILLMORE.

Nay, no corruption, good Colonel: come, the longest
sword carries her. –

They all draw, forgetting DON PEDRO, *being a Spaniard, had
the longest.*

BLUNT. I yield up my interest to you gentlemen, and that
will be revenge sufficient.

WILLMORE (*to* PEDRO). The wench is yours. – [*Aside.*]
Pox of his Toledo, I had forgot that.

FREDERICK. Come, sir, I'll conduct you to the lady.

Exeunt FREDERICK *and* PEDRO.

BELVILE (*aside*). To hinder him will certainly discover her. [*To* WILLMORE.] Dost know, dull beast, what mischief thou hast done?

WILLMORE *walking up and down out of humour.*

WILLMORE. Ay, ay, to trust our fortune to lots, a devil on't; 'twas madness, that's the truth on't.

BELVILE. Oh intolerable sot!

Enter FLORINDA, *running, masked,* PEDRO *after her.* WILLMORE *gazing round her.*

FLORINDA (*aside*). Good Heaven, defend me from discovery.

PEDRO. 'Tis but in vain to fly me, you're fallen to my lot.

BELVILE. Sure she's undiscovered yet, but now I fear there is no way to bring her off.

WILLMORE. Why, what a pox is not this my woman, the same I followed but now?

PEDRO *talking to* FLORINDA, *who walks up and down.*

PEDRO. As if I did not know ye, and your business here.

FLORINDA (*aside*). Good Heaven! I fear he does indeed –

PEDRO. Come, pray be kind, I know you meant to be so when you entered here, for these are proper gentlemen.

WILLMORE. But, sir – perhaps the lady will not be imposed upon, she'll choose her man.

PEDRO. I am better bred, than not to leave her choice free.

Enter VALERIA, *and is surprised at sight of* DON PEDRO.

VALERIA (*aside*). Don Pedro here! There's no avoiding him.

FLORINDA (*aside*). Valeria! Then I'm undone –

VALERIA (*to* PEDRO, *running to him*). Oh, have I found you, sir? – The strangest accident – if I had breath – to tell it.

PEDRO. Speak – is Florinda safe? Hellena well?

VALERIA. Ay, ay, sir – Florinda – is safe [*Aside.*] from any
fears of you.

PEDRO. Why, where's Florinda? – Speak.

VALERIA. Ay, where indeed, sir? I wish I could inform you
– but to hold you no longer in doubt –

FLORINDA (*aside*). Oh, what will she say?

VALERIA. She's fled away in the habit of one of her pages,
sir – but Callis thinks you may retrieve her yet, if you
make haste away; she'll tell you, sir, the rest – (*Aside.*) if
you can find her out.

PEDRO. Dishonourable girl, she has undone my aim – [*To*
BELVILE.] Sir – you see my necessity of leaving you, and
hope you'll pardon it: my sister, I know, will make her
flight to you; and if she do I shall expect she should be
rendered back.

BELVILE. I shall consult my love and honour, sir.

Exit PEDRO.

FLORINDA (*to* VALERIA). My dear preserver, let me
embrace thee.

WILLMORE. What the devil's all this?

BLUNT. Mystery by this light.

VALERIA. Come, come, make haste and get your selves
married quickly, for your brother will return again.

BELVILE. I'm so surprised with fears and joys, so amazed to
find you here in safety, I can scarce persuade my heart
into a faith of what I see –

WILLMORE. Hark ye, Colonel, is this that mistress who has
cost you so many sighs, and me so many quarrels with
you?

BELVILE. It is. – (*To* FLORINDA.) Pray give him the
honour of your hand.

WILLMORE. Thus it must be received then.

Kneels and kisses her hand.

And with it give your pardon too.

FLORINDA. The friend to Belvile may command me anything.

WILLMORE (*aside*). Death, would I might, 'tis a surprising beauty.

BELVILE. Boy, run and fetch a Father instantly.

Exit BOY.

FREDERICK. So, now do I stand like a dog, and have not a syllable to plead my own cause with: by this hand, madam, I was never thoroughly confounded before, nor shall I ever more dare look up with confidence, till you are pleased to pardon me.

FLORINDA. Sir, I'll be reconciled to you on one condition, that you'll follow the example of your friend, in marrying a maid that does not hate you, and whose fortune (I believe) will not be unwelcome to you.

FREDERICK. Madam, had I no inclinations that way, I should obey your kind commands.

BELVILE. Who, Fred marry; he has so few inclinations for womankind, that had he been possessed of paradise, he might have continued there to this day, if no crime but love could have disinherited him.

FREDERICK. Oh, I do not use to boast of my intrigues.

BELVILE. Boast! Why, thou dost nothing but boast; and I dare swear, wert thou as innocent from the sin of the grape, as thou art from the apple, thou might'st yet claim that right in Eden which our first parents lost by too much loving.

FREDERICK. I wish this lady would think me so modest a man.

VALERIA. She would be sorry then, and not like you half so well, and I should be loath to break my word with you; which was, that if your friend and mine agreed, it should be a match between you and I.

She gives him her hand.

FREDERICK. Bear witness, Colonel, 'tis a bargain.

Kisses her hand.

BLUNT (*to* FLORINDA). I have a pardon to beg too; but adsheartlikins I am so out of countenance, that I'm a dog if I can say any thing to purpose.

FLORINDA. Sir, I heartily forgive you all.

BLUNT. That's nobly said, sweet lady. – Belvile, prithee present her her ring again, for I find I have not courage to approach her myself.

Gives him the ring; [BELVILE] *gives it to* FLORINDA.

Enter BOY.

BOY. Sir, I have brought the Father that you sent for.

BELVILE. 'Tis well, and now my dear Florinda, let's fly to complete that mighty joy we have so long wished and sighed for. – Come, Fred, you'll follow?

FREDERICK. Your example, sir, 'twas ever my ambition in war, and must be so in love.

WILLMORE. And must not I see this juggling knot tied?

BELVILE. No, thou shalt do us better service, and be our guàrd, lest Don Pedro's sudden return interrupt the ceremony.

WILLMORE. Content; I'll secure this pass.

Exeunt BELVILE, FLORINDA, FREDERICK *and* VALERIA.

Enter BOY.

BOY (*to* WILLMORE). Sir, there's a lady without would speak to you.

WILLMORE. Conduct her in, I dare not quit my post.

BOY [*to* BLUNT]. And sir, your tailor waits you in your
  chamber.

BLUNT. Some comfort yet, I shall not dance naked at the
  wedding.

Exeunt BLUNT *and* BOY.

Enter again the BOY, *conducting in* ANGELLICA *in a masking
habit and a vizard,* WILLMORE *runs to her.*

WILLMORE. This can be none but my pretty gipsy. – Oh,
  I see you can follow as well as fly. – Come, confess thyself
  the most malicious devil in nature, you think you have
  done my business with Angellica –

ANGELLICA. Stand off, base villain –

She draws a pistol, and holds to his breast.

WILLMORE. Hah, 'tis not she: who art thou? And what's
  thy business?

ANGELLICA. One thou hast injured, and who comes to kill
  thee for't.

WILLMORE. What the devil canst thou mean?

ANGELLICA. By all my hopes to kill thee –

Holds still the pistol to his breast, he going back, she following still.

WILLMORE. Prithee on what acquaintance? For I know
  thee not.

ANGELLICA. Behold this face – so lost to thy
  remembrance!

Pulls off her vizard.

And then call all thy sins about thy soul,
And let 'em die with thee.

WILLMORE. Angellica!

ANGELLICA. Yes, traitor,
  Does not thy guilty blood run shivering through thy veins?
  Hast thou no horror at this sight, that tells thee,
  Thou hast not long to boast thy shameful conquest?

WILLMORE. Faith, no child, my blood keeps its old ebbs
and flows still, and that usual heat too, that could oblige
thee with a kindness, had I but opportunity.

ANGELLICA. Devil! Dost wanton with my pain − have at
thy heart.

WILLMORE. Hold, dear virago! Hold thy hand a little,
I am not now at leisure to be killed − hold and hear me −
(*Aside.*) Death, I think she's in earnest.

ANGELLICA (*aside, turning from him*). Oh if I take not heed,
My coward heart will leave me to his mercy.
[*To* WILLMORE.] − What have you, sir, to say? − But
should I hear thee,
Thou'ldst talk away all that is brave about me:

Follows him with the pistol to his breast.

And I have vowed thy death, by all that's sacred.

WILLMORE. Why then there's an end of a proper
handsome fellow, that might 'a lived to have done good
service yet: that's all I can say to't.

ANGELLICA (*pausingly*). Yet − I would give thee − time for
penitence.

WILLMORE. Faith, child, I thank God I have ever took
care to lead a good, sober, hopeful life, and am of a
religion that teaches me to believe I shall depart in peace.

ANGELLICA. So will the devil: tell me
How many poor believing fools thou hast undone;
How many hearts thou hast betrayed to ruin!
− Yet these are little mischiefs to the ills
Thou'st taught mine to commit: thou'st taught it love!

WILLMORE. Egad, 'twas shrewdly hurt the while.

ANGELLICA. − Love, that has robbed it of its unconcern,
Of all that pride that taught me how to value it.
And in its room a mean submissive passion was conveyed,
That made me humbly bow, which I ne'er did
To any thing but Heaven.

Thou, perjured man, didst this, and with thy oaths,
Which on thy knees thou didst devoutly make,
Softened my yielding heart – and then, I was a slave –
Yet still had been content to've worn my chains,
Worn 'em with vanity and joy for ever,
Hadst thou not broke those vows that put them on.
– 'Twas then I was undone.

All this while follows him with the pistol to his breast.

WILLMORE. Broke my vows! Why, where hast thou lived?
Amongst the gods! For I never heard of mortal man,
That has not broke a thousand vows.

ANGELLICA. Oh, impudence!

WILLMORE.
Angellica! That beauty has been too long tempting.
Not to have made a thousand lovers languish,
Who in the amorous favour, no doubt have sworn
Like me; did they all die in that faith? Still adoring?
I do not think they did.

ANGELLICA. No, faithless man: had I repaid their vows, as
I did thine, I would have killed the ingrateful that had
abandoned me.

WILLMORE. This old General has quite spoiled thee,
nothing makes a woman so vain, as being flattered; your
old lover ever supplies the defects of age, with intolerable
dotage, vast charge, and that which you call constancy;
and attributing all this to your own merits, you domineer,
and throw your favours in's teeth, upbraiding him still
with the defects of age, and cuckold him as often as he
deceives your expectations. But the gay, young, brisk
lover, that brings his equal fires, and can give you dart for
dart, you'll find will be as nice as you sometimes.

ANGELLICA. All this thou'st made me know, for which
I hate thee.
Had I remained in innocent security,
I should have thought all men were born my slaves;
And worn my power like lightning in my eyes,
To have destroyed at pleasure when offended.

But when love held the mirror, the undeceiving glass
Reflected all the weakness of my soul, and made me know,
My richest treasure being lost, my honour,
All the remaining spoil could not be worth
The conqueror's care or value.
– Oh how I fell like a long worshipped idol,
Discovering all the cheat!
Would not the incense and rich sacrifice,
Which blind devotion offered at my altars,
Have fallen to thee?
Why would'st thou then destroy my fancied power?

WILLMORE.
By Heaven, thou'rt brave, and I admire thee strangely.
I wish I were that dull, that constant thing,
Which thou would'st have, and nature never meant me:
I must, like cheerful birds, sing in all groves,
And perch on every bough,
Billing the next kind she that flies to meet me;
Yet after all could build my nest with thee,
Thither repairing when I'd loved my round,
And still reserve a tributary flame.
– To gain your credit, I'll pay you back your charity,
And be obliged for nothing but for love.

Offers her a purse of gold.

ANGELLICA. Oh, that thou wert in earnest!
So mean a thought of me,
Would turn my rage to scorn, and I should pity thee,
And give thee leave to live;
Which for the public safety of our sex,
And my own private injuries, I dare not do.
Prepare –

Follows still, as before.

– I will no more be tempted with replies.

WILLMORE. Sure –

ANGELLICA. Another word will damn thee! I've heard thee
talk too long.

She follows him with the pistol ready to shoot: he retires, still amazed. Enter DON ANTONIO, *his arm in a scarf, and lays hold on the pistol.*

ANTONIO. Hah! Angellica!

ANGELLICA. Antonio! What devil brought thee hither?

ANTONIO. Love and curiosity, seeing your coach at door. Let me disarm you of this unbecoming instrument of death. (*Takes away the pistol.*) Amongst the number of your slaves, was there not one worthy the honour to have fought your quarrel? [*To* WILLMORE.] – Who are you, sir, that are so very wretched to merit death from her?

WILLMORE. One, sir, that could have made a better end of an amorous quarrel without you, than with you.

ANTONIO. Sure, 'tis some rival – hah – the very man took down her picture yesterday – the very same that set on me last night – blest opportunity –

Offers to shoot him.

ANGELLICA. Hold, you're mistaken, sir.

ANTONIO. By Heaven, the very same!
    – Sir, what pretensions have you to this lady?

WILLMORE. Sir, I do not use to be examined, and am ill at all disputes but this –

Draws, ANTONIO *offers to shoot.*

ANGELLICA (*to* WILLMORE). Oh, hold! You see he's armed
        with certain death:
    – And you, Antonio, I command you hold,
    By all the passion you've so lately vowed me.

Enter DON PEDRO, *sees* ANTONIO, *and stays.*

PEDRO (*aside*). Hah, Antonio! And Angellica!

ANTONIO. When I refuse obedience to your will,
    May you destroy me with your mortal hate.
    By all that's holy I adore you so,

That even my rival, who has charms enough
To make him fall a victim to my jealousy,
Shall live, nay, and have leave to love on still.

PEDRO (*aside*). What's this I hear?

ANGELLICA (*pointing to* WILLMORE).
Ah, thus, 'twas thus he talked, and I believed.
– Antonio, yesterday,
I'd not have sold my interest in his heart,
For all the sword has won and lost in battle.
– But now to show my utmost of contempt,
I give thee life – which if thou would'st preserve,
Live where my eyes may never see thee more,
Live to undo someone, whose soul may prove
So bravely constant to revenge my love.

Goes out, ANTONIO *follows, but* PEDRO *pulls him back.*

PEDRO. Antonio – stay.

ANTONIO. Don Pedro –

PEDRO. What coward fear was that prevented thee
From meeting me this morning on the Molo?

ANTONIO. Meet thee?

PEDRO. Yes me; I was the man that dared thee to't.

ANTONIO. Hast thou so often seen me fight in war,
To find no better cause to excuse my absence?
– I sent my sword and one to do thee right,
Finding myself uncapable to use a sword.

PEDRO. But 'twas Florinda's quarrel that we fought,
And you to show how little you esteemed her,
Sent me your rival, giving him your interest.
– But I have found the cause of this affront,
And when I meet you fit for the dispute,
– I'll tell you my resentment.

ANTONIO. I shall be ready, sir, ere long to do you reason.

Exit ANTONIO.

PEDRO. If I could find Florinda, now whilst my anger's high, I think I should be kind, and give her to Belvile in revenge.

WILLMORE. Faith, sir, I know not what you would do, but I believe the priest within has been so kind.

PEDRO. How! My sister married?

WILLMORE. I hope by this time she is, and bedded too, or he has not my longings about him.

PEDRO. Dares he do this? Does he not fear my power?

WILLMORE. Faith not at all. If you will go in, and thank him for the favour he has done your sister, so; if not, sir, my power's greater in this house than yours; I have a damned surly crew here, that will keep you till the next tide, and then clap you on board for prize; my ship lies but a league off the Molo, and we shall show your Donship a damned Tramontana rover's trick.

Enter BELVILE.

BELVILE. This rogue's in some new mischief – hah, Pedro returned!

PEDRO. Colonel Belvile, I hear you have married my sister.

BELVILE. You have heard truth then, sir.

PEDRO. Have I so? Then, sir, I wish you joy.

BELVILE. How!

PEDRO. By this embrace I do, and I am glad on't.

BELVILE. Are you in earnest?

PEDRO. By our long friendship and my obligations to thee, I am. The sudden change I'll give you reasons for anon. Come, lead me to my sister, that she may know I now approve her choice.

Exit BELVILE *with* PEDRO. WILLMORE *goes to follow them. Enter* HELLENA *as before in boy's clothes, and pulls him back.*

WILLMORE. Ha! My gipsy – now a thousand blessings on thee for this kindness. Egad, child, I was e'en in despair of ever seeing thee again; my friends are all provided for within, each man his kind woman.

HELLENA. Hah! I thought they had served me some such trick.

WILLMORE. And I was e'en resolved to go abroad, condemn myself to my lone cabin, and the thoughts of thee.

HELLENA. And could you have left me behind? Would you have been so ill-natured?

WILLMORE. Why, 'twould have broke my heart, child – but since we are met again, I defy foul weather to part us.

HELLENA. And would you be a faithful friend now, if a maid should trust you?

WILLMORE. For a friend I cannot promise, thou art of a form so excellent, a face and humour too good for cold dull friendship; I am parlously afraid of being in love, child, and you have not forgot how severely you have used me.

HELLENA. That's all one, such usage you must still look for, to find out all your haunts, to rail at you to all that love you, till I have made you love only me in your own defence, because nobody else will love you.

WILLMORE. But hast thou no better quality to recommend thyself by?

HELLENA. Faith none, Captain – why, 'twill be the greater charity to take me for thy mistress, I am a lone child, a kind of orphan lover; and why I should die a maid, and in a Captain's hands too, I do not understand.

WILLMORE. Egad, I was never clawed away with broadsides from any female before, thou hast one virtue I adore, good nature; I hate a coy demure mistress, she's as troublesome as a colt, I'll break none; no, give me a mad mistress when mewed, and in flying one I dare trust upon the wing, that whilst she's kind will come to the lure.

HELLENA. Nay, as kind as you will, good Captain, whilst it lasts, but let's lose no time.

WILLMORE. My time's as precious to me, as thine can be; therefore, dear creature, since we are so well agreed, let's retire to my chamber, and if ever thou wert treated with such savoury love. – Come – my bed's prepared for such a guest, all clean and sweet as thy fair self; I love to steal a dish and a bottle with a friend, and hate long graces. – Come, let's retire and fall to.

HELLENA. 'Tis but getting my consent, and the business is soon done; let but old Gaffer Hymen and his priest say Amen to't, and I dare lay my mother's daughter by as proper a fellow as your father's son, without fear or blushing.

WILLMORE. Hold, hold, no bug words, child, priest and Hymen: prithee add a hangman to 'em to make up the consort. – No, no, we'll have no vows but love, child, nor witness but the lover; the kind deity enjoins naught but love and enjoy. Hymen and priest wait still upon portion, and jointure; love and beauty have their own ceremonies. Marriage is as certain a bane to love, as lending money is to friendship: I'll neither ask nor give a vow, though I could be content to turn gipsy, and become a left-handed bridegroom, to have the pleasure of working that great miracle of making a maid a mother, if you durst venture; 'tis upse gipsy that, and if I miss, I'll lose my labour.

HELLENA. And if you do not lose, what shall I get? A cradle full of noise and mischief, with a pack of repentance at my back? Can you teach me to weave incle to pass my time with? 'Tis upse gipsy that, too.

WILLMORE. I can teach thee to weave a true love's knot better.

HELLENA. So can my dog.

WILLMORE. Well, I see we are both upon our guards, and I see there's no way to conquer good nature, but by yielding – here – give me thy hand – one kiss and I am thine –

HELLENA. One kiss! How like my page he speaks; I am resolved you shall have none, for asking such a sneaking sum. – He that will be satisfied with one kiss, will never die of that longing; good friend single-kiss, is all your talking come to this? A kiss, a caudle! Farewell Captain Single-Kiss.

Going out he stays her.

WILLMORE. Nay, if we part so, let me die like a bird upon a bough, at the sheriff's charge. By Heaven, both the Indies shall not buy thee from me. I adore thy humour and will marry thee, and we are so of one humour, it must be a bargain – give me thy hand – (*Kisses her hand.*) and now let the blind ones (love and fortune) do their worst.

HELLENA. Why, God-a-mercy, Captain!

WILLMORE. But hark ye – the bargain is now made; but is it not fit we should know each other's names? That when we have reason to curse one another hereafter, and people ask me who 'tis I give to the devil, I may at least be able to tell what family you came of.

HELLENA. Good reason, Captain; and where I have cause (as I doubt not but I shall have plentiful) that I may know at whom to throw my – blessings – I beseech ye your name.

WILLMORE. I am called Robert the Constant.

HELLENA. A very fine name! Pray was it your falconer or butler that christened you? Do they not use to whistle when they call you?

WILLMORE. I hope you have a better, that a man may name without crossing himself, you are so merry with mine.

HELLENA. I am called Hellena the Inconstant.

Enter PEDRO, BELVILE, FLORINDA, FREDERICK, VALERIA.

PEDRO. Hah! Hellena!

FLORINDA. Hellena!

HELLENA. The very same – hah my brother! Now,
Captain, show your love and courage; stand to your arms,
and defend me bravely, or I am lost for ever.

PEDRO. What's this I hear? False girl, how came you
hither, and what's your business? Speak.

Goes roughly to her.

WILLMORE. Hold off, sir, you have leave to parley only.

Puts himself between.

HELLENA. I had e'en as good tell it, as you guess it. Faith,
brother, my business is the same with all living creatures
of my age, to love and be beloved, and here's the man.

PEDRO. Perfidious maid, hast thou deceived me too,
deceived thy self and Heaven?

HELLENA. 'Tis time enough to make my peace with that,
Be you but kind, let me alone with Heaven.

PEDRO. Belvile, I did not expect this false play from you;
was't not enough you'd gain Florinda (which I pardoned)
but your lewd friends too must be enriched with the spoils
of a noble family?

BELVILE. Faith, sir, I am as much surprised at this as you
can be: yet, sir, my friends are gentlemen, and ought to
be esteemed for their misfortunes, since they have the
glory to suffer with the best of men and kings; 'tis true,
he's a rover of fortune, yet a prince aboard his little
wooden world.

PEDRO. What's this to the maintenance of a woman of her
birth and quality?

WILLMORE. Faith, sir, I can boast of nothing but a sword
which does me right where'er I come, and has defended a
worse cause than a woman's: and since I loved her before
I either knew her birth or name, I must pursue my
resolution, and marry her.

PEDRO [*to* HELLENA]. And is all your holy intent of becoming a nun debauched into a desire of man?

HELLENA. Why – I have considered the matter, brother, and find the three hundred thousand crowns my uncle left me (and you cannot keep from me) will be better laid out in love than in religion, and turn to as good an account – let most voices carry it, for Heaven or the Captain?

ALL (*cry*). A Captain, a Captain!

HELLENA. Look ye, sir, 'tis a clear case.

PEDRO. Oh I am mad – (*Aside.*) if I refuse, my life's in danger. [*To* WILLMORE.] – Come – there's one motive induces me – take her – I shall now be free from fears of her honour; guard it you now, if you can, I have been a slave to't long enough.

Gives her to him.

WILLMORE. Faith, sir, I am of a nation that are of opinion a woman's honour is not worth guarding when she has a mind to part with it.

HELLENA. Well said, Captain.

PEDRO (*to* VALERIA). This was your plot, mistress, but I hope you have married one that will revenge my quarrel to you –

VALERIA. There's no altering destiny, sir.

PEDRO. Sooner than a woman's will, therefore I forgive you all – and wish you may get my father's pardon as easily; which I fear.

Enter BLUNT *dressed in a Spanish habit, looking very ridiculously; his* MAN *adjusting his band.*

MAN. 'Tis very well, sir.

BLUNT. Well, sir, 'dsheartlikins I tell you 'tis damnable ill, sir – a Spanish habit, good Lord! Could the devil and my tailor devise no other punishment for me, but the mode of a nation I abominate?

BELVILE. What's the matter, Ned?

BLUNT. Pray view me round and judge.

Turns round.

BELVILE. I must confess thou art a kind of an odd figure.

BLUNT. In a Spanish habit with a vengeance! I had rather
be in the Inquisition for Judaism, than in this doublet and
breeches; a pillory were an easy collar to this, three
handfuls high; and these shoes too are worse than the
stocks, with the sole an inch shorter than my foot. In fine,
gentlemen, methinks I look altogether like a bag of bays
stuffed full of fool's flesh.

BELVILE. Methinks 'tis well, and makes thee look *en cavalier*.
Come, sir, settle your face, and salute our friends. Lady –

BLUNT (*to* HELLENA). Hah! Say'st thou so, my little rover?
Lady – (if you be one) give me leave to kiss your hand,
and tell you, adsheartlikins, for all I look so, I am your
humble servant. – A pox of my Spanish habit!

Music is heard to play.

WILLMORE. Hark – what's this?

Enter BOY.

BOY. Sir, as the custom is, the gay people in masquerade,
who make every man's house their own, are coming up.

*Enter several men and women in masking habits, with music. They
put themselves in order and dance.*

BLUNT. Adsheartlikins, would 'twere lawful to pull off their
false faces, that I might see if my doxy were not amongst
'em.

BELVILE (*to the* MASKERS). Ladies and gentlemen, since
you are come so apropos, you must take a small collation
with us.

WILLMORE (*to* HELLENA). Whilst we'll to the good man
within, who stays to give us a cast of his office. – Have
you no trembling at the near approach?

HELLENA. No more than you have in an engagement or a tempest.

WILLMORE. Egad, thou'rt a brave girl, and I admire thy love and courage.

Lead on, no other dangers they can dread,
Who venture in the storms o' th' marriage bed.

Exeunt.

Epilogue

The banished cavaliers! A roving blade!
A popish carnival! A masquerade!
The devil's in't if this will please the nation,
In these our blessed times of reformation,
When conventicling is so much in fashion.
And yet –
That mutinous tribe less factions do beget,
Than your continual differing in wit;
Your judgement's (as your passion's) a disease:
Nor muse nor miss your appetite can please;
You're grown as nice as queasy consciences,
Whose each convulsion, when the spirit moves,
Damns everything that maggot disapproves.

With canting rule you would the stage refine,
And to dull method all our sense confine.
With th' insolence of commonwealths you rule,
Where each gay fop, and politic grave fool
On monarch wit impose without control.
As for the last who seldom sees a play,
Unless it be the old Blackfriars way,
Shaking his empty noddle o'er bamboo,
He cries, 'Good faith, these plays will never do.
– Ah, sir, in my young days, what lofty wit,
What high-strained scenes of fighting there were writ:
These are slight airy toys. But tell me, pray,
What has the House of Commons done today?'
Then shows his politics, to let you see

Of state affairs he'll judge as notably,
As he can do of wit and poetry.

The younger sparks, who hither do resort,
Cry, 'Pox o' your genteel things. Give us more sport;
– Damn me, I'm sure 'twill never please the court.'

Such fops are never pleased, unless the play
Be stuffed with fools, as brisk and dull as they:
Such might the half-crown spare, and in a glass
At home behold a more accomplished ass,
Where they may set their cravats, wigs and faces,
And practise all their buffoonery grimaces;
See how this – huff becomes – this damme – stare,
Which they at home may act, because they dare,
But – must with prudent caution do elsewhere.
Oh that our Nokes, or Tony Lee, could show
A fop but half so much to th' life as you.

Postscript

This play had been sooner in print, but for a report about the town (made by some either very malicious or very ignorant) that 'twas *Thomaso* altered; which made the booksellers fear some trouble from the proprietor of that admirable play, which indeed has wit enough to stock a poet, and is not to be pieced or mended by any but the excellent author himself. That I have stolen some hints from it may be a proof, that I valued it more than to pretend to alter it: had I had the dexterity of some poets who are not more expert in stealing than in the art of concealing, and who even that way outdo the Spartan-boys I might have appropriated all to myself, but I, vainly proud of my judgement, hang out the sign of Angellica (the only stolen object) to give notice where a great part of the wit dwelt; though if the play of *The Novella* were as well worth remembering as *Thomaso*, they might (bating the name) have as well said, I took it from thence: I will only say the plot and business (not to boast on't) is my own: as for the words and characters, I leave the reader to judge and compare 'em with *Thomaso*, to whom I recommend the great entertainment of reading it, though had this succeeded ill, I should have had no need of imploring that justice from the critics, who are naturally so kind to any that pretend to usurp their dominion, especially of our sex, they would doubtless have given me the whole honour on't. Therefore I will only say in English what the famous Virgil does in Latin: I make verses, and others have the fame.

THE WAY OF THE WORLD

Dedication

TO THE RIGHT HONOURABLE RALPH
EARL OF MOUNTAGUE ETC.

My Lord,

Whether the world will arraign me of vanity or not, that I
have presumed to dedicate this comedy to your Lordship, I
am yet in doubt: though it may be it is some degree of
vanity even to doubt of it. One who has at any time had the
honour of your Lordship's conversation, cannot be supposed
to think very meanly of that which he would prefer to your
perusal; yet it were to incur the imputation of too much
sufficiency to pretend to such a merit as might abide the test
of your Lordship's censure.

Whatever value may be wanting to this play while yet it is
mine, will be sufficiently made up to it when it is once
become your Lordship's; and it is my security that I cannot
have overrated it more by my dedication than your Lordship
will dignify it by your patronage.

That it succeeded on the stage was almost beyond my
expectation; for but little of it was prepared for that general
taste which seems now to be predominant in the palates of
our audience.

Those characters which are meant to be ridiculous in most
of our comedies are of fools so gross that, in my humble
opinion, they should rather disturb than divert the well-
natured and reflecting part of an audience; they are rather
objects of charity than contempt; and instead of moving our
mirth, they ought very often to excite our compassion.

This reflection moved me to design some characters which
should appear ridiculous not so much through a natural folly
(which is incorrigible, and therefore not proper for the stage)

as through an affected wit: a wit, which at the same time
that it is affected, is also false. As there is some difficulty in
the formation of a character of this nature, so there is some
hazard which attends the progress of its success upon the
stage. For many come to a play so over-charged with
criticism that they very often let fly their censure, when
through their rashness they have mistaken their aim. This I
had occasion lately to observe; for this play had been acted
two or three days before some of these hasty judges could
find the leisure to distinguish betwixt the character of a
Witwoud and a Truewit.

I must beg your Lordship's pardon for this digression from
the true course of this epistle; but that it may not seem
altogether impertinent, I beg that I may plead the occasion
of it, in part of that excuse of which I stand in need for
recommending this comedy to your protection. It is only by
the countenance of your Lordship, and the few so qualified,
that such who write with care and pains can hope to be
distinguished, for the prostituted name of poet promiscuously
levels all that bear it.

Terence, the most correct writer in the world, had a Scipio
and a Lelius, if not to assist him, at least to support him in
his reputation; and notwithstanding his extraordinary merit,
it may be their countenance was not more than necessary.

The purity of his style, the delicacy of his turns, and the
justness of his characters, were all of them beauties which the
greater part of his audience were incapable of tasting; some
of the coarsest strokes of Plautus, so severally censured by
Horace, were more likely to affect the multitude; such who
come with expectation to laugh out the last act of a play,
and are better entertained with two or three unseasonable
jests, than with the artful solution of the fable.

As Terence excelled in his performances, so had he great
advantages to encourage his undertakings, for he built most
on the foundations of Menander: his plots were generally
modelled, and his characters ready drawn to his hand. He
copied Menander; and Menander had no less light in the
formation of his characters from the observations of
Theophrastus, of whom he was a disciple; and Theophrastus,

it is known, was not only the disciple but the immediate successor of Aristotle, the first and greatest judge of poetry. These were great models to design by; and the further advantage which Terence possessed towards giving his plays the due ornaments of purity of style, and justness of manners, was not less considerable from the freedom of conversation which was permitted him with Lelius and Scipio, two of the greatest and most polite men of his age. And indeed, the privilege of such a conversation is the only certain means of attaining to the perfection of dialogue.

If it has happened in any part of this comedy that I have gained a turn of style or expression more correct, or at least more corrigible than in those which I have formerly written, I must, with equal pride and gratitude, ascribe it to the honour of your Lordship's admitting me into your conversation, and that of a society where everybody else was so well worthy of you, in your retirement last summer from the town, for it was immediately after that this comedy was written. If I have failed in my performance, it is only to be regretted, where there were so many not inferior either to a Scipio or a Lelius, that there should be one wanting equal to the capacity of a Terence.

If I am not mistaken, poetry is almost the only art which has not yet laid claim to your Lordship's patronage. Architecture, and painting, to the great honour of our country, have flourished under your influence and protection. In the mean time, poetry, the eldest sister of all arts, and parent of most, seems to have resigned her birthright by having neglected to pay her duty to your Lordship, and by permitting others of a later extraction to prepossess that place in your esteem to which none can pretend a better title. Poetry, in its nature, is sacred to the good and great; the relation between them is reciprocal, and they are ever propitious to it. It is the privilege of poetry to address to them, and it is their prerogative alone to give it protection.

This received maxim is a general apology for all writers who consecrate their labours to great men. But I could wish at this time that this address were exempted from the common pretence of all dedications; and that, as I can distinguish your Lordship even among the most deserving, so this offering might become remarkable by some particular instance of respect, which should assure your Lordship that I am, with all due sense of your extreme worthiness and humanity,

My LORD,

Your Lordship's most obedient and most obliged humble servant,

WILL. CONGREVE.

Prologue

Spoken by Mr Betterton.

Of those few fools, who with ill stars are cursed,
Sure scribbling fools, called poets, fare the worst;
For they're a sort of fools which Fortune makes,
And after she has made 'em fools, forsakes.
With Nature's oafs 'tis quite a different case,
For Fortune favours all her idiot race;
In her own nest the cuckoo eggs we find,
O'er which she broods to hatch the changeling kind.
No portion for her own she has to spare,
So much she dotes on her adopted care.

Poets are bubbles, by the town drawn in,
Suffered at first some trifling stakes to win;
But what unequal hazards do they run!
Each time they write, they venture all they've won;
The squire that's buttered still, is sure to be undone.
This author, heretofore, has found your favour,
But pleads no merit from his past behaviour.
To build on that might prove a vain presumption,
Should grants to poets made admit resumption;
And in Parnassus he must lose his seat,
If that be found a forfeited estate.

He owns, with toil he wrought the following scenes,
But if they're naught ne'er spare him for his pains;
Damn him the more; have no commiseration
For dullness on mature deliberation.
He swears he'll not resent one hissed-off scene,
Nor, like those peevish wits, his play maintain,
Who, to assert their sense, your taste arraign.
Some plot we think he has, and some new thought;
Some humour too, no farce; but that's a fault.

Satire, he thinks, you ought not to expect;
For so reformed a town, who dares correct?
To please this time has been his sole pretence;
He'll not instruct, lest it should give offence.
Should he by chance a knave or fool expose,
That hurts none here; sure here are none of those.
In short our play shall (with your leave to show it)
Give you one instance of a passive poet.
Who to your judgments yields all resignation;
So save or damn, after your own discretion.

Dramatis Personae

MEN

FAINALL, *in love with* MRS MARWOOD

MIRABELL, *in love with* MRS MILLAMANT

WITWOUD, } *followers of* MRS MILLAMANT
SIR PETULANT,

WILFULL WITWOUD, *half-brother to* WITWOUD,
  and nephew to LADY WISHFORT

WAITWELL, *servant to* MIRABELL

WOMEN

LADY WISHFORT, *enemy to* MIRABELL, *for having falsely
  pretended love to her*

MRS MILLAMANT, *a fine lady, niece to* LADY WISHFORT,
  and loves MIRABELL

MRS MARWOOD, *friend to* MR FAINALL, *and likes*
  MIRABELL

MRS FAINALL, *daughter to* LADY WISHFORT, *and wife to*
  FAINALL, *formerly friend to* MIRABELL

FOIBLE, *woman to* LADY WISHFORT

MINCING, *woman to* MRS MILLAMANT

Dancers, Footmen, and Attendants

The scene: London

The time: equal to that of the presentation

ACT ONE

A chocolate-house.

MIRABELL *and* FAINALL *rising from cards.* BETTY *waiting.*

MIRABELL. You are a fortunate man, Mr Fainall.

FAINALL. Have we done?

MIRABELL. What you please. I'll play on to entertain you.

FAINALL. No, I'll give you your revenge another time, when you are not so indifferent; you are thinking of something else now, and play too negligently. The coldness of a losing gamester lessens the pleasure of the winner. I'd no more play with a man that slighted his ill fortune, than I'd make love to a woman who undervalued the loss of her reputation.

MIRABELL. You have a taste extremely delicate, and are for refining on your pleasures.

FAINALL. Prithee, why so reserved? Something has put you out of humour.

MIRABELL. Not at all. I happen to be grave today, and you are gay; that's all.

FAINALL. Confess, Millamant and you quarrelled last night after I left you. My fair cousin has some humours that would tempt the patience of a Stoic. What, some coxcomb came in and was well received by her, while you were by?

MIRABELL. Witwoud and Petulant; and what was worse, her aunt, your wife's mother, my evil genius; or to sum up all in her own name, my old Lady Wishfort came in.

FAINALL. Oh there it is then! She has a lasting passion for you, and with reason. What, then my wife was there?

MIRABELL. Yes, and Mrs Marwood, and three or four more whom I never saw before. Seeing me, they all put on their grave faces, whispered one another; then complained aloud of the vapours, and after fell into a profound silence.

FAINALL. They had a mind to be rid of you.

MIRABELL. For which reason I resolved not to stir. At last the good old lady broke through her painful taciturnity with an invective against long visits. I would not have understood her, but Millamant joining in the argument, I rose and with a constrained smile told her, I thought nothing was so easy as to know when a visit began to be troublesome. She reddened and I withdrew, without expecting her reply.

FAINALL. You were to blame to resent what she spoke only in compliance with her aunt.

MIRABELL. She is more mistress of herself than to be under the necessity of such a resignation.

FAINALL. What? Though half her fortune depends upon her marrying with my lady's approbation?

MIRABELL. I was then in such a humour that I should have been better pleased if she had been less discreet.

FAINALL. Now I remember, I wonder not they were weary of you; last night was one of their cabal nights; they have 'em three times a week, and meet by turns at one another's apartments, where they come together like the coroner's inquest, to sit upon the murdered reputations of the week. You and I are excluded; and it was once proposed that all the male sex should be excepted; but somebody moved that to avoid scandal there might be one man of the community; upon which motion Witwoud and Petulant were enrolled members.

MIRABELL. And who may have been the foundress of this sect? My Lady Wishfort, I warrant, who publishes her detestation of mankind, and full of the vigour of fifty-five, declares for a friend and ratafia, and let posterity shift for itself, she'll breed no more.

FAINALL. The discovery of your sham addresses to her, to conceal your love to her niece, has provoked this separation. Had you dissembled better, things might have continued in the state of nature.

MIRABELL. I did as much as man could, with any reasonable conscience; I proceeded to the very last act of flattery with her, and was guilty of a song in her commendation. Nay, I got a friend to put her into a lampoon, and compliment her with the imputation of an affair with a young fellow, which I carried so far that I told her the malicious town took notice that she had grown fat of a sudden; and when she lay in of a dropsy, persuaded her she was reported to be in labour. The devil's in't, if an old woman is to be flattered further, unless a man should endeavour downright personally to debauch her; and that my virtue forbad me. But for the discovery of that amour I am indebted to your friend, or your wife's friend, Mrs Marwood.

FAINALL. What should provoke her to be your enemy, without she has made you advances which you have slighted? Women do not easily forgive omissions of that nature.

MIRABELL. She was always civil to me till of late. I confess I am not one of those coxcombs who are apt to interpret a woman's good manners to her prejudice, and think that she who does not refuse 'em everything, can refuse 'em nothing.

FAINALL. You are a gallant man, Mirabell; and though you may have cruelty enough not to satisfy a lady's longing, you have too much generosity not to be tender of her honour. Yet you speak with an indifference which seems to be affected, and confesses you are conscious of a negligence.

MIRABELL. You pursue the argument with a distrust that seems to be unaffected, and confesses you are conscious of a concern for which the lady is more indebted to you than your wife.

FAINALL. Fie, fie, friend, if you grow censorious I must leave you. I'll look upon the gamesters in the next room.

MIRABELL. Who are they?

FAINALL. Petulant and Witwoud. (*To* BETTY.) Bring me some chocolate.

Exit.

MIRABELL. Betty, what says your clock?

BETTY. Turned of the last canonical hour, sir. (*Exit.*)

MIRABELL. How pertinently the jade answers me! (*Looking on his watch.*) Ha? almost one o'clock! Oh, y'are come —

Enter a SERVANT.

Well, is the grand affair over? You have been something tedious.

SERVANT. Sir, there's such coupling at Pancras that they stand behind one another, as 'twere in a country dance. Ours was the last couple to lead up, and no hopes appearing of dispatch, besides the parson growing hoarse, we were afraid his lungs would have failed before it came to our turn; so we drove round to Duke's Place, and there they were riveted in a trice.

MIRABELL. So, so, you are sure they are married.

SERVANT. Married and bedded, sir; I am witness.

MIRABELL. Have you the certificate?

SERVANT. Here it is, sir.

MIRABELL. Has the tailor brought Waitwell's clothes home, and the new liveries?

SERVANT. Yes, sir.

MIRABELL. That's well. Do you go home again, d'ye hear, and adjourn the consummation till farther order. Bid Waitwell shake his ears, and Dame Partlet rustle up her feathers, and meet me at one o'clock by Rosamond's

Pond, that I may see her before she returns to her lady; and as you tender your ears, be secret.

Exit SERVANT.

Re-enter FAINALL.

FAINALL. Joy of your success, Mirabell; you look pleased.

MIRABELL. Ay. I have been engaged in a matter of some sort of mirth which is not yet ripe for discovery. I am glad this is not a cabal night. I wonder, Fainall, that you who are married, and of consequence should be discreet, will suffer your wife to be of such a party.

FAINALL. Faith, I am not jealous. Besides, most who are engaged are women and relations; and for the men, they are of a kind too contemptible to give scandal.

MIRABELL. I am of another opinion. The greater the coxcomb, always the more the scandal; for a woman who is not a fool can have but one reason for associating with a man that is.

FAINALL. Are you jealous as often as you see Witwoud entertained by Millamant?

MIRABELL. Of her understanding I am, if not of her person.

FAINALL. You do her wrong; for to give her her due, she has wit.

MIRABELL. She has beauty enough to make any man think so, and complaisance enough not to contradict him who shall tell her so.

FAINALL. For a passionate lover, methinks you are a man somewhat too discerning in the failings of your mistress.

MIRABELL. And for a discerning man, somewhat too passionate a lover; for I like her with all her faults; nay, like her for her faults. Her follies are so natural, or so artful, that they become her; and those affectations which in another woman would be odious, serve but to make her more agreeable. I'll tell thee, Fainall, she once used me with that insolence, that in revenge I took her to pieces; sifted her, and separated her failings; I studied 'em, and got 'em by rote. The catalogue was so large that I was not without hopes one day or other to hate her heartily: to which end I so used myself to think of 'em that at length, contrary to my design and expectation, they gave me every hour less and less disturbance, till in a few days it became habitual to me to remember 'em without being displeased. They are now grown as familiar to me as my own frailties; and in all probability, in a little time longer I shall like 'em as well.

FAINALL. Marry her, marry her. Be half as well acquainted with her charms as you are with her defects, and my life on't, you are your own man again.

MIRABELL. Say you so?

FAINALL. Ay, ay, I have experience; I have a wife, and so forth.

Enter MESSENGER.

MESSENGER. Is one Squire Witwoud here?

BETTY. Yes; what's your business?

MESSENGER. I have a letter for him, from his brother Sir Wilfull, which I am charged to deliver into his own hands.

BETTY. He's in the next room, friend; that way.

Exit MESSENGER.

MIRABELL. What, is the chief of that noble family in town, Sir Wilfull Witwoud?

FAINALL. He is expected today. Do you know him?

MIRABELL. I have seen him. He promises to be an extraordinary person; I think you have the honour to be related to him.

FAINALL. Yes; he is half-brother to this Witwoud by a former wife, who was sister to my Lady Wishfort, my wife's mother. If you marry Millamant, you must call cousins too.

MIRABELL. I had rather be his relation than his
acquaintance.

FAINALL. He comes to town in order to equip himself for
travel.

MIRABELL. For travel! Why, the man that I mean is above
forty!

FAINALL. No matter for that; 'tis for the honour of England
that all Europe should know we have blockheads of all
ages.

MIRABELL. I wonder there is not an act of parliament to
save the credit of the nation and prohibit the exportation
of fools.

FAINALL. By no means, 'tis better as 'tis. 'Tis better to
trade with a little loss, than to be quite eaten up with
being overstocked.

MIRABELL. Pray, are the follies of this knight errant and
those of the squire his brother anything related?

FAINALL. Not at all; Witwoud grows by the knight like a
medlar grafted on a crab. One will melt in your mouth,
and t'other set your teeth on edge; one is all pulp, and
the other all core.

MIRABELL. So one will be rotten before he be ripe, and
the other will be rotten without ever being ripe at all.

FAINALL. Sir Wilfull is an odd mixture of bashfulness and
obstinacy. But when he's drunk, he's as loving as the
monster in *The Tempest*, and much after the same manner.
To give t'other his due, he has something of good nature,
and does not always want wit.

MIRABELL. Not always; but as often as his memory fails
him, and his commonplace of comparisons. He is a fool
with a good memory and some few scraps of other folks'
wit. He is one whose conversation can never be approved,
yet it is now and then to be endured. He has indeed one
good quality, he is not exceptious; for he so passionately
affects the reputation of understanding raillery, that he will

construe an affront into a jest, and call downright rudeness and ill language, satire and fire.

FAINALL. If you have a mind to finish his picture, you have an opportunity to do it at full length. Behold the original!

Enter WITWOUD.

WITWOUD. Afford me your compassion, my dears! Pity me, Fainall, Mirabell, pity me!

MIRABELL. I do, from my soul.

FAINALL. Why, what's the matter?

WITWOUD. No letters for me, Betty?

BETTY. Did not the messenger bring you one but now, sir?

WITWOUD. Ay, but no other?

BETTY. No, sir.

WITWOUD. That's hard, that's very hard. A messenger, a mule, a beast of burden, he has brought me a letter from the fool my brother, as heavy as a panegyric in a funeral sermon, or a copy of commendatory verses from one poet to another. And what's worse, 'tis as sure a forerunner of the author as an epistle dedicatory.

MIRABELL. A fool, and your brother, Witwoud!

WITWOUD. Ay, ay, my half-brother. My half-brother he is, no nearer, upon honour.

MIRABELL. Then 'tis possible he may be but half a fool.

WITWOUD. Good, good, Mirabell *le drôle*! Good, good, hang him, don't let's talk of him. Fainall, how does your lady? Gad, I say anything in the world to get this fellow out of my head. I beg pardon that I should ask a man of pleasure and the town, a question at once so foreign and domestic. But I talk like an old maid at a marriage, I don't know what I say; but she's the best woman in the world.

FAINALL. 'Tis well you don't know what you say, or else your commendation would go near to make me either vain or jealous.

WITWOUD. No man in town lives well with a wife but Fainall. Your judgment, Mirabell?

MIRABELL. You had better step and ask his wife if you would be credibly informed.

WITWOUD. Mirabell.

MIRABELL. Ay.

WITWOUD. My dear, I ask ten thousand pardons. Gad, I have forgot what I was going to say to you.

MIRABELL. I thank you heartily, heartily.

WITWOUD. No, but prithee excuse me; my memory is such a memory.

MIRABELL. Have a care of such apologies, Witwoud; for I never knew a fool but he affected to complain either of the spleen or his memory.

FAINALL. What have you done with Petulant?

WITWOUD. He's reckoning his money – my money it was. I have no luck today.

FAINALL. You may allow him to win of you at play, for you are sure to be too hard for him at repartee; since you monopolise the wit that is between you, the fortune must be his of course.

MIRABELL. I don't find that Petulant confesses the superiority of wit to be your talent, Witwoud.

WITWOUD. Come, come, you are malicious now, and would breed debates. Petulant's my friend, and a very honest fellow, and a very pretty fellow, and has a smattering – faith and troth, a pretty deal of an odd sort of a small wit. Nay, I'll do him justice. I'm his friend, I won't wrong him neither. And if he had but any judgment in the world, he would not be altogether contemptible. Come come, don't detract from the merits of my friend.

FAINALL. You don't take your friend to be over-nicely bred?

WITWOUD. No, no, hang him, the rogue has no manners at all, that I must own. No more breeding than a bumbaily, that I grant you. 'Tis pity, faith; the fellow has fire and life.

MIRABELL. What, courage?

WITWOUD. Hum, faith, I don't know as to that; I can't say as to that. Yes, faith, in a controversy he'll contradict anybody.

MIRABELL. Though 'twere a man whom he feared, or a woman whom he loved.

WITWOUD. Well, well, he does not always think before he speaks; we have all our failings. You are too hard upon him, you are, faith. Let me excuse him; I can defend most of his faults, except one or two. One he has, that's the truth on't, if he were my brother, I could not acquit him. That, indeed, I could wish were otherwise.

MIRABELL. Ay, marry, what's that, Witwoud?

WITWOUD. O, pardon me. Expose the infirmities of my friend? No, my dear, excuse me there.

FAINALL. What, I warrant he's unsincere, or 'tis some such trifle.

WITWOUD. No, no, what if he be? 'Tis no matter for that; his wit will excuse that. A wit should no more be sincere than a woman constant. One argues a decay of parts, as t'other of beauty.

MIRABELL. Maybe you think him too positive?

WITWOUD. No, no, his being positive is an incentive to argument, and keeps up conversation.

FAINALL. Too illiterate?

WITWOUD. That! that's his happiness. His want of learning gives him the more opportunities to show his natural parts.

MIRABELL. He wants words.

WITWOUD. Ay, but I like him for that now; for his want of words gives me the pleasure very often to explain his meaning.

FAINALL. He s impudent.

WITWOUD. No; that's not it.

MIRABELL. Vain.

WITWOUD. No.

MIRABELL. What, he speaks unseasonable truths sometimes, because he has not wit enough to invent an evasion?

WITWOUD. Truths! Ha, ha, ha! No, no, since you will have it, I mean he never speaks truth at all, that's all. He will lie like a chambermaid, or a woman of quality's porter. Now that is a fault.

Enter a COACHMAN.

COACHMAN. Is Master Petulant here, mistress?

BETTY. Yes.

COACHMAN. Three gentlewomen in the coach would speak with him.

FAINALL. O brave Petulant; three!

BETTY. I'll tell him.

COACHMAN. You must bring two dishes of chocolate and a glass of cinnamon water.

Exit BETTY *and* COACHMAN.

WITWOUD. That should be for two fasting strumpets, and a bawd troubled with wind. Now you may know what the three are.

MIRABELL. You are very free with your friend's acquaintance.

WITWOUD. Ay, ay, friendship without freedom is as dull as love without enjoyment, or wine without toasting. But to tell you a secret, these are trulls that he allows coach-hire, and something more, by the week, to call on him once a day at public places.

MIRABELL. How!

WITWOUD. You shall see he won't go to 'em because there's no more company here to take notice of him. Why this is nothing to what he used to do; before he found out this way, I have known him call for himself.

FAINALL. Call for himself? What dost thou mean?

WITWOUD. Mean, why he would slip you out of this chocolate-house, just when you had been talking to him; as soon as your back was turned – whip, he was gone. Then trip to his lodging, clap on a hood and scarf and mask, slap into a hackney-coach, and drive hither to the door again in a trice, where he would send in for himself, that I mean, call for himself, wait for himself, nay, and what's more, not finding himself, sometimes leave a letter for himself.

MIRABELL. I confess this is something extraordinary. I believe he waits for himself now, he is so long à-coming. Oh, I ask his pardon.

Enter PETULANT.

BETTY. Sir, the coach stays.

PETULANT. Well, well, I come. 'Sbud, a man had as good be a professed midwife as a professed whoremaster at this rate! To be knocked up and raised at all hours, and in all places. Pox on 'em, I won't come. D'ye hear, tell 'em I won't come. Let 'em snivel and cry their hearts out.

FAINALL. You are very cruel, Petulant.

PETULANT. All's one, let it pass. I have a humour to be cruel.

MIRABELL. I hope they are not persons of condition that you use at this rate.

PETULANT. Condition? Condition's a dried fig, if I am not in humour. By this hand, if they were your – a – a – your what-d'ye-call-'ems themselves, they must wait or rub off, if I want appetite.

MIRABELL. What-d'ye-call-'ems! What are they, Witwoud?

WITWOUD. Empresses, my dear; by your what-d'ye-call-'ems he means Sultana queens.

PETULANT. Ay, Roxolanas.

MIRABELL. Cry you mercy.

FAINALL. Witwoud says they are

PETULANT. What does he say th'are?

WITWOUD. I? Fine ladies, I say.

PETULANT. Pass on, Witwoud. Harkee, by this light his relations: two co-heiresses his cousins, and an old aunt that loves caterwauling better than a conventicle.

WITWOUD. Ha, ha, ha! I had a mind to see how the rogue would come off. Ha, ha, ha! Gad, I can't be angry with him, if he said they were my mother and my sisters.

MIRABELL. No!

WITWOUD. No; the rogue's wit and readiness of invention charm me; dear Petulant!

BETTY. They are gone, sir, in great anger.

PETULANT. Enough, let 'em trundle. Anger helps complexion, saves paint.

FAINALL. This continence is all dissembled; this is in order to have something to brag of the next time he makes court to Millamant, and swear he has abandoned the whole sex for her sake.

MIRABELL. Have you not left your impudent pretensions there yet? I shall cut your throat sometime or other, Petulant, about that business.

PETULANT. Ay, ay, let that pass. There are other throats to be cut –

MIRABELL. Meaning mine, sir?

PETULANT. Not I – I mean nobody – I know nothing. But there are uncles and nephews in the world, and they may be rivals – what then? All's one for that.

MIRABELL. How! Harkee Petulant, come hither. Explain, or I shall call your interpreter.

PETULANT. Explain? I know nothing. Why, you have an uncle, have you not, lately come to town, and lodges by my Lady Wishfort's?

MIRABELL. True.

PETULANT. Why, that's enough. You and he are not friends; and if he should marry and have a child, you may be disinherited, ha?

MIRABELL. Where hast thou stumbled upon all this truth?

PETULANT. All's one for that. Why then, say I know something.

MIRABELL. Come, thou art an honest fellow, Petulant, and shalt make love to my mistress, thou shalt, i'faith. What hast thou heard of my uncle?

PETULANT. I? Nothing I. If throats are to be cut, let swords clash. Snug's the word; I shrug and am silent.

MIRABELL. O raillery, raillery. Come, I know thou art in the women's secrets. What, you're a cabalist; I know you stayed at Millamant's last night, after I went. Was there any mention made of my uncle, or me? Tell me. If thou hadst but good nature equal to thy wit, Petulant, Tony Witwoud, who is now thy competitor in fame, would show as dim by thee as a dead whiting's eye by a pearl of orient. He would no more be seen by thee than Mercury is by the sun. Come, I'm sure thou wilt tell me.

PETULANT. If I do, will you grant me common sense then, for the future?

MIRABELL. Faith, I'll do what I can for thee; and I'll pray that heaven may grant it thee in the meantime.

PETULANT. Well, harkee .

MIRABELL *and* PETULANT *talk apart.*

FAINALL. Petulant and you both will find Mirabell as warm a rival as a lover.

WITWOUD. Pshaw! pshaw! That she laughs at Petulant is plain. And for my part, but that it is almost a fashion to admire her, I should. Harkee, to tell you a secret, but let it go no further – between friends, I shall never break my heart for her.

FAINALL. How!

WITWOUD. She's handsome; but she's a sort of an uncertain woman.

FAINALL. I thought you had died for her.

WITWOUD. Umh – no –

FAINALL. She has wit.

WITWOUD. 'Tis what she will hardly allow anybody else. Now, demme, I should hate that, if she were as handsome as Cleopatra. Mirabell is not so sure of her as he thinks for.

FAINALL. Why do you think so?

WITWOUD. We stayed pretty late there last night, and heard something of an uncle to Mirabell, who is lately come to town, and is between him and the best part of his estate. Mirabell and he are at some distance, as my Lady Wishfort has been told; and you know she hates Mirabell worse than a Quaker hates a parrot, or than a fishmonger hates a hard frost. Whether this uncle has seen Mrs Millamant or not, I cannot say; but there were items of such a treaty being in embryo, and if it should come to life, poor Mirabell would be in some sort unfortunately fobbed, i'faith.

FAINALL. 'Tis impossible Millamant should hearken to it.

WITWOUD. Faith, my dear, I can't tell; she's a woman, and a kind of a humorist.

MIRABELL. And this is the sum of what you could collect last night?

PETULANT. The quintessence. Maybe Witwoud knows
more; he stayed longer. Besides, they never mind him;
they say anything before him.

MIRABELL. I thought you had been the greatest favourite.

PETULANT. Ay, *tête à tête*, but not in public, because I make
remarks.

MIRABELL. Do you?

PETULANT. Ay, ay, pox, I'm malicious, man. Now he's soft
you know; they are not in awe of him. The fellow's well-
bred; he's what you call a – what-d'ye-call-'em – a fine
gentleman; but he's silly withal.

MIRABELL. I thank you, I know as much as my curiosity
requires. Fainall, are you for the Mall?

FAINALL. Ay, I'll take a turn before dinner.

WITWOUD. Ay, we'll all walk in the park; the ladies talked
of being there.

MIRABELL. l thought you were obliged to watch for your
brother Sir Wilfull's arrival.

WITWOUD. No, no, he comes to his aunt's, my Lady
Wishfort. Pox on him, I shall be troubled with him too;
what shall I do with the fool?

PETULANT. Beg him for his estate, that I may beg you
afterwards, and so have but one trouble with you both.

WITWOUD. O rare Petulant! Thou art as quick as a fire in
a frosty morning; thou shalt to the Mall with us, and we'll
be very severe.

PETULANT. Enough. I'm in a humour to be severe.

MIRABELL. Are you? Pray then walk by yourselves – let
not us be accessory to your putting the ladies out of
countenance with your senseless ribaldry, which you roar
out aloud as often as they pass by you; and when you
have made a handsome woman blush, then you think you
have been severe.

PETULANT. What, what? Then let 'em either show their innocence by not understanding what they hear, or else show their discretion by not hearing what they would not be thought to understand.

MIRABELL. But hast not thou then sense enough to know that thou ought'st to be most ashamed thyself, when thou hast put another out of countenance?

PETULANT. Not I, by this hand. I always take blushing either for a sign of guilt, or ill breeding.

MIRABELL. I confess you ought to think so. You are in the right, that you may plead the error of your judgment in defence of your practice.

Where modesty's ill manners, 'tis but fit

That impudence and malice pass for wit.

Exeunt.

ACT TWO

St James's Park.

Enter MRS FAINALL *and* MRS MARWOOD.

MRS FAINALL. Ay, ay, dear Marwood, if we will be happy, we must find the means in ourselves, and among ourselves. Men are ever in extremes, either doting or averse. While they are lovers, if they have fire and sense, their jealousies are insupportable; and when they cease to love (we ought to think at least) they loathe. They look upon us with horror and distaste; they meet us like the ghosts of what we were, and as such fly from us.

MRS MARWOOD. True, 'tis an unhappy circumstance of life, that love should ever die before us; and that the man so often should outlive the lover. But say what you will, 'tis better to be left than never to have been loved. To pass our youth in dull indifference, to refuse the sweets of life because they once must leave us, is as preposterous as to wish to have been born old, because we one day must be old. For my part, my youth may wear and waste, but it shall never rust in my possession.

MRS FAINALL. Then it seems you dissemble an aversion to mankind, only in compliance with my mother's humour.

MRS MARWOOD. Certainly. To be free, I have no taste of those insipid dry discourses with which our sex of force must entertain themselves apart from men. We may affect endearments to each other, profess eternal friendships, and seem to dote like lovers; but 'tis not in our natures long to persevere. Love will resume his empire in our breasts, and every heart, or soon or late, receive and readmit him as its lawful tyrant.

MRS FAINALL. Bless me, how have I been deceived! Why, you profess a libertine!

MRS MARWOOD. You see my friendship by my freedom. Come, be as sincere, acknowledge that your sentiments agree with mine.

MRS FAINALL. Never.

MRS MARWOOD. You hate mankind?

MRS FAINALL. Heartily, inveterately.

MRS MARWOOD. Your husband?

MRS FAINALL. Most transcendently. Ay, though I say it, meritoriously.

MRS MARWOOD. Give me your hand upon it.

MRS FAINALL. There.

MRS MARWOOD. I join with you; what I have said has been to try you.

MRS FAINALL. Is it possible? Dost thou hate those vipers, men?

MRS MARWOOD. I have done hating em, and am now come to despise 'em; the next thing I have to do, is eternally to forget 'em.

MRS FAINALL. There spoke the spirit of an Amazon, a Penthesilea.

MRS MARWOOD. And yet I am thinking sometimes to carry my aversion further.

MRS FAINALL. How?

MRS MARWOOD. Faith, by marrying; if I could but find one that loved me very well and would be thoroughly sensible of ill usage, I think I should do myself the violence of undergoing the ceremony.

MRS FAINALL. You would not make him a cuckold?

MRS MARWOOD. No; but I'd make him believe I did, and that's as bad.

MRS FAINALL. Why, had not you as good do it?

MRS MARWOOD. Oh, if he should ever discover it, he would then know the worst, and be out of his pain; but I would have him ever to continue upon the rack of fear and jealousy.

MRS FAINALL. Ingenious mischief! Would thou wert married to Mirabell.

MRS MARWOOD. Would I were.

MRS FAINALL. You change colour.

MRS MARWOOD. Because I hate him.

MRS FAINALL. So do I; but I can hear him named. But what reason have you to hate him in particular?

MRS MARWOOD. I never loved him; he is, and always was, insufferably proud.

MRS FAINALL. By the reason you give for your aversion, one would think it dissembled; for you have laid a fault to his charge of which his enemies must acquit him.

MRS MARWOOD. Oh, then it seems you are one of his favourable enemies. Methinks you look a little pale, and now you flush again.

MRS FAINALL. Do I? I think I am a little sick o' the sudden.

MRS MARWOOD. What ails you?

MRS FAINALL. My husband. Don't you see him? He turned short upon me unawares, and has almost overcome me.

Enter FAINALL *and* MIRABELL.

MRS MARWOOD. Ha, ha, ha; he comes opportunely for you.

MRS FAINALL. For you, for he has brought Mirabell with him.

FAINALL. My dear.

MRS FAINALL. My soul.

FAINALL. You don't look well today, child.

MRS FAINALL. D'ye think so?

MIRABELL. He is the only man that does, madam.

MRS FAINALL. The only man that would tell me so at least; and the only man from whom I could hear it without mortification.

FAINALL. Oh, my dear, I am satisfied of your tenderness; I know you cannot resent anything from me; especially what is an effect of my concern.

MRS FAINALL. Mr Mirabell, my mother interrupted you in a pleasant relation last night; I would fain hear it out.

MIRABELL. The persons concerned in that affair have yet a tolerable reputation; I am afraid Mr Fainall will be censorious.

MRS FAINALL. He has a humour more prevailing than his curiosity and will willingly dispense with the hearing of one scandalous story, to avoid giving an occasion to make another by being seen to walk with his wife. This way Mr Mirabell, and I dare promise you will oblige us both.

Exeunt MRS FAINALL *and* MIRABELL.

FAINALL. Excellent creature! Well sure if I should live to be rid of my wife, I should be a miserable man.

MRS MARWOOD. Ay!

FAINALL. For having only that one hope, the accomplishment of it, of consequence, must put an end to all my hopes; and what a wretch is he who must survive his hopes! Nothing remains when that day comes, but to sit down and weep like Alexander, when he wanted other worlds to conquer.

MRS MARWOOD. Will you not follow 'em?

FAINALL. Faith, I think not.

MRS MARWOOD. Pray let us; I have a reason.

FAINALL. You are not jealous?

MRS MARWOOD. Of whom?

FAINALL. Of Mirabell.

MRS MARWOOD. If I am, is it inconsistent with my love
to you that I am tender of your honour?

FAINALL. You would intimate then, as if there were a
fellow-feeling between my wife and him.

MRS MARWOOD. I think she does not hate him to that
degree she would be thought.

FAINALL. But he, I fear, is too insensible.

MRS MARWOOD. It may be you are deceived.

FAINALL. It may be so. I do now begin to apprehend it.

MRS MARWOOD. What?

FAINALL. That I have been deceived madam, and you are
false.

MRS MARWOOD. That I am false! What mean you?

FAINALL. To let you know I see through all your little arts.
Come, you both love him, and both have equally
dissembled your aversion. Your mutual jealousies of one
another have made you clash till you have both struck
fire. I have seen the warm confession reddening on your
cheeks and sparkling from your eyes.

MRS MARWOOD. You do me wrong.

FAINALL. I do not. 'Twas for my ease to oversee and
wilfully neglect the gross advances made him by my wife;
that by permitting her to be engaged, I might continue
unsuspected in my pleasures, and take you oftener to my
arms in full security. But could you think, because the
nodding husband would not wake, that e'er the watchful
lover slept?

MRS MARWOOD. And wherewithal can you reproach me?

FAINALL. With infidelity, with loving of another, with love
of Mirabell.

MRS MARWOOD. 'Tis false. I challenge you to show an instance that can confirm your groundless accusation. I hate him.

FAINALL. And wherefore do you hate him? He is insensible, and your resentment follows his neglect. An instance? The injuries you have done him are a proof: your interposing in his love. What cause had you to make discoveries of his pretended passion? To undeceive the credulous aunt, and be the officious obstacle of his match with Millamant?

MRS MARWOOD. My obligations to my lady urged me. I had professed a friendship to her, and could not see her easy nature so abused by that dissembler.

FAINALL. What, was it conscience then? Professed a friendship! Oh the pious friendships of the female sex!

MRS MARWOOD. More tender, more sincere, and more enduring than all the vain and empty vows of men, whether professing love to us, or mutual faith to one another.

FAINALL. Ha, ha, ha! You are my wife's friend too.

MRS MARWOOD. Shame and ingratitude! Do you reproach me? You, you upbraid me! Have I been false to her through strict fidelity to you, and sacrificed my friendship to keep my love inviolate? And have you the baseness to charge me with the guilts unmindful of the merit! To you it should be meritorious that I have been vicious. And do you reflect that guilt upon me, which should lie buried in your bosom?

FAINALL. You misinterpret my reproof. I meant but to remind you of the slight account you once could make of strictest ties, when set in competition with your love to me.

MRS MARWOOD. 'Tis false, you urged it with deliberate malice. 'Twas spoke in scorn, and I never will forgive it.

FAINALL. Your guilt, not your resentment, begets your rage. If yet you loved, you could forgive a jealousy; but you are stung to find you are discovered.

MRS MARWOOD. It shall be all discovered. You too shall be discovered. Be sure you shall. I can but be exposed. If I do it myself, I shall prevent your baseness.

FAINALL. Why, what will you do?

MRS MARWOOD. Disclose it to your wife; own what has passed between us.

FAINALL. Frenzy!

MRS MARWOOD. By all my wrongs I'll do't. I'll publish to the world the injuries you have done me, both in my fame and fortune. With both I trusted you, you bankrupt in honour, as indigent of wealth.

FAINALL. Your fame I have preserved. Your fortune has been bestowed as the prodigality of your love would have it, in pleasures which we both have shared. Yet had not you been false, I had ere this repaid it. 'Tis true! Had you permitted Mirabell with Millamant to have stolen their marriage, my lady had been incensed beyond all means of reconcilement; Millamant had forfeited the moiety of her fortune, which then would have descended to my wife. And wherefore did I marry, but to make lawful prize of a rich widow's wealth, and squander it on love and you?

MRS MARWOOD. Deceit and frivolous pretence.

FAINALL. Death, am I not married? What's pretence? Am I not imprisoned, fettered? Have I not a wife? Nay a wife that was a widow, a young widow, a handsome widow; and would be again a widow, but that I have a heart of proof, and something of a constitution to bustle through the ways of wedlock and this world. Will you yet be reconciled to truth and me?

MRS MARWOOD. Impossible. Truth and you are inconsistent. I hate you, and shall for ever.

FAINALL. For loving you?

MRS MARWOOD. I loathe the name of love after such usage; and next to the guilt with which you would asperse me, I scorn you most. Farewell.

FAINALL. Nay, we must not part thus.

MRS MARWOOD. Let me go.

FAINALL. Come, I'm sorry.

MRS MARWOOD. I care not, let me go. Break my hands, do! I'd leave 'em to get loose.

FAINALL. I would not hurt you for the world. Have I no other hold to keep you here?

MRS MARWOOD. Well, I have deserved it all.

FAINALL. You know I love you.

MRS MARWOOD. Poor dissembling! Oh, that – well, it is not yet –

FAINALL. What? What is it not? What is it not yet? It is not yet too late

MRS MARWOOD. No, it is not yet too late – I have that comfort.

FAINALL. It is, to love another.

MRS MARWOOD. But not to loathe, detest, abhor mankind, myself, and the whole treacherous world.

FAINALL. Nay, this is extravagance. Come, I ask your pardon. No tears. I was to blame; I could not love you and be easy in my doubts. Pray, forbear. I believe you; I'm convinced I've done you wrong, and any way, every way, will make amends. I'll hate my wife yet more, damn her. I'll part with her, rob her of all she's worth, and we'll retire somewhere, anywhere, to another world. I'll marry thee; be pacified. 'Sdeath, they come; hide your face, your tears. You have a mask; wear it a moment. This way, this way. Be persuaded.

Exeunt.

Enter MIRABELL *and* MRS FAINALL.

MRS FAINALL. They are here yet.

MIRABELL. They are turning into the other walk.

MRS FAINALL. While I only hated my husband, I could bear to see him; but since I have despised him, he's too offensive.

MIRABELL. Oh, you should hate with prudence.

MRS FAINALL. Yes, for I have loved with indiscretion.

MIRABELL. You should have just so much disgust for your husband as may be sufficient to make you relish your lover.

MRS FAINALL. You have been the cause that I have loved without bounds, and would you set limits to that aversion of which you have been the occasion? Why did you make me marry this man?

MIRABELL. Why do we daily commit disagreeable and dangerous actions? To save that idol, reputation. If the familiarities of our loves had produced that consequence of which you were apprehensive, where could you have fixed a father's name with credit, but on a husband? I knew Fainall to be a man lavish of his morals, an interested and professing friend, a false and a designing lover; yet one whose wit and outward fair behaviour have gained a reputation with the town enough to make that woman stand excused who has suffered herself to be won by his addresses. A better man ought not to have been sacrificed to the occasion; a worse had not answered to the purpose. When you are weary of him, you know your remedy.

MRS FAINALL. I ought to stand in some degree of credit with you, Mirabell.

MIRABELL. In justice to you, I have made you privy to my whole design, and put it in your power to ruin or advance my fortune.

MRS FAINALL. Whom have you instructed to represent your pretended uncle?

MIRABELL. Waitwell, my servant.

MRS FAINALL. He is an humble servant to Foible, my mother's woman, and may win her to your interest.

MIRABELL. Care is taken for that – she is won and worn by this time. They were married this morning.

MRS FAINALL. Who?

MIRABELL. Waitwell and Foible. I would not tempt my servant to betray me by trusting him too far. If your mother, in hopes to ruin me, should consent to marry my pretended uncle, he might, like Mosca in *The Fox*, stand upon terms; so I made him sure beforehand.

MRS FAINALL. So, if my poor mother is caught in a contract, you will discover the imposture betimes, and release her by producing a certificate of her gallant's former marriage.

MIRABELL. Yes, upon condition she consent to my marriage with her niece, and surrender the moiety of her fortune in her possession.

MRS FAINALL. She talked last night of endeavouring at a match between Millamant and your uncle.

MIRABELL. That was by Foible's direction, and my instruction, that she might seem to carry it more privately.

MRS FAINALL. Well, I have an opinion of your success, for I believe my lady will do anything to get a husband; and when she has this, which you have provided for her, I suppose she will submit to anything to get rid of him.

MIRABELL. Yes, I think the good lady would marry anything that resembled a man, though 'twere no more than what a butler could pinch out of a napkin.

MRS FAINALL. Female frailty! We must all come to it, if we live to be old, and feel the craving of a false appetite when the true is decayed.

MIRABELL. An old woman's appetite is depraved like that of a girl. 'Tis the green sickness of a second childhood, and, like the faint offer of a latter spring, serves but to usher in the fall, and withers in an affected bloom.

MRS FAINALL. Here's your mistress.

Enter MRS MILLAMANT, WITWOUD, *and* MINCING.

MIRABELL. Here she comes, i'faith, full sail, with her fan spread and her streamers out, and a shoal of fools for tenders. Ha, no, I cry her mercy.

MRS FAINALL. I see but one poor empty sculler, and he tows her woman after him.

MIRABELL. You seem to be unattended, madam. You used to have the *beau monde* throng after you, and a flock of gay, fine perukes hovering round you.

WITWOUD. Like moths about a candle. I had like to have lost my comparison for want of breath.

MILLAMANT. Oh, I have denied myself airs today. I have walked as I fast through the crowd –

WITWOUD. As a favourite in disgrace; and with as few followers.

MILLAMANT. Dear Mr Witwoud, truce with your similitudes; for I am as sick of 'em –

WITWOUD. As a physician of a good air. I cannot help it madam, though 'tis against myself.

MILLAMANT. Yet again! Mincing, stand between me and his wit.

WITWOUD. Do, Mrs Mincing, like a screen before a great fire. I confess I do blaze today; I am too bright.

MRS FAINALL. But dear Millamant, why were you so long?

MILLAMANT. Long! Lord, have I not made violent haste? I have asked every living thing I met for you; I have enquired after you as after a new fashion.

WITWOUD. Madam, truce with your similitudes. No, you met her husband, and did not ask him for her.

MIRABELL. By your leave, Witwoud, that were like enquiring after an old fashion, to ask a husband for his wife.

WITWOUD. Hum; a hit, a hit, a palpable hit, I confess it.

MRS FAINALL. You were dressed before I came abroad.

MILLAMANT. Ay, that's true. Oh, but then I had –
Mincing, what had I? Why was I so long?

MINCING. Oh mem, your la'ship stayed to peruse a
pecquet of letters.

MILLAMANT. Oh, ay, letters – I had letters – I am
persecuted with letters – I hate letters. Nobody knows
how to write letters; and yet one has 'em, one does not
know why. They serve one to pin up one's hair.

WITWOUD. Is that the way? Pray madam, do you pin up
your hair with all your letters? I find I must keep copies.

MILLAMANT. Only with those in verse, Mr Witwoud. I
never pin up my hair with prose. I fancy one's hair would
not curl if it were pinned up with prose. I think I tried
once, Mincing.

MINCING. Oh mem, I shall never forget it.

MILLAMANT. Ay, poor Mincing tift and tift all the
morning.

MINCING. Till I had the cremp in my fingers I'll vow,
mem. And all to no purpose. But when your la'ship pins
it up with poetry, it sits so pleasant the next day as
anything, and is so pure and so crips.

WITWOUD. Indeed, so crips?

MINCING. You're such a critic Mr Witwoud.

MILLAMANT. Mirabell, did not you take exceptions last
night? Oh, ay, and went away. Now I think on't, I'm
angry. No, now I think on't I'm pleased, for I believe I
gave you some pain.

MIRABELL. Does that please you?

MILLAMANT. Infinitely; I love to give pain.

MIRABELL. You would affect a cruelty which is not in your
nature; your true vanity is in the power of pleasing.

MILLAMANT. Oh, I ask your pardon for that. One's
cruelty is one's power, and when one parts with one's
cruelty, one parts with one's power; and when one has
parted with that, I fancy one's old and ugly.

MIRABELL. Ay, ay, suffer your cruelty to ruin the object of
your power, to destroy your lover and then how vain,
how lost a thing you'll be! Nay, 'tis true: you are no
longer handsome when you've lost your lover; your beauty
dies upon the instant. For beauty is the lover's gift; 'tis he
bestows your charms, your glass is all a cheat. The ugly
and the old, whom the looking-glass mortifies, yet after
commendation can be flattered by it, and discover beauties
in it; for that reflects our praises, rather than your face.

MILLAMANT. Oh, the vanity of these men! Fainall, d'ye
hear him? If they did not commend us, we were not
handsome! Now you must know they could not commend
one, if one was not handsome. Beauty the lover's gift –
Lord, what is a lover, that it can give? Why, one makes
lovers as fast as one pleases, and they live as long as one
pleases, and they die as soon as one pleases; and then, if
one pleases, one makes more.

WITWOUD. Very pretty. Why, you make no more of
making of lovers, madam, than of making so many card-
matches.

MILLAMANT. One no more owes one's beauty to a lover,
than one's wit to an echo. They can but reflect what we
look and say; vain empty things if we are silent or unseen,
and want a being.

MIRABELL. Yet to those two vain empty things you owe
two of the greatest pleasures of your life.

MILLAMANT. How so?

MIRABELL. To your lover you owe the pleasure of hearing
yourselves praised; and to an echo the pleasure of hearing
yourselves talk.

WITWOUD. But I know a lady that loves talking so
incessantly she won't give an echo fair play; she has that

everlasting rotation of tongue, that an echo must wait till she dies before it can catch her last words.

MILLAMANT. Oh, fiction! Fainall, let us leave these men.

MIRABELL (*aside to* MRS FAINALL). Draw off Witwoud.

MRS FAINALL. Immediately. I have a word or two for Mr Witwoud.

MIRABELL. I would beg a little private audience too –

Exit WITWOUD *and* MRS FAINALL.

You had the tyranny to deny me last night, though you knew I came to impart a secret to you that concerned my love.

MILLAMANT. You saw I was engaged.

MIRABELL. Unkind. You had the leisure to entertain a herd of fools; things who visit you from their excessive idleness, bestowing on your easiness that time which is the encumbrance of their lives. How can you find delight in such society? It is impossible they should admire you; they are not capable. Or if they were, it should be to you as a mortification; for sure, to please a fool is some degree of folly.

MILLAMANT. I please myself. Besides, sometimes to converse with fools is for my health.

MIRABELL. Your health! Is there a worse disease than the conversation of fools?

MILLAMANT. Yes, the vapours; fools are physics for it, next to assafoetida.

MIRABELL. You are not in a course of fools?

MILLAMANT. Mirabell, if you persist in this offensive freedom you'll displease me. I think I must resolve, after all, not to have you; we shan't agree.

MIRABELL. Not in our physic, it may be.

MILLAMANT. And yet our distemper in all likelihood will be the same; for we shall be sick of one another. I shan't

endure to be reprimanded, nor instructed; 'tis so dull to
act always by advice, and so tedious to be told of one's
faults − I can't bear it. Well, I won't have you Mirabell −
I'm resolved − I think − you may go. Ha, ha, ha! What
would you give, that you could help loving me?

MIRABELL. I would give something that you did not know
I could not help it.

MILLAMANT. Come, don't look grave then. Well, what do
you say to me?

MIRABELL. I say that a man may as soon make a friend
by his wit, or a fortune by his honesty, as win a woman
with plain dealing and sincerity.

MILLAMANT. Sententious Mirabell! Prithee, don't look with
that violent and inflexible wise face, like Solomon at the
dividing of the child in an old tapestry hanging.

MIRABELL. You are merry, madam, but I would persuade
you for one moment to be serious.

MILLAMANT. What, with that face? No, if you keep your
countenance, 'tis impossible I should hold mine. Well,
after all, there is something very moving in a lovesick
face. Ha, ha, ha! Well, I won't laugh; don't be peevish.
Heigho! Now I'll be melancholy, as melancholy as a
watchlight. Well, Mirabell, if ever you will win me, woo
me now. Nay, if you are so tedious, fare you well; I see
they are walking away.

MIRABELL. Can you not find in the variety of your
disposition one moment −

MILLAMANT. To hear you tell me that Foible's married,
and your plot like to speed? No.

MIRABELL. But how came you to know it?

MILLAMANT. Unless by the help of the devil, you can't
imagine; unless she should tell me herself. Which of the
two it may have been, I will leave you to consider; and
when you have done thinking of that, think of me.

Exit.

MIRABELL. I have something more – gone! Think of you? To think of a whirlwind, though 'twere in a whirlwind, were a case of more steady contemplation; a very tranquillity of mind and mansion. A fellow that lives in a windmill has not a more whimsical dwelling than the heart of a man that is lodged in a woman. There is no point of the compass to which they cannot tum, and by which they are not turned; and by one as well as another, for motion, not method is their occupation. To know this, and yet continue to be in love, is to be made wise from the dictates of reason, and yet persevere to play the fool by the force of instinct. Oh, here come my pair of turtles. What, billing so sweetly? Is not Valentine's day over with you yet?

Enter WAITWELL *and* FOIBLE.

Sirrah Waitwell, why sure you think you were married for your own recreation, and not for my conveniency.

WAITWELL. Your pardon, sir. With submission, we have indeed been solacing in lawful delights; but still with an eye to business, sir. I have instructed her as well as I could. If she can take your directions as readily as my instructions, sir, your affairs are in a prosperous way.

MIRABELL. Give you joy, Mrs Foible.

FOIBLE. Oh las, sir, I'm so ashamed. I'm afraid my lady has been in a thousand inquietudes for me. But I protest, sir, I made as much haste as I could.

WAITWELL. That she did indeed, sir. It was my fault that she did not make more.

MIRABELL. That I believe.

FOIBLE. But I told my lady as you instructed me, sir: that I had a prospect of seeing Sir Rowland your uncle, and that I would put her ladyship's picture in my pocket to show him; which I'll be sure to say has made him so enamoured of her beauty, that he bums with impatience to lie at her ladyship's feet and worship the original.

MIRABELL. Excellent Foible! Matrimony has made you eloquent in love.

WAITWELL. I think she has profited, sir. I think so.

FOIBLE. You have seen Madam Millamant, sir?

MIRABELL. Yes.

FOIBLE. I told her, sir, because I did not know that you might find an opportunity; she had so much company last night.

MIRABELL. Your diligence will merit more. In the meantime –

Gives money.

FOIBLE. Oh dear sir, your humble servant.

WAITWELL. Spouse.

MIRABELL. Stand off, sir, not a penny Go on and prosper, Foible; the lease shall be made good and the farm stocked, if we succeed.

FOIBLE. I don't question your generosity, sir; and you need not doubt of success. If you have no more commands, sir, I'll be gone; I'm sure my lady is at her toilet, and can't dress till I come. (*Looking out.*) Oh dear, I'm sure that was Mrs Marwood that went by in a mask; if she has seen me with you I'm sure she'll tell my lady. I'll make haste home and prevent her. Your servant, sir. B'w'y, Waitwell.

Exit FOIBLE.

WAITWELL. Sir Rowland, if you please. The jade's so pert upon her preferment she forgets herself.

MIRABELL. Come sir, will you endeavour to forget yourself, and transform into Sir Rowland?

WAITWELL. Why sir, it will be impossible I should remember myself. Married, knighted, and attended all in one day! 'Tis enough to make any man forget himself. The difficulty will be how to recover my acquaintance and familiarity with my former self, and fall from my transformation to a reformation into Waitwell. Nay, I shan't be quite the same Waitwell, neither – for now I remember me, I am married, and can't be my own man again.

Ay there's the grief; that's the sad change of life;

To lose my title, and yet keep my wife.

Exeunt.

ACT THREE

A Room in Lady Wishfort's House.

LADY WISHFORT *at her toilet,* PEG *waiting.*

LADY WISHFORT. Merciful, no news of Foible yet?

PEG. No, madam.

LADY WISHFORT. I have no more patience. If I have not
fretted myself till I am pale again, there's no veracity in
me. Fetch me the red – the red, do you hear, sweetheart?
An arrant ash colour, as I'm a person. Look you how this
wench stirs! Why dost thou not fetch me a little red?
Did'st thou not hear me, Mopus?

PEG. The red ratafia does your ladyship mean, or the cherry
brandy?

LADY WISHFORT. Ratafia, fool? No, fool. Not the ratafia,
fool – grant me patience! I mean the Spanish paper, idiot;
complexion, darling. Paint, paint, paint; dost thou
understand that, changeling, dangling thy hands like
bobbins before thee? Why dost thou not stir, puppet?
Thou wooden thing upon wires!

PEG. Lord, madam, your ladyship is so impatient. I cannot
come at the paint, madam; Mrs Foible has locked it up,
and carried the key with her.

LADY WISHFORT. A pox take you both! Fetch me the
cherry brandy then. (*Exit* PEG.) I'm as pale and as faint, I
look like Mrs Qualmsick, the curate's wife, that's always
breeding. Wench, come, come, wench, what art thou
doing? Sipping? Tasting? Save thee, dost thou not know
the bottle?

Enter PEG *with a bottle and china cup.*

PEG. Madam, I was looking for a cup.

LADY WISHFORT. A cup, save thee. And what a cup hast thou brought! Dost thou take me for a fairy, to drink out of an acorn? Why didst thou not bring thy thimble? Hast thou ne'er a brass thimble clinking in thy pocket with a bit of nutmeg? I warrant thee. Come, fill, fill. So – again. (*One knocks.*) See who that is. Set down the bottle first. Here, here, under the table. What, wouldst thou go with the bottle in thy hand like a tapster? As I'm a person, this wench has lived in an inn upon the road before she came to me, like Maritornes the Asturian in *Don Quixote*. No Foible yet?

PEG. No, madam; Mrs Marwood.

LADY WISHFORT. Oh, Marwood, let her come in. Come in, good Marwood.

Enter MRS MARWOOD.

MRS MARWOOD. I'm surprised to find your ladyship in *déshabille* at this time of day.

LADY WISHFORT. Foible's a lost thing; has been abroad since morning, and never heard of since.

MRS MARWOOD. I saw her but now, as I came masked through the park, in conference with Mirabell.

LADY WISHFORT. With Mirabell! You call my blood into my face with mentioning that traitor. She durst not have the confidence. I sent her to negotiate an affair in which if I'm detected I'm undone. If that wheedling villain has wrought upon Foible to detect me, I'm ruined. Oh my dear friend, I'm a wretch of wretches if I'm detected.

MRS MARWOOD. Oh madam, you cannot suspect Mrs Foible's integrity.

LADY WISHFORT. Oh, he carries poison in his tongue that would corrupt integrity itself. If she has given him an opportunity, she has as good as put her integrity into his hands. Ah, dear Marwood, what's integrity to an opportunity? Hark! I hear her. Go, you thing, and send

her in. (*Exit* PEG.) Dear friend, retire into my closet, that
I may examine her with more freedom. You'll pardon me,
dear friend; I can make bold with you. There are books
over the chimney – Quarles and Prynne, and the *Short
View of the Stage*, with Bunyan's works, to entertain you.

Exit MARWOOD.

Enter FOIBLE.

O Foible, where hast thou been? What hast thou been
doing?

FOIBLE. Madam, I have seen the party.

LADY WISHFORT. But what hast thou done?

FOIBLE. Nay, 'tis your ladyship has done, and are to do; I
have only promised. But a man so enamoured – so
transported! Well, here it is, all that is left; all that is not
kissed away. Well, if worshipping of pictures be a sin, poor
Sir Rowland, I say.

LADY WISHFORT. The miniature has been counted like.
But hast thou not betrayed me, Foible? Hast thou not
detected me to that faithless Mirabell? What hadst thou to
do with him in the park? Answer me, he has got nothing
out of thee?

FOIBLE (*aside*). So, the devil has been beforehand with me.
What shall I say? Alas, madam, could I help it, if I met
that confident thing? Was I in fault? If you had heard
how he used me, and all upon your ladyship's account,
I'm sure you would not suspect my fidelity. Nay, if that
had been the worst, I could have borne; but he had a
fling at your ladyship too, and then I could not hold, but
i'faith I gave him his own.

LADY WISHFORT. Me? What did the filthy fellow say?

FOIBLE. Oh madam, 'tis a shame to say what he said, with
his taunts and his fleers, tossing up his nose. 'Humh!' says
he, 'what, you are ahatching some plot,' says he, 'you are
so early abroad, or catering,' says he, 'ferreting for some
disbanded officer, I warrant. Half-pay is but thin

subsistence,' says he. 'Well, what pension does your lady propose? Let me see,' says he. 'What, she must come down pretty deep, now she's superannuated,' says he, 'and – '

LADY WISHFORT. Ods my life, I'll have him, I'll have him murdered. I'll have him poisoned. Where does he eat? I'll marry a drawer to have him poisoned in his wine. I'll send for Robin from Locket's immediately.

FOIBLE. Poison him? Poisoning's too good for him. Starve him madam, starve him; marry Sir Rowland and get him disinherited. Oh, you would bless yourself to hear what he said.

LADY WISHFORT. A villain! Superannuated!

FOIBLE. 'Humh,' says he, 'I hear you are laying designs against me too,' says he, 'and Mrs Millamant is to marry my uncle' (he does not suspect a word of your ladyship); 'but,' says he, 'I'll fit you for that, I warrant you,' says he. 'I'll hamper you for that,' says he, 'you and your old frippery too,' says he, 'I'll handle you – '

LADY WISHFORT. Audacious villain! 'handle' me, would he durst! 'Frippery? Old frippery!' Was there ever such a foul-mouthed fellow? I'll be married tomorrow, I'll be contracted tonight!

FOIBLE. The sooner the better madam.

LADY WISHFORT. Will Sir Rowland be here, sayest thou? When, Foible?

FOIBLE. Incontinently, madam. No new sheriff's wife expects the return of her husband after knighthood with that impatience in which Sir Rowland burns for the dear hour of kissing your ladyship's hands after dinner.

LADY WISHFORT. 'Frippery! Superannuated frippery!' I'll frippery the villain; I'll reduce him to frippery and rags! A tatterdemalion! I hope to see him hung with tatters, like a Long Lane penthouse or a gibbet thief. A slander-mouthed railer. I warrant the spendthrift prodigal's in debt as much as the million lottery, or the whole court upon a birthday. I'll spoil his credit with his tailor. Yes, he shall have my niece with her fortune, he shall.

FOIBLE. He! I hope to see him lodge in Ludgate first, and angle into Blackfriars for brass farthings with an old mitten.

LADY WISHFORT. Ay dear Foible; thank thee for that, dear Foible. He has put me out of all patience. I shall never recompose my features to receive Sir Rowland with any economy of face. This wretch has fretted me that I am absolutely decayed. Look, Foible.

FOIBLE. Your ladyship has frowned a little too rashly, indeed, madam. There are some cracks discernible in the white varnish.

LADY WISHFORT. Let me see the glass. Cracks, say'st thou? Why I am arrantly flayed. I look like an old peeled wall. Thou must repair me Foible, before Sir Rowland comes, or I shall never keep up to my picture.

FOIBLE. I warrant you, madam. A little art once made your picture like you, and now a little of the same art must make you like your picture. Your picture must sit for you, madam.

LADY WISHFORT. But art thou sure Sir Rowland will not fail to come? Or will a' not fail when he does come? Will he be importunate, Foible, and push? For if he should not be importunate, I shall never break decorums. I shall die with confusion, if I am forced to advance – oh no, I can never advance. I shall swoon if he should expect advances. No, I hope Sir Rowland is better bred than to put a lady to the necessity of breaking her forms. I won't be too coy neither – I won't give him despair – but a little disdain is not amiss; a little scorn is alluring.

FOIBLE. A little scorn becomes your ladyship.

LADY WISHFORT. Yes, but tenderness becomes me best – a sort of a dyingness. You see that picture has a sort of a – ha, Foible? A swimminess in the eyes. Yes, I'll look so – my niece affects it, but she wants features. Is Sir Rowland handsome? Let my toilet be removed – I'll dress above. I'll receive Sir Rowland here. Is he handsome? Don't answer me. I won't know; I'll be surprised. I'll be taken by surprise.

FOIBLE. By storm, madam. Sir Rowland's a brisk man.

LADY WISHFORT. Is he! Oh then he'll importune, if he's a brisk man. I shall save decorums if Sir Rowland importunes. I have a mortal terror at the apprehension of offending against decorums. Nothing but importunity can surmount decorums. Oh, I'm glad he's a brisk man. Let my things be removed, good Foible. (*Exit.*)

Enter MRS FAINALL.

MRS FAINALL. Oh Foible, I have been in a fright, lest I should come too late. That devil Marwood saw you in the park with Mirabell, and I'm afraid will discover it to my lady.

FOIBLE. Discover what, madam?

MRS FAINALL. Nay, nay, put not on that strange face. I am privy to the whole design, and know that Waitwell, to whom thou wert this morning married, is to personate Mirabell's uncle, and as such, winning my lady, to involve her in those difficulties from which Mirabell only must release her, by his making his conditions to have my cousin and her fortune left to her own disposal.

FOIBLE. Oh dear madam, I beg your pardon. It was not my confidence in your ladyship that was deficient; but I thought the former good correspondence between your ladyship and Mr Mirabell might have hindered his communicating this secret.

MRS FAINALL. Dear Foible, forget that.

FOIBLE. Oh dear madam, Mr Mirabell is such a sweet winning gentleman – but your ladyship is the pattern of generosity. Sweet lady, to be so good! Mr Mirabell cannot choose but be grateful. I find your ladyship has his heart still. Now, madam, I can safely tell your ladyship our success. Mrs Marwood had told my lady, but I warrant

I managed myself. I turned it all for the better. I told my
lady that Mr Mirabell railed at her. I laid horrid things to
his charge, I'll vow; and my lady is so incensed, that she'll
be contracted to Sir Rowland tonight, she says. I warrant
I worked her up, that he may have her for asking for, as
they say of a Welsh maidenhead.

MRS FAINALL. Oh rare Foible!

FOIBLE. Madam, I beg your ladyship to acquaint Mr
Mirabell of his success. I would be seen as little as
possible to speak to him. Besides, I believe Madam
Marwood watches me. She has a month's mind, but I
know Mr Mirabell can't abide her. (*Enter* FOOTMAN.)
John, remove my lady's toilet. Madam, your servant. My
lady is so impatient, I fear she'll come for me if I stay.

MRS FAINALL. I'll go with you up the back stairs, lest I
should meet her.

Exeunt.

Enter MRS MARWOOD.

MRS MARWOOD. Indeed, Mrs Engine, is it thus with you?
Are you become a go-between of this importance? Yes, I
shall watch you. Why this wench is the *passe-partout*, a very
master key to everybody's strongbox. My friend Fainall,
have you carried it so swimmingly? I thought there was
something in it; but it seems it's over with you. Your
loathing is not from a want of appetite then, but from a
surfeit. Else you could never be so cool to fall from a
principal to be an assistant; to procure for him! 'A pattern
of generosity,' that I confess. Well, Mr Fainall, you
have met with your match. Oh man, man! Woman,
woman! The devil's an ass; if I were a painter, I would
draw him like an idiot, a driveller, with a bib and bells.
Man should have his head and horns, and woman the
rest of him. Poor simple fiend! 'Madam Marwood has a
month's mind, but he can't abide her.' 'Twere better for
him you had not been his confessor in that affair, without
you could have kept his counsel closer. I shall not prove
another pattern of generosity and stalk for him, till he

takes his stand to aim at a fortune. He has not obliged
me to that with those excesses of himself; and now I'll
have none of him. Here comes the good lady, panting
ripe, with a heart full of hope and a head full of care, like
any chemist upon the day of projection.

Enter LADY WISHFORT.

LADY WISHFORT. O dear Marwood, what shall I say for
this rude forgetfulness? But my dear friend is all goodness.

MRS MARWOOD. No apologies, dear madam. I have been
very well entertained.

LADY WISHFORT. As I'm a person, I am in a very chaos
to think I should so forget myself. But I have such an olio
of affairs really I know not what to do. (*Calls.*) Foible! I
expect my nephew, Sir Wilfull, every moment too – why,
Foible – he means to travel for improvement.

MRS MARWOOD. Methinks Sir Wilfull should rather think
of marrying than travelling at his years. I hear he is
turned of forty.

LADY WISHFORT. Oh, he's in less danger of being spoiled
by his travels. I am against my nephew's marrying too
young. It will be time enough when he comes back and
has acquired discretion to choose for himself.

MRS MARWOOD. Methinks Mrs Millamant and he would
make a very fit match. He may travel afterwards. 'Tis a
thing very usual with young gentlemen.

LADY WISHFORT. I promise you I have thought on't; and
since 'tis your judgment, I'll think on't again, I assure you
I will; I value your judgment extremely. On my word, I'll
propose it.

Enter FOIBLE.

Come, come Foible, I had forgot my nephew will be here
before dinner. I must make haste.

FOIBLE. Mr Witwoud and Mr Petulant are come to dine
with your ladyship.

LADY WISHFORT. Oh dear, I can't appear till I'm
dressed. Dear Marwood, shall I be free with you again,
and beg you to entertain 'em? I'll make all imaginable
haste. Dear friend, excuse me.

Exit LADY WISHFORT *and* FOIBLE.

Enter MRS MILLAMANT *and* MINCING.

MILLAMANT. Sure never anything was so unbred as that
odious man. Marwood, your servant.

MRS MARWOOD. You have a colour; what's the matter?

MILLAMANT. That horrid fellow, Petulant, has provoked
me into a flame. I have broke my fan! Mincing, lend me
yours; is not all the powder out of my hair?

MRS MARWOOD. No. What has he done?

MILLAMANT. Nay, he has done nothing; he has only
talked. Nay, he has said nothing neither; but he has
contradicted everything that has been said. For my part, I
thought Witwoud and he would have quarrelled.

MINCING. I vow mem, I thought once they would have fit.

MILLAMANT. Well, 'tis a lamentable thing, I'll swear, that
one has not the liberty of choosing one's acquaintance as
one does one's clothes.

MRS MARWOOD. If we had the liberty, we should be as
weary of one set of acquaintance, though never so good,
as we are of one suit, though never so fine. A fool and a
doily stuff would now and then find days of grace, and be
worn for variety.

MILLAMANT. I could consent to wear 'em, if they would
wear alike, but fools never wear out – they are such
drap-du-Berry things, without one could give 'em to one's
chambermaid after a day or two.

MRS MARWOOD. 'Twere better so indeed. Or what think
you of the playhouse? A fine gay glossy fool should be
given there, like a new masking habit, after the
masquerade is over, and we have done with the disguise.

For a fool's visit is always a disguise, and never admitted
by a woman of wit but to blind her affair with a lover of
sense. If you would but appear barefaced now, and own
Mirabell, you might as easily put off Petulant and
Witwoud as your hood and scarf. And indeed 'tis time, for
the town has found it; the secret is grown too big for the
pretence. 'Tis like Mrs Primly's great belly; she may lace
it down before, but it burnishes on her hips. Indeed,
Millamant, you can no more conceal it than my Lady
Strammel can her face, that goodly face, which in
defiance of her Rhenish-wine tea, will not be
comprehended in a mask.

MILLAMANT. I'll take my death, Marwood, you are more
censorious than a decayed beauty, or a discarded toast;
Mincing, tell the men they may come up. My aunt is not
dressing; their folly is less provoking than your malice.
(*Exit* MINCING.) 'The town has found it.' What has it
found? That Mirabell loves me is no more a secret than it
is a secret that you discovered it to my aunt, or than the
reason why you discovered it is a secret.

MRS MARWOOD. You are nettled.

MILLAMANT. You're mistaken. Ridiculous!

MRS MARWOOD. Indeed my dear, you'll tear another fan
if you don't mitigate those violent airs.

MILLAMANT. Oh silly! Ha, ha, ha! I could laugh
immoderately. Poor Mirabell! His constancy to me has
quite destroyed his complaisance for all the world beside.
I swear, I never enjoined it him to be so coy. If I had the
vanity to think he would obey me, I would command him
to show more gallantry. 'Tis hardly well bred to be so
particular on one hand, and so insensible on the other. But
I despair to prevail, and so let him follow his own way.
Ha, ha, ha! Pardon me, dear creature, I must laugh, ha,
ha, ha, though I grant you 'tis a little barbarous, ha, ha, ha!

MRS MARWOOD. What pity 'tis, so much fine raillery,
and delivered with so significant gesture, should be so
unhappily directed to miscarry.

MILLAMANT. Ha? Dear creature, I ask your pardon – I swear I did not mind you.

MRS MARWOOD. Mr Mirabell and you both may think it a thing impossible, when I shall tell him, by telling you –

MILLAMANT. Oh dear, what? For it is the same thing if I hear it, ha, ha, ha!

MRS MARWOOD. That I detest him, hate him, madam.

MILLAMANT. Oh madam, why so do I – and yet the creature loves me, ha, ha, ha! How can one forbear laughing to think of it? I am a sybil if I am not amazed to think what he can see in me. I'll take my death, I think you are handsomer – and within a year or two as young. If you could but stay for me, I should overtake you – but that cannot be. Well, that thought makes me melancholy. Now I'll be sad.

MRS MARWOOD. Your merry note may be changed sooner than you think.

MILLAMANT. D'ye say so? Then I'm resolved I'll have a song to keep up my spirits.

Enter MINCING.

MINCING. The gentlemen stay but to comb, madam, and will wait on you.

MILLAMANT. Desire Mrs – , that is in the next room, to sing the song I would have learned yesterday. You shall hear it madam not that there's any great matter in it, but 'tis agreeable to my humour.

Song, set by Mr John Eccles, and sung by Mrs Hodgson.

I

Love's but the frailty of the mind,
    When 'tis not with ambition joined;
A sickly flame, which if not fed, expires;
And feeding, wastes in self-consuming fires.

II

'Tis not to wound a wanton boy
Or am'rous youth, that gives the joy;
But 'tis the glory to have pierced a swain,
For whom inferior beauties sighed in vain.

III

Then I alone the conquest prize,
When I insult a rival's eyes;
If there's delight in love, 'tis when I see
That heart which others bleed for, bleed for me.

Enter PETULANT *and* WITWOUD.

MILLAMANT. Is your animosity composed, gentlemen?

WITWOUD. Raillery, raillery, madam; we have no
animosity. We hit off a little wit now and then, but no
animosity. The falling out of wits is like the falling out of
lovers; we agree in the main, like treble and bass. Ha,
Petulant?

PETULANT. Ay, in the main – but when I have a humour
to contradict.

WITWOUD. Ay, when he has a humour to contradict, then
I contradict too. What, I know my cue. Then we
contradict one another like two battledores; for
contradictions beget one another like Jews.

PETULANT. If he says black's black, if I have a humour to
say 'tis blue, let that pass; all's one for that. If I have a
humour to prove it, it must be granted.

WITWOUD. Not positively must but it may, it may.

PETULANT. Yes, it positively must, upon proof positive.

WITWOUD. Ay, upon proof positive it must; but upon
proof presumptive it only may. That's a logical distinction
now, madam.

MRS MARWOOD. I perceive your debates are of
importance and very learnedly handled.

PETULANT. Importance is one thing, and learning's another; but a debate's a debate, that I assert.

WITWOUD. Petulant's an enemy to learning; he relies altogether on his parts.

PETULANT. No, I'm no enemy to learning; it hurts not me.

MRS MARWOOD. That's a sign indeed it's no enemy to you.

PETULANT. No, no, it's no enemy to anybody but them that have it.

MILLAMANT. Well, an illiterate man's my aversion. I wonder at the impudence of any illiterate man to offer to make love.

WITWOUD. That I confess I wonder at too.

MILLAMANT. Ah! to marry an ignorant that can hardly read or write.

PETULANT. Why should a man be ever the further from being married though he can't read, any more than he is from being hanged? The Ordinary's paid for setting the psalm, and the parish priest for reading the ceremony. And for the rest which is to follow in both cases, a man may do it without book so all's one for that.

MILLAMANT. D'ye hear the creature? Lord, here's company; I'll be gone.

Exeunt MILLAMANT *and* MINCING.

WITWOUD. In the name of Bartlemew and his fair, what have we here?

MRS MARWOOD. 'Tis your brother, I fancy. Don't you know him?

WITWOUD. Not I – yes, I think it is he – I've almost forgot him; I have not seen him since the Revolution.

Enter SIR WILFULL WITWOUD *in a country riding habit, and* SERVANT *to* LADY WISHFORT.

SERVANT. Sir, my lady's dressing. Here's company, if you please to walk in, in the mean time.

SIR WILFULL. Dressing! What, it's but morning here, I warrant with you, in London. We should count it towards afternoon in our parts, down in Shropshire. Why then, belike my aunt han't dined yet – ha, friend?

SERVANT. Your aunt, sir?

SIR WILFULL. My aunt, sir, yes my aunt, sir, and your lady, sir; your lady is my aunt, sir. Why, what, dost thou not know me, friend? Why then send somebody here that does. How long hast thou lived with thy lady, fellow, ha?

SERVANT. A week, sir; longer than anybody in the house, except my lady's woman.

SIR WILFULL. Why then, belike thou dost not know thy lady if thou seest her, ha, friend?

SERVANT. Why truly, sir, I cannot safely swear to her face in a morning, before she is dressed. 'Tis like I may give a shrewd guess at her by this time.

SIR WILFULL. Well, prithee try what thou canst do; if thou canst not guess, enquire her out, dost hear fellow? And tell her, her nephew, Sir Wilfull Witwoud, is in the house.

SERVANT. I shall, sir.

SIR WILFULL. Hold ye, hear me, friend; a word with you in your ear. Prithee who are these gallants?

SERVANT. Really sir, I can't tell; here come so many here, 'tis hard to know 'em all.

Exit SERVANT.

SIR WILFULL. Oons, this fellow knows less than a starling; I don't think a' knows his own name.

MRS MARWOOD. Mr Witwoud, your brother is not behindhand in forgetfulness; I fancy he has forgot you too.

WITWOUD. I hope so. The devil take him that remembers first, I say.

SIR WILFULL. Save you, gentlemen and lady.

MRS MARWOOD. For shame, Mr Witwoud; why won't you speak to him? And you, sir.

WITWOUD. Petulant, speak.

PETULANT. And you, sir.

SIR WILFULL. No offence, I hope. (*Salutes* MRS MARWOOD.)

MRS MARWOOD. No, sure sir.

WITWOUD. This is a vile dog, I see that already. No offence! Ha, ha, ha! To him, to him, Petulant! Smoke him.

PETULANT. It seems as if you had come a journey, sir, hem, hem. (*Surveying him round.*)

SIR WILFULL. Very likely, sir, that it may seem so.

PETULANT. No offence, I hope, sir.

WITWOUD. Smoke the boots, the boots, Petulant, the boots! Ha, ha, ha.

SIR WILFULL. Maybe not, sir; thereafter as 'tis meant, sir.

PETULANT. Sir, I presume upon the information of your boots.

SIR WILFULL. Why, 'tis like you may, sir. If you are not satisfied with the information of my boots, sir, if you will step to the stable, you may enquire further of my horse, sir!

PETULANT. Your horse, sir! Your horse is an ass, sir!

SIR WILFULL. Do you speak by way of offence, sir?

MRS MARWOOD. The gentleman's merry, that's all, sir. (*Aside.*) 'Slife, we shall have a quarrel betwixt an horse and an ass, before they find one another out. (*Aloud.*) You must not take anything amiss from your friends, sir. You are among your friends here, though it may be you don't know it. If I am not mistaken, you are Sir Wilfull Witwoud.

SIR WILFULL. Right, lady; I am Sir Wilfull Witwoud, so I write myself; no offence to anybody, I hope; and nephew to the Lady Wishfort of this mansion.

MRS MARWOOD. Don t you know this gentleman, sir?

SIR WILFULL. Hum! What, sure 'tis not − yea, by'r lady, but 'tis. 'S'heart, I know not whether 'tis or no − yea but 'tis by the Rekin. Brother Anthony! What Tony, i'faith! What, dost thou not know me? By'r Lady, nor I thee, thou art so becravatted, and beperiwigged. 'S'heart, why dost not speak? Art thou o'erjoyed?

WITWOUD. Odso, brother, is it you? Your servant, brother.

SIR WILFULL. Your servant! Why, yours, sir. Your servant again, 's'heart, and your friend and servant to that, and a (*Puff*.) and a flapdragon for your service, sir; and a hare's foot, and a hare's scut for your service, sir, an you be so cold and so courtly!

WITWOUD. No offence, I hope, brother.

SIR WILFULL. 'S'heart, sir, but there is, and much offence. A pox, is this your Inns o' Court breeding, not to know your friends and your relations, your elders, and your betters?

WITWOUD. Why, brother Wilfull of Salop, you may be as short as a Shrewsbury cake, if you please, but I tell you, 'tis not modish to know relations in town. You think you're in the country, where great lubberly brothers slobber and kiss one another when they meet, like a call of serjeants. 'Tis not the fashion here; 'tis not indeed, dear brother.

SIR WILFULL. The fashion's a fool; and you're a fop, dear brother. 'S'heart, I've suspected this. By'r Lady I conjectured you were a fop since you began to change the style of your letters, and write in a scrap of paper gilt round the edges, no broader than a subpoena. I might expect this, when you left off 'Honoured Brother', and 'hoping you are in good health', and so forth, to begin with a 'Rat me, knight, I'm so sick of a last night's debauch'; ods heart, and then tell a familiar tale of a cock and a bull, and a whore and a bottle, and so conclude. You could write news before you were out of your time, when you lived with honest Pumplenose the attorney of Furnival's Inn; you could entreat to be remembered then to your friends round the Rekin. We could have gazettes then, and *Dawk's Letter*, and the weekly bill, till of late days.

PETULANT. 'Slife, Witwoud, were you ever an attorney's clerk? Of the family of the Furnivals? Ha, ha, ha!

WITWOUD. Ay, ay, but that was for a while. Not long, not long; pshaw, I was not in my own power then. An orphan, and this fellow was my guardian; ay, ay, I was glad to consent to that man to come to London. He had the disposal of me then. If I had not agreed to that, I might have been bound 'prentice to a felt-maker in Shrewsbury; this fellow would have bound me to a maker of felts!

SIR WILFULL. 'S'heart, and better than to be bound to a maker of fops, where, I suppose, you have served your time, and now you may set up for yourself.

MRS MARWOOD. You intend to travel, sir, as I'm informed.

SIR WILFULL. Belike I may, madam. I may chance to sail upon the salt seas, if my mind hold.

PETULANT. And the wind serve.

SIR WILFULL. Serve or not serve, I shan't ask licence of you, sir; nor the weathercock your companion. I direct my discourse to the lady, sir. 'Tis like my aunt may have told you, madam. Yes, I have settled my concerns, I may say now, and am minded to see foreign parts. If and how that the peace holds, whereby, that is, taxes abate.

MRS MARWOOD. I thought you had designed for France at all adventures.

SIR WILFULL. I can't tell that; 'tis like I may, and 'tis like I may not. I am somewhat dainty in making a resolution, because when I make it I keep it. I don't stand shill I, shall I, then; if I say't, I'll do't. But I have thoughts to tarry a small matter in town, to learn somewhat of your lingo first, before I cross the seas. I'd gladly have a spice of your French, as they say, whereby to hold discourse in foreign countries.

MRS MARWOOD. Here is an academy in town for that use.

SIR WILFULL. There is? 'Tis like there may.

MRS MARWOOD. No doubt you will return very much improved.

WITWOUD. Yes, refined, like a Dutch skipper from a whale-fishing.

Enter LADY WISHFORT *and* FAINALL.

LADY WISHFORT. Nephew, you are welcome.

SIR WILFULL. Aunt, your servant.

FAINALL. Sir Wilfull, your most faithful servant.

SIR WILFULL. Cousin Fainall, give me your hand.

LADY WISHFORT. Cousin Witwoud, your servant; Mr Petulant, your servant. Nephew, you are welcome again. Will you drink anything after your journey, nephew, before you eat? Dinner's almost ready.

SIR WILFULL. I'm very well, I thank you, aunt; however, I thank you for your courteous offer. 'S'heart, I was afraid you would have been in the fashion too, and have remembered to have forgot your relations. Here's your cousin Tony, belike I mayn't call him brother for fear of offence.

LADY WISHFORT. Oh he's a rallier, nephew – my cousin's a wit, and your great wits always rally their best friends to choose. When you have been abroad, nephew, you'll understand raillery better.

FAINALL *and* MRS MARWOOD *talk apart.*

SIR WILFULL. Why then let him hold his tongue in the meantime, and rail when that day comes.

Enter MINCING.

MINCING. Mem, I come to acquaint your la'ship that dinner is impatient.

SIR WILFULL. Impatient? Why then belike it won't stay till I pull off my boots. Sweetheart, can you help me to a pair of slippers? My man's with his horses, I warrant.

LADY WISHFORT. Fie, fie, nephew, you would not pull off your boots here. Go down into the hall; dinner shall stay for you. My nephew's a little unbred; you'll pardon him, madam. Gentlemen, will you walk? Marwood?

MRS MARWOOD. I'll follow you, madam, before Sir Wilfull is ready.

MRS MARWOOD *and* FAINALL *remain*.

FAINALL. Why then, Foible's a bawd, an errant, rank, matchmaking bawd. And I, it seems, am a husband, a rank husband; and my wife a very arrant, rank wife – all in the way of the world. 'Sdeath, to be an anticipated cuckold, a cuckold in embryo! Sure I was born with budding antlers like a young satyr, or a citizen's child. 'Sdeath to be outwitted, to be out-jilted, out-matrimonied! If I had kept my speed like a stag, 'twere somewhat, but to crawl after, with my horns, like a snail, and outstripped by my wife – 'tis scurvy wedlock.

MRS MARWOOD. Then shake it off. You have often wished for an opportunity to part, and now you have it. But first, prevent their plot; the half of Millamant's fortune is too considerable to be parted with, to a foe, to Mirabell.

FAINALL. Damn him! That had been mine, had you not made that fond discovery. That had been forfeited, had they been married. My wife had added lustre to my horns by that increase of fortune; I could have worn 'em tipped with gold, though my forehead had been furnished like a deputy lieutenant's hall.

MRS MARWOOD. They may prove a cap of maintenance to you still, if you can away with your wife. And she's no worse than when you had her – I dare swear she had given up her game before she was married.

FAINALL. Hum! That may be; she might throw up her cards; but I'll be hanged if she did not put Pam in her pocket.

MRS MARWOOD. You married her to keep you; and if you can contrive to have her keep you better than you expected, why should you not keep her longer than you intended?

FAINALL. The means, the means.

MRS MARWOOD. Discover to my lady your wife's conduct; threaten to part with her. My lady loves her, and will come to any composition to save her reputation. Take the opportunity of breaking it, just upon the discovery of this imposture. My lady will be enraged beyond bounds, and sacrifice niece and fortune and all at that conjuncture. And let me alone to keep her warm; if she should flag in her part, I will not fail to prompt her.

FAINALL. Faith, this has an appearance.

MRS MARWOOD. I'm sorry I hinted to my lady to endeavour a match between Millamant and Sir Wilfull; that may be an obstacle.

FAINALL. Oh, for that matter leave me to manage him; I'll disable him for that. He will drink like a Dane; after dinner, I'll set his hand in.

MRS MARWOOD. Well, how do you stand affected towards your lady?

FAINALL. Why, faith, I'm thinking of it. Let me see. I am married already, so that's over. My wife has played the jade with me; well, that's over too. I never loved her, or if I had, why that would have been over too by this time. Jealous of her I cannot be, for I am certain; so there's an end of jealousy. Weary of her I am, and shall be. No, there's no end of that; no, no, that were too much to hope. Thus far concerning my repose. Now for my reputation. As to my own, I married not for it; so that's out of the question. And as to my part in my wife's, why she had parted with hers before; so bringing none to me, she can take none from me. 'Tis against all rule of play that I should lose to one who has not wherewithal to stake.

MRS MARWOOD. Besides, you forget, marriage is honourable.

FAINALL. Hum! Faith, and that's well thought on; marriage is honourable, as you say; and if so, wherefore should cuckoldom be a discredit, being derived from so honourable a root?

MRS MARWOOD. Nay I know not; if the root be honourable, why not the branches?

FAINALL. So, so; why this point's clear. Well, how do we proceed?

MRS MARWOOD. I will contrive a letter which shall be delivered to my lady at the time when that rascal who is to act Sir Rowland is with her. It shall come as from an unknown hand – for the less I appear to know of the truth, the better I can play the incendiary. Besides, I would not have Foible provoked if I could help it, because you know she knows some passages. Nay, I expect all will come out; but let the mine be sprung first, and then I care not if I'm discovered.

FAINALL. If the worst come to the worst, I'll turn my wife to grass. I have already a deed of settlement of the best part of her estate, which I wheedled out of her; and that you shall partake at least.

MRS MARWOOD. I hope you are convinced that I hate Mirabell now; you'll be no more jealous?

FAINALL. Jealous, no – by this kiss. Let husbands be jealous; but let the lover still believe. Or, if he doubt, let it be only to endear his pleasure and prepare the joy that follows, when he proves his mistress true. But let

husbands' doubts convert to endless jealousy; or if they
have belief let it corrupt to superstition and blind
credulity. I am single, and will herd no more with 'em.
True, I wear the badge; but I'll disown the order. And
since I take my leave of 'em, I care not if I leave 'em a
common motto to their common crest:

All husbands must or pain or shame endure;

The wise too jealous are, fools too secure.

Exeunt.

ACT FOUR

Scene continues.

Enter LADY WISHFORT *and* FOIBLE.

LADY WISHFORT. Is Sir Rowland coming, sayest thou, Foible? and are things in order?

FOIBLE. Yes madam. I have put waxlights in the sconces, and placed the footmen in a row in the hall, in their best liveries, with the coachman and postilion to fill up the equipage.

LADY WISHFORT. Have you pullvilled the coachman and postilion, that they may not stink of the stable when Sir Rowland comes by?

FOIBLE. Yes, madam.

LADY WISHFORT. And are the dancers and the music ready, that he may be entertained in all points with correspondence to his passion?

FOIBLE. All is ready, madam.

LADY WISHFORT. And – well – and how do I look, Foible?

FOIBLE. Most killing well, madam.

LADY WISHFORT. Well, and how shall I receive him? In what figure shall I give his heart the first impression? There is a great deal in the first impression. Shall I sit? No, I won't sit – I'll walk; ay, I'll walk from the door upon his entrance, and then turn full upon him. No, that will be too sudden. I'll lie – ay, I'll lie down. I'll receive him in my little dressing-room; there's a couch – yes, yes, I'll give the first impression on a couch. I won't lie neither, but loll and lean upon one elbow, with one foot a

little dangling off, jogging in a thoughtful way. Yes – and
then as soon as he appears, start, ay, start and be
surprised, and rise to meet him in a pretty disorder. Yes.
Oh, nothing is more alluring than a levée from a couch in
some confusion. It shows the foot to advantage, and
furnishes with blushes and recomposing airs beyond
comparison. Hark! There's a coach.

FOIBLE. 'Tis he, madam.

LADY WISHFORT. Oh dear, has my nephew made his
addresses to Millamant? I ordered him.

FOIBLE. Sir Wilfull is set in to drinking, madam, in the
parlour.

LADY WISHFORT. Ods my life, I'll send him to her. Call
her down, Foible; bring her hither. I'll send him as I go.
When they are together, then come to me, Foible, that I
may not be too long alone with Sir Rowland.

Exit.

Enter MRS MILLAMANT, *and* MRS FAINALL.

FOIBLE. Madam, I stayed here to tell your ladyship that Mr
Mirabell has waited this half hour for an opportunity to
talk with you, though my lady's orders were to leave you
and Sir Wilfull together. Shall I tell Mr Mirabell that you
are at leisure?

MILLAMANT. No – what would the dear man have? I am
thoughtful, and would amuse myself – bid him come
another time.

There never yet was woman made,

Nor shall, but to be curs'd.

(*Repeating and walking about.*) That's hard!

MRS FAINALL. You are very fond of Sir John Suckling
today, Millamant, and the poets.

MILLAMANT. He? Ay, and filthy verses; so I am.

FOIBLE. Sir Wilfull is coming, madam. Shall I send Mr
Mirabell away?

MILLAMANT. Ay, if you please, Foible, send him away –
or send him hither just as you will, dear Foible. I think
I'll see him; shall I? Ay, let the wretch come.

Exit FOIBLE.

Thyrsis a youth of the inspir'd train –

Repeating.

Dear Fainall, entertain Sir Wilfull. Thou hast philosophy
to undergo a fool, thou art married and hast patience. I
would confer with my own thoughts.

MRS FAINALL. I am obliged to you, that you would make
me your proxy in this affair; but I have business of my
own.

Enter SIR WILFULL.

O Sir Wilfull, you are come at the critical instant. There's
your mistress up to the ears in love and contemplation;
pursue your point, now or never.

SIR WILFULL. Yes; my aunt would have it so. I would
gladly have been encouraged with a bottle or two,
because I'm somewhat wary at first, before I am
acquainted. But I hope after a time, I shall break my
mind – that is, upon further acquaintance – so for the
present, cousin, I'll take my leave. If so be you'll be so
kind to make my excuse, I'll return to my company

This while MILLAMANT *walks about repeating to herself.*

MRS FAINALL. Oh fie, Sir Wilfull! What, you must not be
daunted.

SIR WILFULL. Daunted? No, that's not it, it is not so much
for that for if so be that I set on't, I'll do't. But only for
the present, 'tis sufficient till further acquaintance, that's
all – your servant.

MRS FAINALL. Nay, I'll swear you shall never lose so
favourable an opportunity, if I can help it. I'll leave you
together and lock the door.

Exit.

SIR WILFULL. Nay, nay cousin – I have forgot my gloves – what d'ye do? 'S'heart, a' has locked the door indeed, I think! Nay, cousin Fainall, open the door! Pshaw, what a vixen trick is this? Nay, now a' has seen me too. Cousin, I made bold to pass through as it were – I think this door's enchanted.

MILLAMANT (*repeating*).
I prithee spare me, gentle boy,
Press me no more for that slight toy.

SIR WILFULL. Anan? Cousin, your servant.

MILLAMANT. That foolish trifle of a heart –

Sir Wilfull!

SIR WILFULL. Yes – your servant. No offence I hope, cousin.

MILLAMANT (*repeating*).
I swear it will not do its part,
Tho' thou dost thine, employ'st thy power and art.
Natural, easy Suckling!

SIR WILFULL. Anan? Suckling? No such suckling neither, cousin, nor stripling; I thank heaven, I'm no minor.

MILLAMANT. Ah rustic! Ruder than Gothic.

SIR WILFULL. Well, well, I shall understand your lingo one of these days, cousin; in the meanwhile, I must answer in plain English.

MILLAMANT. Have you any business with me, Sir Wilfull?

SIR WILFULL. Not at present, cousin. Yes, I made bold to see, to come and know if that how you were disposed to fetch a walk this evening, if so be that I might not be troublesome, I would have sought a walk with you.

MILLAMANT. A walk? What then?

SIR WILFULL. Nay, nothing – only for the walk's sake, that's all.

MILLAMANT. I nauseate walking; 'tis a country diversion, I loathe the country and everything that relates to it.

SIR WILFULL. Indeed! Hah! Look ye, look ye, you do? Nay, 'tis like you may. Here are choice of pastimes here in town, as plays and the like; that must be confessed indeed.

MILLAMANT. Ah, *l'étourdie!* I hate the town too.

SIR WILFULL. Dear heart, that's much. Hah! that you should hate 'em both! Hah! 'Tis like you may; there are some can't relish the town, and others can't away with the country. 'Tis like you may be one of those, cousin.

MILLAMANT. Ha, ha, ha! Yes, 'tis like I may. You have nothing further to say to me?

SIR WILFULL. Not at present, cousin. 'Tis like when I have an opportunity to be more private, I may break my mind in some measure – I conjecture you partly guess – however, that's as time shall try; but spare to speak and spare to speed, as they say.

MILLAMANT. If it is of no great importance, Sir Wilfull, you will oblige me to leave me; I have just now a little business

SIR WILFULL. Enough, enough, cousin; yes, yes, all a case when you're disposed, when you're disposed. Now's as well as another time; and another time as well as now. All's one for that. Yes, yes, if your concerns call you, there's no haste; it will keep cold, as they say. Cousin, your servant. I think this door's locked.

MILLAMANT. You may go this way, sir.

SIR WILFULL. Your servant; then with your leave I'll return to my company. (*Exit.*)

MILLAMANT. Ay, ay; ha, ha, ha!

Like Phoebus sung the no less am'rous boy.

Enter MIRABELL.

MIRABELL.
   – Like Daphne she as lovely and as coy.

Do you lock yourself up from me, to make my search
more curious? Or is this pretty artifice contrived, to signify
that here the chase must end and my pursuit be crowned,
for you can fly no further?

MILLAMANT. Vanity! No – I'll fly and be followed to the
last moment. Though I am upon the very verge of
matrimony, I expect you should solicit me as much as if I
were wavering at the grate of a monastery, with one foot
over the threshold. I'll be solicited to the very last, nay,
and afterwards.

MIRABELL. What, after the last?

MILLAMANT. Oh, I should think I was poor and had
nothing to bestow if I were reduced to an inglorious ease,
and freed from the agreeable fatigues of solicitation.

MIRABELL. But do not you know that when favours are
conferred upon instant and tedious solicitation, that they
diminish in their value, and that both the giver loses the
grace, and the receiver lessens his pleasure?

MILLAMANT. It may be in things of common application,
but never sure in love. Oh, I hate a lover that can dare to
think he draws a moment's air independent on the bounty
of his mistress. There is not so impudent a thing in nature
as the saucy look of an assured man, confident of success.
The pedantic arrogance of a very husband has not so
pragmatical an air. Ah! I'll never marry, unless I am first
made sure of my will and pleasure.

MIRABELL. Would you have 'em both before marriage? Or
will you be contented with the first now, and stay for the
other till after grace?

MILLAMANT. Ah, don't be impertinent. My dear liberty,
shall I leave thee? My faithful solitude, my darling
contemplation, must I bid you then adieu? Ay-h adieu,
my morning thoughts, agreeable wakings, indolent
slumbers, all ye *douceurs*, ye *sommeils du matin*, adieu. I can't
do't, 'tis more than impossible. Positively Mirabell, I'll lie
abed in a morning as long as I please.

MIRABELL. Then I'll get up in a morning as early as I please.

MILLAMANT. Ah, idle creature, get up when you will – and d'ye hear, I won't be called names after I'm married; positively I won't be called names.

MIRABELL. Names!

MILLAMANT. Ay, as wife, spouse, my dear, joy, jewel, love, sweetheart, and the rest of that nauseous cant in which men and their wives are so fulsomely familiar. I shall never bear that. Good Mirabell, don't let us be familiar or fond, nor kiss before folks, like my Lady Fadler and Sir Francis; nor go to Hyde Park together the first Sunday in a new chariot, to provoke eyes and whispers, and then never to be seen there together again, as if we were proud of one another the first week, and ashamed of one another for ever after. Let us never visit together, nor go to a play together, but let us be very strange and well-bred; let us be as strange as if we had been married a great while, and as well bred as if we were not married at all.

MIRABELL. Have you any more conditions to offer? Hitherto your demands are pretty reasonable.

MILLAMANT. Trifles. As liberty to pay and receive visits to and from whom I please, to write and receive letters, without interrogatories or wry faces on your part. To wear what I please, and choose conversation with regard only to my own taste; to have no obligation upon me to converse with wits that I don't like, because they are your acquaintance, or to be intimate with fools, because they may be your relations. Come to dinner when I please; dine in my dressing-room when I'm out of humour, without giving a reason. To have my closet inviolate; to be sole empress of my tea-table, which you must never presume to approach without first asking leave. And lastly, wherever I am, you shall always knock at the door before you come in. These articles subscribed, if I continue to endure you a little longer, I may by degrees dwindle into a wife.

MIRABELL. Your bill of fare is something advanced in this latter account. Well, have I liberty to offer conditions – that when you are dwindled into a wife, I may not be beyond measure enlarged into a husband?

MILLAMANT. You have free leave; propose your utmost, speak and spare not.

MIRABELL. I thank you. *Inprimis* then, I covenant that your acquaintance be general; that you admit no sworn confidante, or intimate of your own sex; no she-friend to screen her affairs under your countenance and tempt you to make trial of a mutual secrecy. No decoy duck to wheedle you a fop, scrambling to the play in a mask; then bring you home in a pretended fright, when you think you shall be found out – and rail at me for missing the play, and disappointing the frolic, which you had to pick me up and prove my constancy.

MILLAMANT. Detestable *inprimis!* I go to the play in a mask!

MIRABELL. *Item*, I article that you continue to like your own face, as long as I shall. And while it passes current with me, that you endeavour not to new coin it. To which end, together with all vizards for the day, I prohibit all masks for the night, made of oiled skins and I know not what – hog's bones, hare's gall, pig-water, and the marrow of a roasted cat. In short, I forbid all commerce with the gentlewoman in what-d'ye-call-it Court. *Item*, I shut my doors against all bawds with baskets, and pennyworths of muslin, china, fans, atlases, etc, etc. *Item*, when you shall be breeding –

MILLAMANT. Ah! Name it not.

MIRABELL. Which may be presumed, with a blessing on our endeavours –

MILLAMANT. Odious endeavours!

MIRABELL. I denounce against all straitlacing, squeezing for a shape, till you mould my boy's head like a sugarloaf; and instead of a manchild, make me the father to a crooked billet. Lastly, to the dominion of the tea-table I submit – but with proviso that you exceed not in your province, but restrain yourself to native and simple tea-table drinks, as tea, chocolate and coffee. As likewise to genuine and authorised tea-table talk, such as mending of fashions, spoiling reputations, railing at absent friends, and so forth; but that on no account you encroach upon the men's prerogative, and presume to drink healths, or toast fellows; for prevention of which, I banish all foreign forces, all auxiliaries to the tea-table, as orange-brandy, all aniseed, cinnamon, citron and Barbadoes waters, together with ratafia and the most noble spirit of clary. But for cowslip wine, poppy-water and all dormitives, those I allow. These provisos admitted, in other things I may prove a tractable and complying husband.

MILLAMANT. Oh horrid provisos! Filthy strong waters! I toast fellows, odious men! I hate your odious provisos.

MIRABELL. Then we're agreed. Shall I kiss your hand upon the contract? And here comes one to be a witness to the sealing of the deed.

Enter MRS FAINALL.

MILLAMANT. Fainall, what shall I do? Shall I have him? I think I must have him.

MRS FAINALL. Ay, ay, take him, take him, what should you do?

MILLAMANT. Well then – I'll take my death I'm in a horrid fright – Fainall, I shall never say it – well – I think – I'll endure you.

MRS FAINALL. Fie, fie, have him, have him, and tell him so in plain terms; for I am sure you have a mind to him.

MILLAMANT. Are you? I think I have – and the horrid man looks as if he thought so too. Well, you ridiculous thing you, I'll have you. I won't be kissed, nor I won't be thanked. Here, kiss my hand though. So, hold your tongue now, and don't say a word.

MRS FAINALL. Mirabell, there's a necessity for your obedience; you have neither time to talk nor stay. My mother is coming; and in my conscience if she should see you, would fall into fits, and maybe not recover time enough to return to Sir Rowland, who as Foible tells me is in a fair way to succeed. Therefore spare your ecstasies for another occasion, and slip down the backstairs, where Foible waits to consult you.

MILLAMANT. Ay, go, go. In the meantime I suppose you have said something to please me.

MIRABELL. I am all obedience. (*Exit* MIRABELL.)

MRS FAINALL. Yonder Sir Wilfull's drunk, and so noisy that my mother has been forced to leave Sir Rowland to appease him; but he answers her only with singing and drinking. What they have done by this time I know not, but Petulant and he were upon quarrelling as I came by.

MILLAMANT. Well, if Mirabell should not make a good husband, I am a lost thing, for I find I love him violently.

MRS FAINALL. So it seems, when you mind not what's said to you. If you doubt him, you had best take up with Sir Wilfull.

MILLAMANT. How can you name that superannuated lubber? Foh! (*Enter* WITWOUD *from drinking.*)

MRS FAINALL. So, is the fray made up, that you have left em?

WITWOUD. Left 'em? I could stay no longer. I have laughed like ten christenings – I am tipsy with laughing. If I had stayed any longer I should have burst – I must have been let out and pieced in the sides like an unsized camlet. Yes, yes, the fray is composed; my lady came in like a *noli prosequi* and stopped their proceedings.

MILLAMANT. What was the dispute?

WITWOUD. That's the jest, there was no dispute, they could neither of 'em speak for rage, and so fell a-sputtering at one another like two roasting apples.

Enter PETULANT *drunk.*

Now Petulant, all's over, all's well? Gad, my head begins
to whim it about – why dost thou not speak? Thou art
both as drunk and as mute as a fish.

PETULANT. Look you, Mrs Millamant, if you can love me,
dear nymph say it – and that's the conclusion – pass on,
or pass off that's all.

WITWOUD. Thou hast uttered volumes, folios, in less than
decimo sexto, my dear Lacedemonian. Sirrah Petulant,
thou art an epitomiser of words.

PETULANT. Witwoud – you are an annihilator of sense.

WITWOUD. Thou art a retailer of phrases, and dost deal in
remnants of remnants, like a maker of pin-cushions – thou
art in truth, metaphorically speaking, a speaker of
shorthand.

PETULANT. Thou art, without a figure, just one half of an
ass, and Baldwin yonder, thy half-brother, is the rest. A
gemini of asses split would make just four of you.

WITWOUD. Thou dost bite, my dear mustardseed; kiss me
for that.

PETULANT. Stand off! I'll kiss no more males – I have
kissed your twin yonder in a humour of reconciliation, till
he (*Hiccup.*) rises upon my stomach like a radish.

MILLAMANT. Eh, filthy creature – what was the quarrel?

PETULANT. There was no quarrel – there might have been
a quarrel.

WITWOUD. If there had been words enow between 'em to
have expressed provocation, they had gone together by
the ears like a pair of castanets.

PETULANT. You were the quarrel.

MILLAMANT. Me!

PETULANT. If I have a humour to quarrel, I can make less
matters conclude premises. If you are not handsome, what

then, if I have a humour to prove it? If I shall have my reward, say so; if not, fight for your face the next time yourself – I'll go sleep.

WITWOUD. Do, wrap thyself up like a woodlouse and dream revenge. And hear me, if thou canst learn to write by tomorrow morning, pen me a challenge. I'll carry it for thee.

PETULANT. Carry your mistress's monkey a spider – go flea dogs, and read romances – I'll go to bed to my maid. (*Exit.*)

MRS FAINALL. He's horridly drunk. How came you all in this pickle?

WITWOUD. A plot, a plot, to get rid of the knight – your husband's advice; but he sneaked off.

Enter LADY WISHFORT *and* SIR WILFULL *drunk.*

LADY WISHFORT. Out upon't, out upon't, at years of discretion, and comport yourself at this rantipole rate.

SIR WILFULL. No offence, aunt.

LADY WISHFORT. Offence? As I'm a person, I'm ashamed of you. Fogh! how you stink of wine! D'ye think my niece will ever endure such a borachio! You're an absolute borachio.

SIR WILFULL. Borachio!

LADY WISHFORT. At a time when you should commence an amour and put your best foot foremost –

SIR WILFULL. 'S'heart, an you grutch me your liquor, make a bill. Give me more drink, and take my purse. (*Sings.*)

> Prithee fill me the glass
> Till it laugh in my face,
> With ale that is potent and mellow;
>
> He that whines for a lass
> Is an ignorant ass,
> For a bumper has not its fellow.

But if you would have me marry my cousin – say the
word, and I'll do't – Wilfull will do't, that's the word –
Wilfull will do't; that's my crest – my motto I have forgot.

LADY WISHFORT. My nephew's a little overtaken, cousin,
but 'tis with drinking your health. O' my word you are
obliged to him.

SIR WILFULL. *In vino veritas* aunt. If I drunk your health
today cousin – I am a borachio. But if you have a mind
to be married, say the word, and send for the piper,
Wilfull will do't. If not, dust it away, and let's have t'other
round – Tony! Odsheart, where's Tony? Tony's an honest
fellow, but he spits after a bumper, and that's a fault.

Sings.

We'll drink, and we'll never ha' done, boys,
Put the glass then around with the sun, boys,
Let Apollo's example invite us;

For he's drunk every night,
And that makes him so bright,
That he's able next morning to light us.

The sun's a good pimple, an honest soaker, he has a
cellar at your Antipodes. If I travel, aunt, I touch at your
Antipodes – your Antipodes are a good rascally sort of
topsy-turvy fellows – if I had a bumper, I'd stand upon
my head and drink a health to 'em. A match or no
match, cousin with the hard name? Aunt, Wilfull will do't;
if she has her maidenhead, let her look to't – if she has
not, let her keep her own counsel in the meantime, and
cry out at the nine months' end.

MILLAMANT. Your pardon, madam, I can stay no longer.
Sir Wilfull grows very powerful. Egh, how he smells! I
shall be overcome if I stay. Come, cousin.

Exeunt MILLAMANT *and* MRS FAINALL.

LADY WISHFORT. Smells! He would poison a tallow-
chandler and his family. Beastly creature, I know not what
to do with him. Travel, quoth 'a! Ay, travel, travel, get

thee gone, get thee but far enough, to the Saracens or the
Tartars or the Turks, for thou are not fit to live in a
Christian commonwealth, thou beastly pagan.

SIR WILFULL. Turks? No; no Turks, aunt: your Turks are
infidels, and believe not in the grape. Your Mahometan,
your Mussulman, is a dry stinkard – no offence, aunt. My
map says that your Turk is not so honest a man as your
Christian – I cannot find by the map that your Mufti is
orthodox – whereby it is a plain case, that orthodox is a
hard word, aunt, and (*Hiccup.*) Greek for claret. (*Sings.*)

> To drink is a Christian diversion,
> Unknown to the Turk and the Persian:
> Let Mahometan fools
> Live by heathenish rules,
> And be damned over tea cups and coffee!
>
> But let British lads sing,
> Crown a health to the king,
> And a fig for your Sultan and Sophy!

Ah Tony!

Enter FOIBLE, *and whispers* LADY WISHFORT.

LADY WISHFORT. Sir Rowland impatient? Good lack!
what shall I do with this beastly tumbril? – Go lie down
and sleep, you sot, or as I'm a person, I'll have you
bastinadoed with broomsticks. Call up the wenches.

Exit FOIBLE.

SIR WILFULL. Ahey! Wenches, where are the wenches?

LADY WISHFORT. Dear cousin Witwoud, get him away,
and you will bind me to you inviolably. I have an affair of
moment that invades me with some precipitation. You will
oblige me to all futurity.

WITWOUD. Come, knight. Pox on him, I don't know what
to say to him. Will you go to a cock-match?

SIR WILFULL. With a wench, Tony? Is she a shakebag,
sirrah? Let me bite your cheek for that.

WITWOUD. Horrible! He has a breath like a bagpipe. Ay, ay, come, will you march, my Salopian?

SIR WILFULL. Lead on, little Tony – I'll follow thee, my Anthony, my Tantony, sirrah, thou shalt be my Tantony, and I'll be thy pig.

And a fig for your Sultan and Sophy.

Exit singing with WITWOUD.

LADY WISHFORT. This will never do. It will never make a match at least before he has been abroad.

Enter WAITWELL, *disguised as* SIR ROWLAND.

Dear Sir Rowland, I am confounded with confusion at the retrospection of my own rudeness, I have more pardons to ask than the Pope distributes in the year of Jubilee. But I hope where there is likely to be so near an alliance, we may unbend the severity of decorum and dispense with a little ceremony.

WAITWELL. My impatience, madam, is the effect of my transport; and till I have the possession of your adorable person, I am tantalized on a rack, and do but hang, madam, on the tenter of expectation.

LADY WISHFORT. You have excess of gallantry, Sir Rowland, and press things to a conclusion with a most prevailing vehemence. But a day or two for decency of marriage –

WAITWELL. For decency of funeral, madam. The delay will break my heart – or if that should fail, I shall be poisoned. My nephew will get an inkling of my designs and poison me, and I would willingly starve him before I die – I would gladly go out of the world with that satisfaction. That would be some comfort to me, if I could but live so long as to be revenged on that unnatural viper.

LADY WISHFORT. Is he so unnatural say you? Truly I would contribute much both to the saving of your life and the accomplishment of your revenge. Not that I respect myself; though he has been a perfidious wretch to me.

WAITWELL. Perfidious to you!

LADY WISHFORT. Oh Sir Rowland, the hours that he has died away at my feet, the tears that he has shed, the oaths that he has sworn, the palpitations that he has felt, the trances, and the tremblings, the ardours and the ecstasies, the kneelings and the risings, the heart-heavings and the hand-grippings, the pangs and the pathetic regards of his protesting eyes! Oh, no memory can register.

WAITWELL. What, my rival! Is the rebel my rival? 'A dies.

LADY WISHFORT. No, don't kill him at once Sir Rowland, starve him gradually, inch by inch.

WAITWELL. I'll do't. In three weeks he shall be barefoot; in a month out at knees with begging an alms. He shall starve upward and upward, till he has nothing living but his head, and then go out in a stink like a candle's end upon a save-all.

LADY WISHFORT. Well, Sir Rowland, you have the way. You are no novice in the labyrinth of love; you have the clue. But as I am a person, Sir Rowland, you must not attribute my yielding to any sinister appetite, or indigestion of widowhood; nor impute my complacency to any lethargy of continence. I hope you do not think me prone to any iteration of nuptials –

WAITWELL. Far be it from me –

LADY WISHFORT. If you do, I protest I must recede – or think that I have made a prostitution of decorums, but in the vehemence of compassion, and to save the life of a person of so much importance

WAITWELL. I esteem it so

LADY WISHFORT. Or else you wrong my condescension

WAITWELL. I do not, I do not –

LADY WISHFORT. Indeed you do –

WAITWELL. I do not, fair shrine of virtue –

LADY WISHFORT. If you think the least scruple of carnality was an ingredient –

WAITWELL. Dear madam, no. You are all camphire and frankincense, all chastity and odour –

LADY WISHFORT. Or that –

Enter FOIBLE.

FOIBLE. Madam, the dancers are ready, and there's one with a letter, who must deliver it into your own hands.

LADY WISHFORT. Sir Rowland, will you give me leave? Think favourably, judge candidly, and conclude you have found a person who would suffer racks in honour's cause, dear Sir Rowland, and will wait on you incessantly. (*Exit.*)

WAITWELL. Fie, fie! What a slavery have I undergone. Spouse, hast thou any cordial? I want spirits.

FOIBLE. What a washy rogue art thou, to pant thus for a quarter of an hour's lying and swearing to a fine lady!

WAITWELL. Oh, she is the antidote to desire. Spouse, thou wilt fare the worse for't. I shall have no appetite to iteration of nuptials this eight-and-forty hours. By this hand I'd rather be a chairman in the dog-days than act Sir Rowland till this time tomorrow.

Enter LADY WISHFORT *with a letter.*

LADY WISHFORT. Call in the dancers. Sir Rowland, we'll sit if you please, and see the entertainment.

Dance.

Now with your permission Sir Rowland, I will peruse my letter. I would open it in your presence, because I would not make you uneasy. If it should make you uneasy, I would burn it. Speak, if it does – but you may see by the superscription it is like a woman's hand.

FOIBLE (*to him*). By heaven! Mrs Marwood's – I know it – my heart aches – get it from her.

WAITWELL. A woman's hand? No, madam, that's no woman's hand; I see that already. That's somebody whose throat must be cut.

LADY WISHFORT. Nay Sir Rowland, since you give me a proof of your passion by your jealousy, I promise you I'll make you a return, by a frank communication. You shall see it – we'll open it together. Look you here.

(*Reads.*) – Madam, though unknown to you (look you there, 'tis from nobody that I know) – I have that honour for your character, that I think myself obliged to let you know you are abused. He who pretends to be Sir Rowland is a cheat and a rascal –

Oh heavens! what's this?

FOIBLE. Unfortunate. All's ruined.

WAITWELL. How, how, let me see, let me see – (*Reading.*) A rascal, and disguised and suborned for that imposture – Oh villainy, Oh villainy! – by the contrivance of –

LADY WISHFORT. I shall faint, I shall die, I shall die, oh!

FOIBLE (*to him*). Say 'tis your nephew's hand – quickly – his plot, swear, swear it –

WAITWELL. Here s a villain! Madam, don't you perceive it, don't you see it?

LADY WISHFORT. Too well, too well! I have seen too much.

WAITWELL. I told you at first I knew the hand. A woman's hand? The rascal writes a sort of a large hand, your Roman hand. I saw there was a throat to be cut presently. If he were my son, as he is my nephew, I'd pistol him

FOIBLE. Oh treachery! But are you sure, Sir Rowland, it is his writing?

WAITWELL. Sure? Am I here? Do I live? Do I love this pearl of India? I have twenty letters in my pocket from him in the same character.

LADY WISHFORT. How!

FOIBLE. Oh, what luck it is, Sir Rowland, that you were present at this juncture! This was the business that brought Mr Mirabell disguised to Madam Millamant this afternoon. I thought something was contriving when he stole by me and would have hid his face.

LADY WISHFORT. How, how! I heard the villain was in the house indeed, and now I remember, my niece went away abruptly when Sir Wilfull was to have made his addresses.

FOIBLE. Then, then, madam, Mr Mirabell waited for her in her chamber; but I would not tell your ladyship to discompose you when you were to receive Sir Rowland.

WAITWELL. Enough! His date is short.

FOIBLE. No, good Sir Rowland, don't incur the law.

WAITWELL. Law? I care not for law. I can but die, and 'tis in a good cause. My lady shall be satisfied of my truth and innocence, though it cost me my life.

LADY WISHFORT. No, dear Sir Rowland, don't fight, if you should be killed I must never show my face, or be hanged. Oh, consider my reputation, Sir Rowland. No, you shan't fight. I'll go in and examine my niece; I'll make her confess. I conjure you Sir Rowland, by all your love, not to fight.

WAITWELL. 1 am charmed madam, I obey. But some proof you must let me give you; I'll go for a black box which contains the writings of my whole estate, and deliver that into your hands.

LADY WISHFORT. Ay, dear Sir Rowland, that will be some comfort; bring the black box.

WAITWELL. And may I presume to bring a contract to be signed this night? May I hope so far?

LADY WISHFORT. Bring what you will; but come alive, pray come alive. Oh this is a happy discovery.

WAITWELL. Dead or alive I'll come and married we will be in spite of treachery; ay, and get an heir that shall defeat the last remaining glimpse of hope in my abandoned nephew. Come, my buxom widow.

Ere long you shall substantial proof receive

That I'm an arrant knight –

FOIBLE (*aside*). Or arrant knave.

Exeunt.

ACT FIVE

Scene continues.

LADY WISHFORT *and* FOIBLE.

LADY WISHFORT. Out of my house, out of my house, thou viper, thou serpent, that I have fostered, thou bosom traitress, that I raised from nothing – begone, begone, begone, go, go – that I took from washing of old gauze and weaving of dead hair, with a bleak blue nose, over a chafing-dish of starved embers and dining behind a traverse rag, in a shop no bigger than a bird-cage – go, go, starve again, do, do.

FOIBLE. Dear madam, I'll beg pardon on my knees.

LADY WISHFORT. Away, out, out! Go set up for yourself again do, drive a trade, do, with your three pennyworth of small ware, flaunting upon a pack-thread, under a brandy-seller's bulk, or against a dead wall by a ballad-monger. Go hang out an old frisoneer gorget, with a yard of yellow colberteen again, do. An old gnawed mask, two rows of pins and a child's fiddle; a glass necklace with the beads broken, and a quilted nightcap with one ear! Go, go, drive a trade – these were your commodities, you treacherous trull, this was your merchandise you dealt in when I took you into my house, placed you next myself, and made you governante of my whole family. You have forgot this, have you, now you have feathered your nest?

FOIBLE. No, no, dear madam. Do but hear me, have but a moment's patience – I'll confess all. Mr Mirabell seduced me; I am not the first that he has wheedled with his dissembling tongue. Your ladyship's own wisdom has been deluded by him, then how should I, a poor ignorant, defend myself? Oh madam, if you knew but what he

promised me, and how he assured me your ladyship
should come to no damage. Or else the wealth of the
Indies should not have bribed me to conspire against so
good, so sweet, so kind a lady as you have been to me.

LADY WISHFORT. 'No damage?' What, to betray me, to
marry me to a cast serving-man; to make me a receptacle,
an hospital for a decayed pimp? 'No damage?' Oh thou
frontless impudence, more than a big-bellied actress.

FOIBLE. Pray do but hear me madam, he could not marry
your ladyship, madam. No indeed, his marriage was to
have been void in law, for he was married to me first, to
secure your ladyship. He could not have bedded your
ladyship; for if he had consummated with your ladyship,
he must have run the risk of the law and been put upon
his clergy. Yes indeed, I enquired of the law in that case
before I would meddle or make.

LADY WISHFORT. What, then I have been your property,
have I? I have been convenient to you it seems, while you
were catering for Mirabell. I have been broker for you?
What, have you made a passive bawd of me? This
exceeds all precedent; I am brought to fine uses, to
become a botcher of secondhand marriages between
Abigails and Andrews! I'll couple you. Yes, I'll baste you
together, you and your Philander. I'll Duke's Place you, as
I'm a person. Your turtle is in custody already; you shall
coo in the same cage, if there be constable or warrant in
the parish.

Exit.

FOIBLE. Oh that ever I was born! Oh that I was ever
married! A bride, ay, I shall be a Bridewell bride. Oh!

Enter MRS FAINALL.

MRS FAINALL. Poor Foible, what's the matter?

FOIBLE. Oh madam, my lady's gone for a constable; I shall
be had to a justice, and put to Bridewell to beat hemp.
Poor Waitwell's gone to prison already.

MRS FAINALL. Have a good heart, Foible; Mirabell's gone to give security for him. This is all Marwood's and my husband's doing.

FOIBLE. Yes, yes, I know it, madam. She was in my lady's closet, and overheard all that you said to me before dinner. She sent the letter to my lady, and that missing effect, Mr Fainall laid this plot to arrest Waitwell when he pretended to go for the papers; and in the meantime Mrs Marwood declared all to my lady.

MRS FAINALL. Was there no mention made of me in the letter? My mother does not suspect my being in the confederacy? I fancy Marwood has not told her, though she has told my husband.

FOIBLE. Yes, madam, but my lady did not see that part. We stifled the letter before she read so far. Has that mischievous devil told Mr Fainall of your ladyship then?

MRS FAINALL. Ay, all's out, my affair with Mirabell, everything discovered. This is the last day of our living together, that's my comfort.

FOIBLE. Indeed madam, and so 'tis a comfort if you knew all. He has been even with your ladyship; which I could have told you long enough since, but I love to keep peace and quietness by my good will; I had rather bring friends together than set 'em at distance. But Mrs Marwood and he are nearer related than ever their parents thought for.

MRS FAINALL. Say'st thou so, Foible? Canst thou prove this?

FOIBLE. I can take my oath of it, madam; so can Mrs Mincing. We have had many a fair word from Madam Marwood, to conceal something that passed in our chamber one evening when you were at Hyde Park and we were thought to have gone a-walking; but we went up unawares, though we were sworn to secrecy too. Madam Marwood took a book and swore us upon it; but it was but a book of verses and poems – so as long as it was not a Bible oath, we may break it with a safe conscience.

MRS FAINALL. This discovery is the most opportune thing I could wish. Now, Mincing?

Enter MINCING.

MINCING. My lady would speak with Mrs Foible, mem. Mr Mirabell is with her; he has set your spouse at liberty, Mrs Foible, and would have you hide yourself in my lady's closet till my old lady's anger is abated. Oh, my old lady is in a perilous passion at something Mr Fainall has said. He swears, and my old lady cries. There's a fearful hurricane, I vow. He says, mem, how that he'll have my lady's fortune made over to him, or he'll be divorced.

MRS FAINALL. Does your lady and Mirabell know that?

MINCING. Yes, mem; they have sent me to see if Sir Wilfull be sober, and to bring him to them. My lady is resolved to have him, I think, rather than lose such a vast sum as six thousand pound. Oh, come Mrs Foible, I hear my old lady.

MRS FAINALL. Foible, you must tell Mincing that she must prepare to vouch when I call her.

FOIBLE. Yes, yes madam.

MINCING. Oh yes, mem, I'll vouch anything for your ladyship's service, be what it will.

Exeunt MINCING *and* FOIBLE.

Enter LADY WISHFORT *and* MARWOOD.

LADY WISHFORT. Oh my dear friend, how can I enumerate the benefits that I have received from your goodness? To you I owe the timely discovery of the false vows of Mirabell; to you the detection of the impostor Sir Rowland. And now you are become an intercessor with my son-in-law, to save the honour of my house, and compound for the frailties of my daughter. Well, friend, you are enough to reconcile me to the bad world, or else I would retire to deserts and solitudes, and feed harmless sheep by groves and purling streams. Dear Marwood, let us leave the world, and retire by ourselves and be shepherdesses.

MRS MARWOOD. Let us first dispatch the affair in hand, madam; we shall have leisure to think of retirement afterwards. Here is one who is concerned in the treaty.

LADY WISHFORT. Oh daughter, daughter, is it possible thou shouldst be my child, bone of my bone, and flesh of my flesh, and as I may say, another me, and yet transgress the most minute particle of severe virtue? Is it possible you should lean aside to iniquity, who have been cast in the direct mould of virtue? I have not only been a mould but a pattern for you, and a model for you, after you were brought into the world.

MRS FAINALL. I don't understand your ladyship.

LADY WISHFORT. Not understand? Why, have you not been naught? Have you not been sophisticated? Not understand? Here I am ruined to compound for your caprices and your cuckoldoms. I must pawn my plate and my jewels and ruin my niece, and all little enough –

MRS FAINALL. I am wronged and abused, and so are you. 'Tis a false accusation, as false as hell, as false as your friend there, ay, or your friend's friend, my false husband.

MRS MARWOOD. My friend, Mrs Fainall? Your husband my friend? What do you mean?

MRS FAINALL. I know what I mean madam, and so do you; and so shall the world at a time convenient.

MRS MARWOOD. I am sorry to see you so passionate, madam. More temper would look more like innocence. But I have done. I am sorry my zeal to serve your ladyship and family should admit of misconstruction, or make me liable to affronts. You will pardon me, madam, if I meddle no more with an affair in which I am not personally concerned.

LADY WISHFORT. Oh dear friend, I am so ashamed that you should meet with such returns – you ought to ask pardon on your knees, ungrateful creature. She deserves more from you than all your life can accomplish. Oh, don't leave me destitute in this perplexity! No, stick to me, my good genius.

MRS FAINALL. I tell you, madam, you're abused. Stick to you? Ay, like a leech, to suck your best blood − she'll drop off when she's full. Madam, you shan't pawn a bodkin, nor part with a brass counter in composition for me. I defy 'em all. Let 'em prove their aspersions; I know my own innocence, and dare stand a trial. (*Exit.*)

LADY WISHFORT. Why, if she should be innocent, if she should be wronged after all, ha? I don't know what to think − and I promise you, her education has been unexceptionable. I may say it; for I chiefly made it my own care to initiate her very infancy in the rudiments of virtue, and to impress upon her tender years a young odium and aversion to the very sight of men. Ay, friend, she would ha' shrieked if she had but seen a man, till she was in her teens. As I'm a person 'tis true. She was never suffered to play with a male child, though but in coats; nay, her very babies were of the feminine gender. Oh, she never looked a man in the face but her own father, or the chaplain, and him we made a shift to put upon her for a woman, by the help of his long garments and his sleek face, till she was going in her fifteen.

MRS MARWOOD. 'Twas much she should be deceived so long.

LADY WISHFORT. I warrant you, or she would never have borne to have been catechized by him; and have heard his long lectures against singing and dancing, and such debaucheries, and going to filthy plays, and profane music meetings, where the lewd trebles squeak nothing but bawdy, and the bases roar blasphemy. Oh, she would have swooned at the sight or name of an obscene playbook and can I think after all this, that my daughter can be naught? What, a whore? And thought it excommunication to set her foot within the door of a playhouse. O my dear friend, I can't believe it, no, no. As she says, let him prove it, let him prove it.

MRS MARWOOD. Prove it madam? What, and have your
name prostituted in a public court? Yours and your
daughter's reputation worried at the bar by a pack of
bawling lawyers? To be ushered in with an Oyez of
scandal, and have your case opened by an old fumbling
lecher in a quoif like a man-midwife to bring your
daughter's infamy to light; to be a theme for legal
punsters and quibblers by the statute, and become a jest
against a rule of court, where there is no precedent for a
jest in any record, not even in Doomsday Book; to
discompose the gravity of the bench, and provoke naughty
interrogatories in more naughty law Latin, while the good
judge, tickled with the proceeding, simpers under a grey
beard, and fidges off and on his cushion as if he had
swallowed cantharides, or sat upon cow-itch.

LADY WISHFORT. Oh, tis very hard!

MRS MARWOOD. And then to have my young revellers of
the Temple take notes, like 'prentices at a conventicle; and
after, talk it all over again in commons, or before drawers
in an eating-house.

LADY WISHFORT. Worse and worse.

MRS MARWOOD. Nay, this is nothing; if it would end
here, 'twere well. But it must after this be consigned by
the shorthand writers to the public press; and from thence
be transferred to the hands, nay into the throats and lungs
of hawkers, with voices more licentious than the loud
flounderman's or the woman that cries 'grey peas'. And
this you must hear till you are stunned; nay, you must
hear nothing else for some days.

LADY WISHFORT. Oh, 'tis insupportable! No, no, dear
friend, make it up, make it up; ay, ay, I'll compound. I'll
give up all, myself and my all, my niece and her all, –
anything, everything for composition.

MRS MARWOOD. Nay madam, I advise nothing, I only
lay before you as a friend the inconveniencies which
perhaps you have overseen. Here comes Mr Fainall. If he
will be satisfied to huddle up all in silence, I shall be glad.

You must think I would rather congratulate than condole with you.

Enter FAINALL.

LADY WISHFORT. Ay, ay, I do not doubt it, dear Marwood; no, no, I do not doubt it.

FAINALL. Well, madam, I have suffered myself to be overcome by the importunity of this lady your friend, and am content you shall enjoy your own proper estate during life, on condition you oblige yourself never to marry, under such penalty as I think convenient.

LADY WISHFORT. Never to marry?

FAINALL. No more Sir Rowlands – the next imposture may not be so timely detected.

MRS MARWOOD. That condition, I dare answer, my lady will consent to without difficulty; she has already but too much experienced the perfidiousness of men. Besides, madam, when we retire to our pastoral solitude, we shall bid adieu to all other thoughts.

LADY WISHFORT. Ay, that's true; but in case of necessity, as of health, or some such emergency –

FAINALL. Oh, if you are prescribed marriage, you shall be considered; I will only reserve to myself the power to choose for you. If your physic be wholesome, it matters not who is your apothecary. Next, my wife shall settle on me the remainder of her fortune not made over already, and for her maintenance depend entirely on my discretion.

LADY WISHFORT. This is most inhumanly savage, exceeding the barbarity of a Muscovite husband.

FAINALL. I learned it from his Czarish majesty's retinue, in a winter evening's conference over brandy and pepper, amongst other secrets of matrimony and policy, as they are at present practised in the northern hemisphere. But this must be agreed unto, and that positively. Lastly, I will be endowed, in right of my wife, with that six thousand

pound which is the moiety of Mrs Millamant's fortune in
your possession; and which she has forfeited (as will
appear by the last will and testament of your deceased
husband, Sir Jonathan Wishfort) by her disobedience in
contracting herself against your consent or knowledge, and
by refusing the offered match with Sir Wilfull Witwoud,
which you, like a careful aunt, had provided for her.

LADY WISHFORT. My nephew was *non compos*, and could
not make his addresses.

FAINALL. I come to make demands. I'll hear no objections.

LADY WISHFORT. You will grant me time to consider.

FAINALL. Yes, while the instrument is drawing, to which
you must set your hand till more sufficient deeds can be
perfected; which I will take care shall be done with all
possible speed. In the meanwhile, I will go for the said
instrument, and till my return, you may balance this
matter in your own discretion.

Exit FAINALL.

LADY WISHFORT. This insolence is beyond all precedent,
all parallel; must I be subject to this merciless villain?

MRS MARWOOD. 'Tis severe indeed, madam, that you
should smart for your daughter's wantonness.

LADY WISHFORT. 'Twas against my consent that she
married this barbarian, but she would have him, though
her year was not out. Ah! her first husband, my son
Languish, would not have carried it thus. Well, that was
my choice, this is hers; she is matched now with a
witness. I shall be mad; dear friend, is there no comfort
for me? Must I live to be confiscated at this rebel rate?
Here come two more of my Egyptian plagues too.

Enter MILLAMANT *and* SIR WILFULL.

SIR WILFULL. Aunt, your servant.

LADY WISHFORT. Out caterpillar, call not me aunt; I know
thee not.

SIR WILFULL. I confess I have been a little in disguise, as they say. 'S'heart! and I'm sorry for't. What would you have? I hope I committed no offence, aunt, and if I did, I am willing to make satisfaction; and what can a man say fairer? If I have broke anything, I'll pay for't, an it cost a pound. And so let that content for what's past, and make no more words. For what's to come, to pleasure you I'm willing to marry my cousin. So pray let's all be friends, she and I are agreed upon the matter before a witness.

LADY WISHFORT. How's this, dear niece? Have I any comfort? Can this be true?

MILLAMANT. I am content to be a sacrifice to your repose, madam; and to convince you that I had no hand in the plot, as you were misinformed, I have laid my commands on Mirabell to come in person, and be a witness that I give my hand to this flower of knighthood; and for the contract that passed between Mirabell and me, I have obliged him to make a resignation of it, in your ladyship's presence. He is without, and waits your leave for admittance.

LADY WISHFORT. Well, I'll swear I am something revived at this testimony of your obedience; but I cannot admit that traitor. I fear I cannot fortify myself to support his appearance. He is as terrible to me as a Gorgon; if I see him, I fear I shall turn to stone, petrify incessantly.

MILLAMANT. If you disoblige him, he may resent your refusal and insist upon the contract still. Then 'tis the last time he will be offensive to you.

LADY WISHFORT. Are you sure it will be the last time? If I were sure of that. Shall I never see him again?

MILLAMANT. Sir Wilfull, you and he are to travel together, are you not?

SIR WILFULL. 'S'heart, the gentleman's a civil gentleman, aunt; let him come in. Why, we are sworn brothers and fellow travellers. We are to be Pylades and Orestes, he and I. He is to be my interpreter in foreign parts. He has been overseas once already; and with proviso that I marry

my cousin will cross 'em once again, only to bear me
company. 'S'heart, I'll call him in – an I set on't once, he
shall come in; and see who'll hinder him. (*Exit.*)

MRS MARWOOD. This is precious fooling, if it would pass,
but I'll know the bottom of it.

LADY WISHFORT. O dear Marwood, you are not going?

MARWOOD. Not far, madam; I'll return immediately. (*Exit.*)

Re-enter SIR WILFULL *and* MIRABELL.

SIR WILFULL. Look up man, I'll stand by you; 'sbud an
she do frown, she can't kill you. Besides, harkee, she dare
not frown desperately, because her face is none of her
own. 'S'heart, an she should, her forehead would wrinkle
like the coat of a cream-cheese, but mum for that, fellow
traveller.

MIRABELL. If a deep sense of the many injuries I have
offered to so good a lady, with a sincere remorse, and a
hearty contrition, can but obtain the least glance of
compassion I am too happy. Ah madam, there was a time
– but let it be forgotten. I confess I have deservedly
forfeited the high place I once held, of sighing at your
feet. Nay, kill me not by turning from me in disdain;
I come not to plead for favour; nay, not for pardon. I am
a suppliant only for your pity. I am going where I never
shall behold you more

SIR WILFULL. How, fellow traveller! You shall go by
yourself then.

MIRABELL. Let me be pitied first, and afterwards forgotten
– I ask no more.

SIR WILFULL. By'r Lady, a very reasonable request, and
will cost you nothing, aunt. Come, come, forgive and
forget, aunt, why you must, an you are a Christian.

MIRABELL. Consider, madam, in reality you could not
receive much prejudice; it was an innocent device; though
I confess it had a face of guiltiness. It was at most an
artifice which love contrived, and errors which love

produces have ever been accounted venial. At least think it is punishment enough that I have lost what in my heart I hold most dear, that to your cruel indignation I have offered up this beauty, and with her my peace and quiet; nay, all my hopes of future comfort.

SIR WILFULL. An he does not move me, would I might never be o' the Quorum. An it were not as good a deed as to drink, to give her to him again, I would I might never take shipping. Aunt, if you don't forgive quickly, I shall melt, I can tell you that. My contract went no further than a little mouth-glue, and that's hardly dry; one doleful sigh more from my fellow traveller, and 'tis dissolved.

LADY WISHFORT. Well, nephew, upon your account – ah, he has a false insinuating tongue! Well, sir, I will stifle my just resentment at my nephew's request. I will endeavour what I can to forget, but on proviso that you resign the contract with my niece immediately.

MIRABELL. It is in writing, and with papers of concern; but I have sent my servant for it, and will deliver it to you, with all acknowledgments for your transcendent goodness.

LADY WISHFORT (aside). Oh, he has witchcraft in his eyes and tongue! When I did not see him, I could have bribed a villain to his assassination; but his appearance rakes the embers which have so long lain smothered in my breast.

Enter FAINALL and MRS MARWOOD.

FAINALL. Your date of deliberation, madam, is expired. Here is the instrument; are you prepared to sign?

LADY WISHFORT. If I were prepared, I am not empowered. My niece exerts a lawful claim, having matched herself by my direction to Sir Wilfull.

FAINALL. That sham is too gross to pass on me, though 'tis imposed on you, madam.

MILLAMANT. Sir, I have given my consent.

MIRABELL. And, sir, I have resigned my pretensions.

SIR WILFULL. And, sir, I assert my right; and will maintain it in defiance of you, sir, and of your instrument. 'S'heart an you talk of an instrument, sir, I have an old fox by my thigh shall hack your instrument of ram vellum to shreds, sir! It shall not be sufficient for a mittimus or a tailor's measure. Therefore withdraw your instrument, sir, or by'r Lady, I shall draw mine.

LADY WISHFORT. Hold nephew, hold.

MILLAMANT. Good Sir Wilfull, respite your valour.

FAINALL. Indeed? Are you provided of a guard, with your single Beefeater there? But I'm prepared for you, and insist upon my first proposal. You shall submit your own estate to my management, and absolutely make over my wife's to my sole use, as pursuant to the purport and tenor of this other covenant. (*To* MILLAMANT.) I suppose, madam, your consent is not requisite in this case; nor, Mr Mirabell, your resignation; nor, Sir Wilfull, your right. You may draw your fox if you please, sir, and make a bear-garden flourish somewhere else, for here it will not avail. This, my Lady Wishfort, must be subscribed, or your darling daughter's turned adrift, like a leaky hulk to sink or swim, as she and the current of this lewd town can agree.

LADY WISHFORT. Is there no means, no remedy, to stop my ruin? Ungrateful wretch! Dost thou not owe thy being, thy subsistence, to my daughter's fortune?

FAINALL. I'll answer you when I have the rest of it in my possession.

MIRABELL. But that you would not accept of a remedy from my hands — I own I have not deserved you should owe any obligation to me; or else perhaps I could advise —

LADY WISHFORT. Oh what? what? To save me and my child from ruin, from want, I'll forgive all that's past; nay I'll consent to anything to come, to be delivered from this tyranny.

MIRABELL. Ay, madam; but that is too late, my reward is intercepted. You have disposed of her who only could have made me a compensation for all my services. But be it as it may, I am resolved I'll serve you; you shall not be wronged in this savage manner.

LADY WISHFORT. How! Dear Mr Mirabell, can you be so generous at last? But it is not possible. Harkee, I'll break my nephew's match; you shall have my niece yet, and all her fortune, if you can but save me from this imminent danger.

MIRABELL. Will you? I take you at your word. I ask no more. I must have leave for two criminals to appear.

LADY WISHFORT. Ay, ay, anybody, anybody.

MIRABELL. Foible is one, and a penitent.

Enter MRS FAINALL, FOIBLE, *and* MINCING.

MRS MARWOOD (*to* FAINALL). Oh my shame! (MIRABELL *and* LADY WISHFORT *go to* MRS FAINALL *and* FOIBLE.) These corrupt things are bought and brought hither to expose me.

FAINALL. If it must all come out, why let 'em know it, tis but the way of the world. That shall not urge me to relinquish or abate one tittle of my terms; no, I will insist the more.

FOIBLE. Yes indeed, madam; I'll take my Bible oath of it.

MINCING. And so will I, mem.

LADY WISHFORT. Oh Marwood, Marwood, art thou false? My friend deceive me? Hast thou been a wicked accomplice with that profligate man?

MRS MARWOOD. Have you so much ingratitude and injustice, to give credit against your friend to the aspersions of two such mercenary trulls?

MINCING. 'Mercenary', mem? I scorn your words. 'Tis true we found you and Mr Fainall in the blue garret; by the same token, you swore us to secrecy upon Messalina's poems. 'Mercenary?' No, if we would have been mercenary, we should have held our tongues; you would have bribed us sufficiently.

FAINALL. Go, you are an insignificant thing. Well, what are you the better for this? Is this Mr Mirabell's expedient? I'll be put off no longer. You thing, that was a wife, shall smart for this. I will not leave thee wherewithal to hide thy shame. Your body shall be naked as your reputation.

MRS FAINALL. I despise you and defy your malice. You have aspersed me wrongfully. I have proved your falsehood. Go you and your treacherous – I will not name it – but starve together – perish.

FAINALL. Not while you are worth a groat. Indeed my dear madam, I'll be fooled no longer.

LADY WISHFORT. Ah Mr Mirabell, this is small comfort, the detection of this affair.

MIRABELL. Oh, in good time. Your leave for the other offender and penitent to appear, madam.

Enter WAITWELL *with a box of writings.*

LADY WISHFORT. Oh, Sir Rowland! Well, rascal?

WAITWELL. What your ladyship pleases. I have brought the black box at last, madam.

MIRABELL. Give it me. Madam, you remember your promise.

LADY WISHFORT. Ay, dear sir.

MIRABELL. Where are the gentlemen?

WAITWELL. At hand sir, rubbing their eyes; just risen from sleep.

FAINALL. 'Sdeath, what's this to me? I'll not wait your private concerns.

Enter PETULANT *and* WITWOUD.

PETULANT. How now? What's the matter? Whose hand's out?

WITWOUD. Heyday! What, are you all got together, like players at the end of the last act?

MIRABELL. You may remember, gentlemen, I once requested your hands as witnesses to a certain parchment.

WITWOUD. Ay, I do, my hand I remember. Petulant set his mark.

MIRABELL. You wrong him, his name is fairly written, as shall appear. You do not remember, gentlemen, anything of what that parchment contained?

Undoing the box.

WITWOUD. No.

PETULANT. Not I. I writ. I read nothing.

MIRABELL. Very well; now you shall know. Madam, your promise.

LADY WISHFORT. Ay, ay, sir, upon my honour.

MIRABELL. Mr Fainall, it is now time that you should know that your lady, while she was at her own disposal, and before you had by your insinuations wheedled her out of a pretended settlement of the greatest part of her fortune –

FAINALL. Sir! Pretended!

MIRABELL. Yes, sir. I say that this lady while a widow, having it seems received some cautions respecting your inconstancy and tyranny of temper, which from her own partial opinion and fondness of you, she could never have suspected – she did, I say, by the wholesome advice of friends and of sages learned in the laws of this land, deliver this same as her act and deed to me in trust, and to the uses within mentioned. You may read if you please (*Holding out the parchment.*) though perhaps what is inscribed on the back may serve your occasions.

FAINALL. Very likely, sir. What's here? Damnation! (*Reads.*) A deed of conveyance of the whole estate real of Arabella Languish, widow, in trust to Edward Mirabell. Confusion!

MIRABELL. Even so, sir; 'tis the way of the world, sir, of the widows of the world. I suppose this deed may bear an elder date than what you have obtained from your lady.

FAINALL. Perfidious fiend! Then thus I'll be revenged.
(*Offers to run at* MRS FAINALL.)

SIR WILFULL. Hold, sir, now you may make your bear-garden flourish somewhere else, sir.

FAINALL. Mirabell, you shall hear of this, sir; be sure you shall. Let me pass, oaf!

Exit.

MRS FAINALL. Madam, you seem to stifle your resentment; you had better give it vent.

MRS MARWOOD. Yes, it shall have vent – and to your confusion, or I'll perish in the attempt.

Exit.

LADY WISHFORT. Oh daughter, daughter, 'tis plain thou hast inherited thy mother's prudence.

MRS FAINALL. Thank Mr Mirabell, a cautious friend, to whose advice all is owing.

LADY WISHFORT. Well, Mr Mirabell, you have kept your promise, and I must perform mine. First, I pardon for your sake, Sir Rowland there, and Foible. The next thing is to break the matter to my nephew – and how to do that –

MIRABELL. For that, madam, give yourself no trouble; let me have your consent. Sir Wilfull is my friend; he has had compassion upon lovers and generously engaged a volunteer in this action, for our service, and now designs to prosecute his travels.

SIR WILFULL. 'S'heart aunt, I have no mind to marry. My cousin's a fine lady, and the gentleman loves her and she loves him, and they deserve one another. My resolution is to see foreign parts. I have set on't – and when I'm set on't, I must do't. And if these two gentlemen would travel too, I think they may be spared.

PETULANT. For my part, I say little – I think things are best off or on.

WITWOUD. Egad I understand nothing of the matter – I'm in a maze yet, like a dog in a dancing school.

LADY WISHFORT. Well sir, take her, and with her all the joy I can give you.

MILLAMANT. Why does not the man take me? Would you have me give myself to you over again.

MIRABELL. Ay, and over and over again; for I would have you as often as possibly I can. (*Kisses her hand.*) Well, heaven grant I love you not too well, that's all my fear.

SIR WILFULL. 'S'heart, you'll have him time enough to toy after you're married; or, if you will toy now, let us have a dance in the meantime, that we who are not lovers may have some other employment besides looking on.

MIRABELL. With all my heart, dear Sir Wilfull. What shall we do for music?

FOIBLE. Oh, sir, some that were provided for Sir Rowland's entertainment are yet within call.

A dance.

LADY WISHFORT. As I am a person I can hold out no longer. I have wasted my spirits so today already that I am ready to sink under the fatigue; and I cannot but have some fears upon me yet that my son Fainall will pursue some desperate course.

MIRABELL. Madam, disquiet not yourself on that account. To my knowledge his circumstances are such, he must of force comply. For my part, I will contribute all that in me lies to a reunion. (*To* MRS FAINALL.) In the meantime, madam, let me before these witnesses restore to you this deed of trust. It may be a means, well managed, to make you live easily together.

From hence let those be warned, who mean to wed,
Lest mutual falsehood stain the bridal bed;
For each deceiver to his cost may find,
That marriage frauds too oft are paid in kind.

Exeunt omnes.

Epilogue

Spoken by Mrs Bracegirdle.

After our epilogue this crowd dismisses,
I'm thinking how this play'll be pulled to pieces.
But pray consider ere you doom its fall,
How hard a thing 'twould be to please you all.
There are some critics so with spleen diseased,
They scarcely come inclining to be pleased;
And sure he must have more than mortal skill,
Who pleases anyone against his will.
Then, all bad poets we are sure, are foes,
And how their number's swelled the town well knows;
In shoals I've marked 'em judging in the pit;
Though they're on no pretence for judgment fit,
But that they have been damned for want of wit.
Since when, they, by their own offences taught,
Set up for spies on plays, and finding fault.
Others there are whose malice we'd prevent;
Such who watch plays with scurrilous intent
To mark out who by characters are meant.
And though no perfect likeness they can trace,
Yet each pretends to know the copied face.
These with false glosses feed their own ill nature,
And turn to libel, what was meant a satire.
May such malicious fops this fortune find,
To think themselves alone the fools designed;
If any are so arrogantly vain,
To think they singly can support a scene,
And fumish fool enough to entertain.
For well the learned and the judicious know,
That satire scorns to stoop so meanly low
As any one abstracted fop to show.
For, as when painters form a matchless face,
They from each fair one catch some different grace,

And shining features in one portrait blend,
To which no single beauty must pretend;
So poets oft do in one piece expose
Whole *belles assemblées* of coquettes and beaux.

    Finis.

Glossary

Abigails and Andrews – female and male servants

adsheartlikins, 'sheartlikins – abbreviated forms of 'God's heartlikins', or 'God's little heart', a term of affection, here used simply as an exclamation or catch-phrase by Blunt

angle into Blackfriars with a mitten – prisoners would fish for offerings from passers-by by letting down a mitten on a string

Aniseed Robin – a well-known hermaphrodite

apropos – opportunely, in timely fashion

arithmetical – over-precise

assafoetida – a strong smelling medicine

asseverations – assertions

atlases – silk-satins

B'w'y – [God] be with you

babies – dolls

Baldwin – a traditional name for an ass

bamboo – cane walking-stick

Barbadoes waters – a type of brandy

Bartlemew and his fair – the great fair held on St Bartholomew's Day was notorious for its freak shows

basilisks – legendary monsters whose stare was fatal

bating – other than

beaux garçons – exhausted rakes

beholding – indebted

black-lead – pencil

Blackfriars way – ie, in the style of plays seen at the former Blackfriars playhouse, now regarded as old-fashioned

bona roba – a good (but often showy) dresser

borachio – a drunkard

box – dice box (also with sexual connotations)

Bridewell – a prison

broadsides – a sustained artillery attack from one side of a vessel

bubble, bubbled – fool, gulled

bubbles – dupes

buckram – stiff

bulk – stall

bum baily – 'a bailiff of the meanest kind; one employed in arrests' (Dr Johnson's *Dictionary*)

Bunyan – John Bunyan, Puritan author of *Pilgrim's Progress*

burnishes – fattens

buttered – flattered

cabal – political or literary faction

call of serjeants – a group of barristers who qualified together

camphire – camphor

canonical hour – marriages were supposed to take place between eight in the morning and midday (the canonical hours)

cantharides – Spanish Fly, an aphrodisiac

cap of maintenance – in heraldry, a cap with two points like horns. Part of a series of jokes about the horns traditionally associated with cuckolds

capon – castrated cock (applied to Horner)

Capuchin – hooded friar

Carnival – here, specifically the brief period of celebration immediately preceding the deprivations of Lent

carriage – behaviour

cast of his office – a sign of his role: in the priest's case, to perform a marriage

cast, venture a – take a risk (as in throwing dice)

Castril – the 'angry boy' in Ben Jonson's *The Alchemist*

catering – procuring

caudle – warm gruel

chair-man – sedan chair carrier

chairs – sedan chairs

changeling – fool

chapmen – strolling dealers in cheap goods (sometimes, also their customers)

Chateline's – a French restaurant

Cheapside husband – merchant (citizen) husband

chemist – alchemist

cit – citizen, specifically (often derogatorily) of the City of London

clap – venereal disease

clap, proclaimed – visible signs of venereal disease

clary – a type of brandy

close walks – covered walks

Cock, Dog and Partridge – taverns/eating places. The Countess of Drogheda let Wycherley visit the Cock in Bow Street

colberteen – a type of lace

common house – a tavern restaurant, possibly also a brothel

commonplace – a book in which noteworthy quotations are entered

commons – communal meals

Commonwealth – here, specifically the period of republican rule, from 1649 to 1653

condition – high status

conventicle – a meeting of religious Dissenters

conventicling – going to meetings (conventicles) of religious dissenters

Covent Garden – fashionable area of London, hence 'Covent Garden wife', a fashionable wife

Covent Garden Drollery – book of songs, etc, from plays (1672)

cow-itch – a stinging plant

crazy – sickly

crips – an obsolete or (given the speaker) affected form of 'crisp'

crowd – violin

cuckold – noun: a man whose wife is unfaithful; verb: to have sex with another man's wife

cully – cuckold

curiously – carefully

Damon – rustic shepherd and lover

Dawk's Letter – a newspaper

decimo sexto – (Latin) a very small book, one with each sheet folded into sixteen pages, whereas a folio has one fold

deputy-lieutenant's hall – presumably full of mounted stag's heads. Part of a series of jokes about the horns traditionally associated with cuckolds

diffide in – distrust

discovers – reveals

doily – a light material

domine – (Latin) master

dormitives – sleep-inducing drinks

douceurs – (French) sweetnesses

doze – confuse

drap-du-Berry – coarse cloth from Berry in France

drawer – waiter

drolling – comic

druggets – cheap fabrics

Duke's Place – location of a church where irregular marriages took place

duns – creditors

dust it away – drink it down

éclaircissement – elucidation

Ecole des Filles – a French pornographic book

eighteenpenny place – a gallery in the theatre used by prostitutes

English-French disaster – catching venereal disease (French pox) from an English prostitute

essence – perfume

Essex – then as now a target for Londoners' derogatory jokes

étourdie, l' – (French) the giddy town

exceptious – inclined to take exception, peevish

extempore, mimic good – to imitate verse which better poets can make up as they go along

fadges – succeeds

fadler – fondler

falling sickness – epilepsy

Father – a priest (to perform the marriage)

fidges – fidgets

fine – pay

fishmonger hates a hard frost – since ice makes fishing difficult

fit – an affected pronunciation of 'fought'

Flanders – Spanish possession in the Netherlands, lost to French incursions

flapdragon – a raisin in the game of the same name

foiled – diseased

fox – sword
frank – open, sometimes 'generous'
fresco, in – in the open (fresh) air
frippery – worn out clothes
frisoneer gorget – a type of neck cover
frontless – shameless
fropish – – fretful
Furnivall's Inn – one of the Inns of Court

gemini – twins
grand signior – the Turkish sultan
grate – the barred window between a nun and the outside
    world
grazier – cattle grazer (at market)
grum, grumness – morose, moroseness
grutch – begrudge

hackney – hired
hictius doctius – Latinate magician's patter
hogoes – well-flavoured relishes
honest – chaste
horns – the sign of a cuckold
humour, hit your – caricature you accurately
husband's proper sign – cuckold's horns

'I prithee spare me' – first line of a poem by Sir John Suckling.
    Quoted by Millamant
incle – linen thread
incontinently – immediately
Infanta, portion for the – dowry fit for the Spanish King's
    daughter
inprimis – (Latin) in the first place. A legal term

jealous – used by Sparkish in Act Three of *The Country Wife* to
    mean angry, vehement
Jephthah's daughter – in the biblical Book of Judges, a daughter
    condemned to be sacrificed by her own father, but first
    permitted to bemoan her virgin state
Jubilee – a year in which the Pope offers special dispensations
    of punishments for sins

keepers – men who keep mistresses

Lacedemonian – Spartan, with reference to their traditional brevity

Lanterlu – lanterloo, or loo, is a card game

Lee, Tony – contemporary comic actor

Lelius – a patron of the Latin dramatist Terence

Lewis's – a tavern

'Like Phoebus . . . ' – a line from Waller's *The Story of Phoebus and Daphne, Applied*

Limberham – see *tattle*

Lincoln's Inn Fields – a fashionable meeting place

liquorish – lecherous

Locket's – a well-known tavern

Lombard Street – where goldsmiths had their shops, with connotations of wealth

Long Lane penthouse – a stall in a road notorious for its rag pedlars

Loretto, road to – well-travelled road (leading to a place of pilgrimage on the Adriatic)

Ludgate – Ludgate debtors' prison

maggot – here, contemptuous reference to the inner spiritual voice heeded by religious dissenters

mainly – much

Mar-all, Sir Martin – hero of Dryden's 1667 comedy *Sir Martin Mar-all*, who pretends to sing and play the lute to his mistress while his servant actually performs

marker – scorekeeper (at dice)

medlar grafted on a crab – a type of apple eaten when mushy through decay, grafted on to a sour wild apple eaten when hard

megrim – migraine

Menander – a Greek dramatist

menial – domestic

mercury – treatment for venereal disease

Messalina's poems – probably Mincing's mistake for a 'miscellany of poems', but very appropriate since the historical Messalina was notorious for her sexual activities

mewed – shut up, restrained

mittimus – (Latin) a warrant for imprisonment

moiety – half

moiling – labouring

Molo – stone-built pier

Montague – Ralph Montague (1638- 1709), politician and courtier who made two fortunes by marriage

month's mind – strong desire

Mopus – stupid person

Mosca in The Fox – Volpone's accomplice in Jonson's *Volpone*

motion – puppet (ie, lifeless)

mousled – rumpled, pulled about roughly

Mrs Engine – Mrs Trickery

Mufti – Muslim priest

Mulberry Garden – a fashionable meeting place in St James's Park

murrain – cattle disease

mutinous tribe – ie, religious dissenters, nonconformists

name, forgot my – failed to consider my reputation

nangered – angered

natural – a fool

necessity for a cloak – need a cloak to hide a pregnancy

New Bridge – Nieuwerbrug: Dutch garrison which fell to the French in 1672 (the reference here thus being anachronistic)

New Exchange – a fashionable meeting place

new postures – new pornographic pictures

nightgown – loose gown; dressing gown rather than nightdress

Nokes – contemporary comic actor

noli prosequi – (Latin) phrase used to end legal proceedings

Novella, The – comedy by Richard Brome (1632)

obscenely – openly

occasional – timely

olio – a mixture, from a Spanish stew with varied ingredients

ombre – a card game

Ordinary – the prison chaplain

pack-thread – twine ('flaunting upon a pack-thread' may mean living on a shoestring or could refer to prostitution)

Pall Mall – a fashionable meeting place

pallets – mattresses

Pam – the highest card in the game of loo

Pamplona – Northern Spanish town, guarding a pass through the Pyrenees (in besieging which Belvile served as a mercenary for the French army)

Pancras – a church where irregular marriages took place

Partlet, Dame – the wife of Chanticleer the Cock in Chaucer's *Nun's Priest's Tale*

pass your grants – accept your favours

passe partout – (French) a permit to go anywhere

paw – naughty

Penthesilea – Queen of the Amazons

peruke – wig

Philander – lover

Piazza – a fashionable meeting place in Covent Garden

picaroon – wanderer, often piratical

pieced – enlarged

pies and jays – magpies and jays, meaning fops

piquet – a card game

placehouse – main house on an estate

Prado – promenade, place of fashionable assembly

Prince, the – specifically the exiled Prince Charles, later Charles II

probatum est – (Latin) it has been tested (used on prescriptions)

projection – the last stage of making base metal into gold in alchemy

projector – schemer

propriety – rightful ownership

Prynne – William Prynne, author of *Histriomastix*, a puritan attack on the theatre

pulpit comedian – clergyman

pulvilio – scented powder

pulvilled – perfumed with powder

Pumplenose – Pimplenose

pure – fine

put upon his clergy – criminals who could read and write could claim 'benefit of clergy' to escape the death penalty

Pylades and Orestes – representative faithful friends

Quarles – Francis Quarles, a theological controversialist

quean – hussy

quoif – a lawyer's cap

Quorum – to be 'o' the Quorum' means to be a Justice of the Peace

Rabel's drops – a quack medicine

railleurs – banterers

rally – tease

rantipole – ill mannered

ratafia – a type of brandy

receipts – recipes

Rekin – the Wrekin, a famous hill in Shropshire

roll-wagon – wagon-load, possibly with an obscene reference to a type of china

rooks – cheats or, in context, the victims of cheats

Rosamond's Pond – a meeting place in St James's Park

Roxalana – the wife of the Sultan in William Davenant's *The Siege of Rhodes*

Russell Street – a street in the Covent Garden area

sack – a Spanish wine

Salop – Shropshire

save-all – a type of candle holder

Scipio – a patron of the Latin dramatist Terence

sensible – felt acutely

shake-bag – a kind of fighting cock

'sheartlikins – see *adsheartlikins*

shocks – poodles

shore, common – public sewer

shy – distrustful

signs – shop signs

silly – ignorant

Slighted Maiden – comedy by Sir Robert Stapleton (1663)

Smithfield jade – worn out horse from the well-known London market; jade also means disreputable woman

smoke – mock

snack – share

sommeils du matin – morning drowsinesses

sophisticated – corrupted

Sophy – a Persian ruler

Spanish paper – used for applying rouge

squab – chubby

St James's Fields or *Park* – a fashionable meeting place

stir – fret

strait-lacing – tight corseting

Strammel – a gaunt person

Suckling – Sir John Suckling, the poet. Sir Wilfull thinks he is being called a young pig

sybil – classical prophetess

tallow-chandler – a manufacturer and seller of candles made from tallow

Tantony – shortened form of St Antony, who is often depicted with a pig

Tarugo's Wiles – comedy by Sir Thomas St Serfe (1668)

tattle, limberham – harmless escorts

Theophrastus – ancient Greek author of *Characters*

'There never yet . . . '– first line of a poem by Sir John Suckling. Quoted by Millamant

Thomaso – play by Thomas Killigrew, alleged to have been plagiarised by Behn for *The Rover*

'Thyrsis a youth . . . '– first line of Edmund Waller's *The Story of Phoebus and Daphne, Applied*

tift – arranged

tire-women – ladies' maids

to choose – by choice

Toledo – Spanish sword, long and finely-honed

torch – a boy with a torch

tosses – throws

toused and moused – rumpled and played with

Tramontana – from over the mountains; hence, in Italy, anything to (or from) the north of the Alps

trimmings – clothes

Truewit – a character in Jonson's *Epicene*

turtles – turtle doves, birds associated with love

ungrateful – thankless

unsized camlet – unstiffened material

upse gispsy – like a gipsy; gipsy-style

ure – practice

vex – prevent
vizard-mask – prostitute

wag – stir
watch-night – night light
weekly bill – the weekly record of deaths in the City of London
wether – castrated ram (applied to Horner)
whim it about – spin
Whitehall – the palace of Whitehall
with a witness – with a vengeance
woodcocks – fools
worse than a quaker hates a parrot – since a quaker's sober dress
    and behaviour are seen as contrasting sharply with the
    noise and colour of a parrot

y'vads – i'faith
ycleped – known as, called
year, [he]r – year of mourning